The Crippets.

Leckhampton. 1900

Ted Wilson.

Woman with the Iceberg Eyes

Woman with the Iceberg Eyes:
Oriana F. Wilson

KATHERINE MACINNES

The History Press

Endpapers: 'The Crippets, Leckhampton', 1900, by Edward Wilson. Pencil sketch. (Cheltenham College Archives)

First published 2019

The History Press
97 St George's Place, Cheltenham,
Gloucestershire, GL50 3QB
www.thehistorypress.co.uk

British Library Cataloguing in Publication Data.
A catalogue record for this book is available from the British Library.

ISBN 978 0 7509 9153 7

Typesetting and origination by The History Press
Printed and bound in Great Britain by TJ International Ltd.

'[Oriana] had a strong smile with a hint of the iceberg, and was reserved and friendly at the same time.'
Sara Wheeler, *Cherry: A Life of Apsley Cherry-Garrard*
(Jonathan Cape, 2001)

'Yes, Oriana was so absolutely beautiful, she had piercing blue eyes … even when her eyes went glacial … and she had a lovely smile and when you went into a room you noticed her straight away. There was a charisma about her that was about nobody else … she reminded me of an iceberg … but she had this tremendous heart …'
Eleanor Forbes (née Ferrar) with David Wilson 11 August 1995

'I loved Aunt Ory, she was super.'
Michael and David Wilson, 30 March 1995

'And now we had loose ice all round us and here and there great frozen hummocks, where slabs the size of kitchen tables were thrown one on the other anyhow and so frozen with every hollow and crack and crevice a perfect miracle of blue and green light …'
from Edward Wilson's Antarctic Journal 1901–04, quoted in D&C
Edward Wilson's Antarctic Notebooks (Reardon Publishing, 2011)

'Aunt Ory had iceberg eyes which could freeze you at 20 paces.'
Conversation between the author and David Wilson, Cheltenham, 2011

Contents

Acknowledgements

The mystery and opacity of Oriana's long life meant I often had to turn to others for advice. I would like to acknowledge, with gratitude, the debts I owe the following individuals: Dr David Wilson, Maarten Mowbury, Eleanor Bragge, Nicholas and Christina Bantoft, Toby Garfitt, Kit Bowen, Wayland Kennet, Peter Seaver, Nicola Kearton, Ralph Slater, Anne Strathie, David Elder, Neela Mann, Henrietta Brooks, Valerie Johnston, Sarah Davies Jones, Jan Wood, Lynne Cleaver, Carol O Brien, Jane Bannister, Harriet Lear, Audrey Adams, Jim Craig Gray, Emma Taylor, Jane Mayes, Sarah Strong, Joe Maldonado, Elizabeth Millman, Jennifer Thompson, Ann Rachael Harwood, Benedict Sayers, Sally Cline, Sarah Wheeler, Sue Limb, Charlie Viney, Chrissy McMorris, Alex Waite, Naomi Boneham, Mick Brunt and Lucy Martin.

In New Zealand: Nick Smith, Conservation Minister and Minister for Housing NZ Government, for his recognition of the significance of the hut and support of the restoration project. Also Nicholas Boigelt, Jill Haley, Gillian Painter, Simon Martin, Janet Bray, Allan Campell, Judy Rogers, Alan Robb, David L Harrowfield, Natalie Cadenhead, Joanne Condon, Richard Studholme, Maryann Cowan, Paul Scofield, Ian Church, George Griffiths, Maryann Cowan, Paul H. Jackson, Eva Garbutt and Boo Woodhouse.

Thank you to the following institutions: Scott Polar Research Institute, Copthorne School, Bradfield College, St Andrew's Prep School, Devon Record Office, Cheltenham College, Cheltenham Local Studies Library, The Wilson (formerly Cheltenham Art Gallery and Museum), Cheltenham Festivals, British Library, Royal Geographic Society, Natural History Museum, Bushey Museum and Art Gallery.

In New Zealand: The Press, Canterbury Museum, Alexander Turnbull Library, Ashburton Museum, Oamaru Whitestone Civic Trust, Waitaki Boys High School, North Otago Museum and Geraldine Museum.

Thank you also to the magnificent cast of the theatre play *Love & Death & Mrs Bill* performed at Cheltenham College; and to the staff at Sir Peter Scott's Slimbridge Wildfowl and Wetlands trust – a 'Wilsonian' text book inspired by making that boy ' … interested in Natural History', may they continue to teach it in 'some schools'; and finally I would to thank the Cheltenham Arts Council for a research grant when I was editor of *Perspectives*.

People have often asked why I wanted to write about a 'well-behaved woman' ('well-behaved women don't', as the saying goes, 'make history') and why waste time on one who was so determinedly invisible? I have been motivated by her extraordinary ability to communicate the 'infection of good courage'. There is already proof of how contagious this elusive species of 'courage' is. Features on Ory in everything from *The Lady* to *Cotswold Life* in the UK and *The Press* NZ have resulted in 'a migration' of letters, photographs and memories flying in to roost on my desk – every new 'bird', a fresh delight. May there be (and there may well be) many more! All the mistakes are mine and I am sorry for them. (Ory wanted an 'archangel's draft' for a single letter to King George – I need a fully paid-up choir of angels for this.)

Thank you to my friends and family who have been extraordinary – imagine, if you can, the full range of supportive gestures from cups of tea to camper van journeys around South Island. Thank you particularly to my amazing 'right living' parents Patrick and Hilary. Thank you also to my husband Sebastian and to our children Xander, Jago and Claudie, who have grown up with this book. This is for you.

1

From Battersea to Cheltenham

1897–98

In which Miss Oriana Souper comes up to London as the vicar's eldest daughter, secures independence and a career, whilst engineering an opportunity to bump into the man she has fallen for without losing face or eligibility in the process.

'I have quite made up my mind to remain a bachelor for life,' wrote 25-year-old Edward Wilson in a letter home to his parents, 'I have thought about it a good deal lately, and perhaps I will write a paper on Marriage some day with all the symptoms and signs of acute love. They are very interesting when you come to think of them.'[1]

One April evening in 1897, the warden and his wife, Mr and Mrs Leighton-Hopkins, were dining out. They had left their 22-year-old niece, Miss Oriana Souper (Ory), sitting reading by the fire in the drawing room.[2] She was probably sewing. Life was complicated but embroidery soothed her. Embossing, appliqué and lace work required total absorption, dexterity and skill. Most of the students she had met were Cambridge medics doing a little light charity work in their university holidays. The Caius College Mission was on Holman Road, Battersea, so it was convenient for the hospital and the practical part of the course. Students lived at the Mission in exchange for going out into the Battersea slums and treating the bare-footed street urchins. Ory had visited one house with her aunt earlier that day. Gaggles of children. Croup, adenoids, eczema, fleas and lice, and the smell!

For the last few years she had been unofficial matron at an orphanage in Brixham, Devon, where her father, the Reverend Francis, was head-master. Since the children boarded, it enabled Ory and the rest of her father's staff to control the fleas and lice with strict washing routines. She had been itching to whisk the ragged clothes off those small Battersea children, just for a second, and introduce them to a little carbolic. Today she had longed for the salted air of Devon, the cry of gulls and the fresh onshore breeze. Even the docks with the barrels of fish guts was preferable to the still, close stench of the slums. Beside her on the table stood a vase of narcissi. A young medical student, a Mr Wilson, had given them to Mrs Leighton-Hopkins the evening before. The clean, clear scent cut through the smell of coal, spring triumphing, somehow, through the smoke. It echoed her own feelings. Here at the sharp end of poverty, she had seen gold. Perhaps it was God? She knew that was what she should have been thinking, anyway.

Ory had come up to London to find something to do and instead she had found someone. But now what?

Mr Edward Wilson (Ted) opened the front door. Normally the house was rushing with Caius medics racing between the hospital and the slums, but now it seemed unusually calm. He remembered that the Leighton-Hopkins were having a night off duty.

He had just been giving the slum children a slide show. He did this two nights a week. The hall where he'd given the show was full to bursting and in the seats outside there were children with babes in arms. One little 'brat'[3] had come with a bandage over both eyes.

Ted set about stowing the two boxes he had brought in. One was the Mission's heavy black leather projector with its concertina lens, which claimed to be portable. The other was his medical kit, a wooden box with a leather strap containing liniment, carbolic and ointments. He would need more of the eye ointment. Ted had treated that boy for ophthalmia and blepharitis before the show. At each change of the pictures on the screen, the brat had looked up from under his bandage for a few seconds and then kept his face buried until the next.

Ted's slides were of animals, mostly birds. There were birds in the city, but his birds were different. They were wild, country birds and seeing them, Ted hoped, might bring a little bit of natural beauty into their grime-filled lives. And besides, there was something about beauty that he didn't pretend to understand. 'Love comes to me by one channel only – the recognition of some beauty, whether mental, moral, or physical …'[4] It was one of the great mysteries of God's creation.

He hefted the medical kit box again and made for the stairs. The drawing room door was ajar. There she was, sitting in an armchair reading beside the cheerful fire.

He'd met her the evening before. Mrs Leighton-Hopkins (Mrs 'L-H', also known as 'Mrs Warden') had introduced them. A doctor's son. A vicar's daughter. He hadn't been looking for it, although 'first sight' he now realised was less cliché and more a scientifically accurate way of describing it.[5] Ted recognised his response to beauty was partly responsible. He felt he didn't 'handsome much' himself.[6] He was 25 years old, tall, wiry, with close-cut dark-red hair and a rather crooked smile. He could be identified easily from a distance by his long loping stride.[7] Ory was the same height; she described herself as 'scraggy thin' but she passed for slim in the right layers.[8] She was fine-featured with arresting blue eyes and a heart-shaped face framed with light-brown hair.

Ory was so beautiful that men were known to have given her flowers on impulse, before they even knew her name. And when Ted had first met her, he had been holding narcissi. But he had brought them for Mrs L-H (he could never pass a flower seller) and he had given them to Mrs L-H despite himself. When he'd first met Miss Souper, he'd thought those eyes iceberg-blue, formidable and yet – when she smiled at him, as she did now – they were indescribably warm.[9]

Ted and Ory sat in the fern-fronded oasis of the Mission's private drawing room, and talked. Some considerable time later, the Warden and his wife returned to find the doctor's son and the vicar's daughter sitting chatting. The L-Hs observed good-humouredly that neither of them seemed to have noticed that the fire had long since gone out.

What did they talk about? Was Ted confiding to her that he was considering becoming a 'real' missionary, beyond the Battersea slum nursery slopes to 'Abroad'? Missionary work, Ted knew, 'meant throwing up the chance of a comfortable home practice and the society of all the people you know and the chance of making any money at all, to go and work in an unhealthy tropical climate for the rest of your life.'[10] He thought it irresistible.

Ory, already with a lifetime of experience with the clergy, might have suggested carefully that 'a man can do so much for other men without taking holy orders.'[11] She had been sidestepping the 'Mr Collins' types for years. It was possible, she felt, to be on a mission without being a 'Missionary' with a capital 'M'. Ted agreed. His younger brother, Jim, had followed him to Cambridge and was preparing for ordination – Ted imagined they might go out to Africa probably, together.

They did not discuss singing. Ted was at pains to avoid it. If he had brought up singing, Ory might have guessed that last night, after he had gone upstairs 'to study', he had crept back down and listened. She had a strong clear voice. None of that awful drawing room warbling, and no hymns either – a good smattering of folk tunes and fun. Someone had accompanied her on the piano. At least he thought someone had. Or had she played it herself? She was some musician, of that he was certain, but he couldn't have complimented her now without giving himself away. And so ...

... he probably stuck to what he knew, his default conversation. Birds. Ted's sketches of birds were a way of worshipping God – of praising the astonishing beauty of creation. God was just so much better at it. Man was a fumbling amateur by comparison. Look at churches, for example. Churches were all very well, but they were dark and cold, smelt musty, and abounded in ludicrous brass eagle lecterns.

Ory disagreed. She loved churches. Churches were home and she understood them in the way Ted understood birds. But she was interested in birds, of course. Ted had just drawn a letter to his sister, who wanted to be able to distinguish between swallows and swifts, and house martins.[12] Did Miss Souper know the difference? Perhaps Ted sketched them for her there and then. Sometimes words were too, well, wordy, and it was always difficult to speak when one had birds weaving in and out of the conversation – what was the birding like in Dorset at this time of year?

Some time later Ory returned home to Whitchurch-Canonicorum, Dorset, where her father, the Reverend Francis Souper, a now retired headmaster, was waiting for someone to find him a proper position with a living sufficient to keep his family. Souper was an academic and had read Gilbert White's *Nature Notes* on the mysterious disappearance of swallows during the winter months (where did they go – surely something that small wouldn't fly all the way to Africa?) but Ory had never really given birds much thought.

She didn't have binoculars so she spent much of the following months squinting at the sky. 'Behold the fowls of the air:' *Matthew 6: 26* (Ory had a verse for every occasion, though she made a conscious effort never to say them out loud), 'for they sow not, neither do they reap, nor gather into barns …' After her mother's death, when the 13-year-old Ory was up before dawn getting her brothers and sister ready for school, they'd used it as an excuse for a lie-in. At least until her oldest brother Noel, always adventurous, had escaped to work on a farm in Canada, sowing and reaping for all he was worth. And now this prodigal son (*Luke 15: 11–32*), was back and off to Cambridge with their father's blessing. Ory and her sister, Constance, who'd been Dutiful Daughters, would never be offered such opportunities. Education was expensive. Education was for boys.

Now Ory tramped through Marshwood Vale towards Hardy's Tower, trying to push that Biblical story out of her mind. Fiction. That's what she needed. Thomas Hardy's recent bestseller, *Tess of the D'Urbervilles*, sprang to mind, but Tess had never ventured more than 50 miles from home. Ory had no ambitions to be a passive fictional heroine. On freshly minted May mornings, she began to note that swallows and house martins both had black backs, but the swallow, a longer forked tail, black head and red chin. House martins were white underneath. Swifts were dark brown all over. There was nothing nuanced in her observations.

Ory returned to a vicarage that smelt of mothballs, *Bible* paper and piety. As she began to fill the unforgiving minute with usefulness, she paused and thought of those 'birds of the air' – she knew that life was not about hoarding riches, it was about doing what you were born to do. What, she wondered, had she been born to do? And, in passing, what did 'Africa probably' smell like?

In Battersea, Ted was sitting at the scuffed wooden desk in his friend Abercrombie's study, chain-smoking Piccadilly Virginias. When he had smoked one cigarette until he could feel the heat of the lighted end in his fingers, he lit the next one off it and inhaled. 'Oh, the joy of tobacco.'[13]

'Oriana'. It was an unusual name. She pronounced it Oar-ree-anna. Good initials. 'O Souper.' 'Oh Super!' Probably best that they stayed that way. He inhaled and blew a smoke ring over fellow student Abercrombie's head. The low evening sun lit it like a lunar corona and for a moment it hovered in the air as a perfect circle before disintegrating.

Ted was still divided between a 'positive reek of slum children'[14] and his medical books. He should have been revising for his medical exams on 4 May when, with laconic disinterest, he lent the cigarette against the side of a cheap ash tray, pulled out a sheet of paper and began to write to his mother. It was a month since he'd met Ory and he still couldn't concentrate. He didn't tell his mother any of that – he had standards – but he was, he told her, aware of the 'signs of acute love'. They were 'quite interesting' when you came to think about them. He meant to write 'a paper on it someday'.[15] The thing was to analyse the situation scientifically, to notice the changes to heart and mind, to commit them to paper and then to shelve them and get on with what was directly in front of one. Work. Career. A mission.

But despite himself, whatever Ted felt on meeting Ory, he felt alive. He had been reading Kipling's *The Jungle Book* to the slum children. They hung on his every word. It was as if the energy of the jungle was channelled into the Caius Mission hall. He sometimes thought, when he paused between paragraphs, that you could have heard a feather alight. Writing the next day to his father, he confessed that try as he might to give the thing a scientific name, he now knew how 'Mowgli felt … in the time of the spring running', adding as an afterthought, 'the fitter I feel, the more I swear'.[16] Swearing was good. False piety, as Miss Souper had agreed in their fireside chat, was true blasphemy.

Eventually, as the year wore on, it seemed to Ory in Dorset that she might never hear from Ted again. It had been more than eight months since the fire went out. She could only assume that he was fixed on 'Africa probably', and that he did not require a Mrs Livingstone for company. What could she do?

It was difficult. Her family were 'church mice'.[17] For their sake she needed to make a financial contribution: for her own, she needed to move out. How to earn money discreetly? How to get a job without a formal education? How to become independent yet remain eligible?

Ory was stuck in the classic Victorian conundrum. What would her late mother have advised?

Frances Emmeline, Ory's mother, was always known as 'Fanny'. This was lucky, Frances marrying Francis could have been confusing – there was no way of distinguishing between the endings in speech. Fanny Souper, née Beaumont, was an unusually tall, elegant lady with a ready smile, who had been born to a family of lawyers.[18] Her father, James, was a solicitor based in the family practice at Lincoln's Inn. Fanny had grown up reciting the principles of English law: 'innocent till proved guilty', 'pleading guilty', 'trial by jury', etc. Quietly, from the wings, Fanny had influenced the public school stand on punishment. As an 18-year-old prefect, Ory's father had been inordinately fond of 'swishing'. As headmaster, he later banned it.[19] Why? He was a classicist and yet, in a system steeped in the liberal use of corporal punishment, the Reverend Souper began citing the principles of English law. (The boys had 'pleaded guilty' and therefore were only required to write lines.)[20]

It may have been his undoing. The Educational Establishment regarded him as not just 'different' but a troublemaker, an anarchist, or at the very least a 'faddist of the most irritating kind'.[21] But although he challenged convention in some ways, in others he was an out-and-out traditionalist.

Girls. Ory had been born on 19 October 1874. She was a girl, the only girl in a hard school for boys – a metaphor, perhaps, for the rest of her life. The Reverend Francis Souper assured his wife that Oriana Fanny Souper (named for her paternal grandmother and her mother respectively) would be the first of many. She was the first of eight – six boys and two girls. At roughly two year intervals, Fanny was delivered of Oriana, James, Noel, Constance, Quintus (who died in infancy), Edward, Woodford and Adrian. Oriana was five years older than her sister, Constance.

When Oriana was born, Francis, still in his mid-twenties, had just been appointed headmaster of Bradfield College, the public school in Berkshire where he had been head boy. Since leaving he had acquired a degree at Cambridge, an ordination and a startling black beard. A photographic portrait shows Souper's beard to perfection, but Arthur Leach, author of *History of Bradfield College*, briefly outlines Francis' five-year reign under a chapter headed 'Decline'. Souper would have thought that unfair. 'All I stipulated,' he later wrote in defence of his teaching style, '… was that the boy should not work simply for the examination, but should honestly try to become less of a fool.'[22] It wasn't a winning marketing gambit.

When Ory was 4, her father bought Colstocks Farm in Eastbourne, rechristened it 'The Meads' – and then on second thoughts 'St Andrews' – and advertised it as a 'private school for young gentlemen'. Gentlemen only. Ory's brothers and her ex-pat male cousins were schooled in everything from Greek to German (via 'Gymnastic Exercises &c in wet weather'). Ory and her sister Constance were not, though Ory held her own in school games.

But there were certain principles that applied across the sexes. Souper exhorted them all to chew more, 'If [you] would bite [your] food more, there would follow beneficial results all round – to mind as well as to body. But it is not an easy thing to train a [child] to do this.' However, chewing should be limited because as the nursery saying went: 'Enough is as good as a Feast'. Everyone knew that. 'A flabby state of body,' declared Souper, 'is too often responded to by a flabby state of mind.'[23] There was never going to be a modicum of 'flabbyness' about Ory and her sister – you could hardly see them sideways on, and neither in later life could chew, let alone swallow, their food when stressed.

So other than extreme slenderness of mind and body, what exactly did Souper expect of his daughters? Ory's maternal grandfather was a lawyer, her paternal grandfather, Philip Dottin Souper, was a 'servant of Empire', holding various roles in colonial administration in Trinidad and Mauritius. Philip Souper was a traditionalist, often siding with the planters over their slaves in disputes.[24] Perhaps Francis' stand against convention was partly a way of carving his own path, but some of that traditionalism had rubbed off. Souper's sons *would* go into public service (preferably the Church, or if they must, the Army). His daughters *would* marry (preferably Church types).

After the excitement of meeting Ted in Battersea, there was a loud silence. As 1897 drew to a close, 23-year-old Ory surveyed the wintery Marshwood Vale from the Whitchurch Rectory and knew for certain that she did not want to leap from the frying pan into the fire, out of one rectory into another. There must be more to life?

As Ory saw it, she had three options. They looked the same but there were fundamental differences. The Swallow: a talented pianist, taught by her stepmother, Henrietta Escreet (she had accompanied herself when Ted had listened from the bottom of the Mission stairs), Ory might have given recitals, but only certain kinds of women 'performed' and, in doing so, ruined their chances on the marriage market. The Housemartin: Ory might have taken a more domestic role in a Mission such as the Caius College Mission in Battersea where she had met Ted. But although she was well attuned to the practical side of housekeeping, it was a bit 'below stairs'. The Swift: schools were home. Her father dusted off his address book – he must find something for his eldest daughter 'to do'. But Aunt 'Emmie' Leighton-Hopkins beat him to it.

'There is a girl I have met at Battersea,' wrote Ted in early January 1898, to his parents: 'a Miss Souper who is going to be "Matron" she says, Useful Help I say, to the James' School. You must be kind to her because she is a connection of Mrs Warden. But you will like her I think.'[25]

Later Ory would claim airily that it was 'just one of those coincidences that mould events',[26] that she had accepted the post 'in entire ignorance of any connection of the Wilsons with Cheltenham'.[27] And so it may have been pure and utter coincidence that, through the very lady who had first introduced them, Oriana landed a job less than 500 yards from Ted's front door.

The Vicar's eldest daughter arrived at Cheltenham Spa Station at the beginning of 1898. It was an odd time to start, halfway through the school year, but the Jameses were moving the school upmarket, taking over an imposing 'gent's residence' in Montpellier, the smartest area of town, and it was all hands on deck.

Ory's cab passed genteel terraces of classical houses facing a wide tree-lined road. The trees were January-bare, but in the pleasure gardens teams of gardeners were busy preparing the flower beds. On the far side of Montpellier Gardens were the villas including Westal, the Wilson family home. Beyond that, the tall creamy spires of Cheltenham College where Ted had gone to school.[28] The cab turned right at the Montpellier Rotunda and, almost immediately, pulled up under the towering classical portico of Suffolk Hall. And so independent life began.

Ory made herself useful immediately. First they had to convert the thirteen bedrooms and dressing rooms into dormitories, the tennis lawns into a playground and the coach house and sundry servant rooms into staff accommodation. After a few weeks the smell of fresh paint and sawdust would give way to the familiar odour of sweat and plimsolls and Ory would begin to feel at home. Really, she had been a matron all her life, the difference was now she was being paid.

Mrs James left the running of the school to her daughters, Evelyn and Beatrice. Together with four other assistant teachers, they taught the three Rs to seventeen boys ranging in age from 6 to 12. At Suffolk Hall there were boys from India, Mauritius and even Australia, but for now, they were Ory's boys.

Which is not to say that they were perfect. Her father's school reports for similar boys, though critical, reveal the Souper sense of humour, fully shared by Ory:

Scripture: Foggy.
Arithmetic: The ice is broken. That is all that can be said at present.
Algebra: Very confused, and not a boy who can be easily delivered from his confusion.
Geography: No boy could have done worse …
Latin Grammar: Not secure enough to be of any use.
Latin Exercises: Excruciatingly careless.
English History: Feeble at present, but improving.
French: No grasp of the language, but decidedly improved.
Singing: Flat – very willing and very plucky.
Drawing: Wild.[29]

Ory admired her father's acerbic wit and she could conjure up a report for any given human being based on a sliding scale of her personal ideal of virtues: from simplicity and sincerity at one end, to 'any suspicion of affectation [which] she abhorred'.[30] Although later in life she taught herself to be quite diplomatic, she knew she could be judgemental and tried to check herself, with limited success. She thrived according to her necessaryness – as the term got going she became indispensable.

Cheltenham had emerged as a spa town in 1761 when pigeons had been observed pecking deposits around a saline chalybeate spring. The pigeon became the symbol of the town, and ornamental metal pigeons perched on gate posts, stone pigeons proliferated around wells, over doorways and wooden pigeons perched atop signposts. Pigeons were everywhere. When the Cheltenham census scribe appeared at the Suffolk Hall front door, he could reasonably assume that every occupant would know their place, every pigeon his or her hole.

It was not to be. The first time he asked for Miss Oriana Fanny Souper's 'Profession or Occupation', he was told 'Matron'. He wrote it down. Her name appeared after all the teaching staff but before the boys and servants. As an afterthought, he was asked to prefix it with 'Lady'. But the box was intended for one word! The person dictating insisted. Ory was so much more than a servant and 'Lady' would make that clear. Ory became the 'Lady Matron' but even that didn't seem sufficient. They must put 'Teacher' somewhere; after all, she taught the younger boys for pity's sake?[31] But the box was intended …

The word 'Teach' was squashed along the top. Not 'Teacher', the 'er' was obviously a step too far.[32] Unbeknown to her or the unfortunate census scribe, Ted had predicted this confusion. 'Matron, she says,' he had written to his parents, 'Useful Help, I say.'[33]

Ted's sisters, having dutifully looked out the 'Mrs Warden's connection' as their brother had instructed, invited the 'Lady-Matron-Teach' for tea at Westal. Without compromising her ladylike character, without appearing to be pushy or forward, Ory had done it. She had evolved into an independent woman in her own right. She had a salary. She had a place to live. She had plans.

But Ory was a Victorian woman and even late ones found it difficult to lose their restraint, to embrace success with both hands. There was something borderline immodest about it. 'The ice is broken,' as her father was so fond of saying, 'That is all that can be said at present.' It was 'all rather too easy,' Ory wrote later, 'perhaps it's in preparation for something hard.'[34]

2

Evolution's Logical Conclusion

1898

In which Ory learns that Ted has been diagnosed with pulmonary tuberculosis.
They renew their acquaintance despite this and go 'birding' together.
When Ted leaves for a cure in Norway, they are consciously detached.

When Ory handed her woollen coat to the Wilsons' housekeeper in the Westal hallway, she shivered. Under her coat she wore her off-duty skirt of sky blue.[1] She had met Ted almost a year ago. Seeing him again now, was 'just another one of those coincidences' (she had rehearsed that nonchalant line), but still part of her wondered. It was March, but all the windows were wide open.[2]

Ted, or Mr Wilson to her, was the same but different. None of the vitality that she remembered. He coughed. Perhaps it was the thick yellow smog that curled around the London streets, perhaps it was the Virginias, or perhaps it was overwork. Ory knew from Ted's sisters that their brother never stopped. He worked at the hospital. He worked in the slums. He slept little, ate little and yet, in the minutes between, Ory knew that he bought narcissi and he drew birds.

The tea cooled almost immediately it was poured into the Wedgwood china. Ory could see her breath – was it warmer outside? As the curtains at the French windows stirred in the breeze, Ted carefully filled his lungs and smiled. He told her he was just 'soot-sodden', but not that it was nothing.[3]

It was strange to see him so still. He looked awkward, held. She did not know until much later, that her visit was the first time he'd left his bedroom. Ted asked her about birds and school boys and the Jameses.

He coughed and coughed. She waited until he stopped. She tried not to notice: instinctively she knew he hated 'fashing' (fussing).

But neither of them could pretend to be interested in small talk. Ory wanted to be in the same space as Ted, and talking and tea were the socially acceptable way of achieving this. It is not clear at what stage in the visit she learned that, in London, Dr Rolleston had diagnosed pulmonary tuberculosis – of which, half the sufferers died.[4]

Ory's leather boot heels clicked back along the pavement to Suffolk Hall. She only had to cross one road. This new Ted was vulnerable in a way that the Battersea Ted had been invincible. And, rather insultingly in the circumstances, he really didn't seem to care whether he lived or died; 'with heaven in measurable distance', he had told her, 'he felt remarkably calm.'[5] Well Ted could be calm if he chose to be, Ory could never get to that pitch, there were too many painful memories.

Ted coughed as her mother, Fanny, had coughed. Back then, a decade ago, Ory had been a child, but she remembered that every single breath her mother took had been acutely painful. Later it was diagnosed not as TB, but pneumonia. Fanny had not been in robust health since the birth of Quintus, the child born after Constance, who had died at four months. Infant death was not uncommon: at the end of the nineteenth century, 16 per cent of children did not survive their first birthday. Souper made sure his children could recite 'the Lord gave, and the Lord hath taken away; blessed be the name of the Lord.' *Job 1: 21.*

Fanny had been pregnant for most of her of married life. She approached her eighth confinement with confidence – she was doing her Christian duty and seven times had proved physically equal to the task (now helped by the administration of chloroform, which was, according to Queen Victoria, 'soothing, quieting and delightful beyond measure'). Fanny's eighth child was born a healthy boy, but shortly afterwards, her breathing became laboured and, on 2 April 1888, she died. In Ory's mind, that death was inextricably linked with that of her oldest brother. Shortly after her mother's funeral, 11-year-old James Francis fell over a cliff and was killed. It was unimaginable.

Ory was only just a teenager and yet, with James gone, she was the oldest by some years and became the Sibling Parent. Francis, her father, had been brought up by his Sibling Parent, his sister Sarah, when his parents were abroad. It was not an unusual arrangement in the Souper family except for the fact that Ory was so young. As far as 13-year-old Ory saw it, there seemed to be no alternative. Her education was sacrificed as she threw herself into housekeeping caring for five children ranging in age from 9 years old to newborn. Her childhood was over.

As she walked back to her rooms at Suffolk Hall in Cheltenham, a decade later, the memory of that double bereavement was still fresh. Ory had not been able to save her mother, or her brother, but tubercular Ted was still alive and (whatever *Job 1: 21* had to say on the matter) if she had anything to do with it, he would stay that way. In conjunction with the professionals, Ory would nurse Ted by stealth without 'fashing'. (Often she was the only one he would allow to do so.) Ory was, as Ted observed, 'different'; she had been 'from the first' and he loved her for it.[6] Sometime around now, Ted's nickname for her, the 'Useful Help', became abbreviated by his family to 'the UH'. It was endearingly unfluffy.

Sitting in bed in 1898, the sash fully open beside him, Ted painted a narcissus that he had just been given and read Kipling, 'the best tonic for any illness'.[7] The treatment for TB was fresh air and food. Unlike Ory, Ted didn't mind eating: it was mealtimes he despised – having to tear himself away from doing something more interesting to sit politely at table. It brought out the very worst of the Wilson temper, a trait that his father had noted scientifically [under 'inherited traits'] in the family tree and attributed to his wife's side. But for now, Ted found it was restful to spoon in Cook's plum duff and watch birds swooping past his bedroom window and up around the turrets of Cheltenham College Chapel. In many ways, being home was some compensation for his illness. London in spring time had left him feeling like 'a soda bottle in an oven'.[8]

Ted's father, Dr Edward Thomas Wilson, known as 'Dad', had founded the Delancey Hospital in Cheltenham as an isolation and fever hospital, one of the few in the country. He had a personal interest in contagion. Nellie, Ted's sister, had died of typhoid while nursing an epidemic in Leicester and both the doctors, the invalid and his dad, respected Dr Rolleston's tubercular diagnosis.

Dad prided himself on his renaissance approach to science and had won prizes for his early research into genetic inheritance with his paper on family faculties.[9] But he was equally interested in others. Where, for example, did Miss Souper get her elegant height from? Both her parents were tall, her youngest brother Adrian was six-foot five in his socks! And her extreme slenderness, was this nature or 'nurture'? That was more difficult to explain. Blue eyes? Both parents or just one – and what about her nose? Her nose? Yes, her nose ...

Well, that came somehow from Aunt Connie. Her father had a Roman nose, her mother, a perfectly normal nose, but Ory had this slightly beaky affair and so did her mother's sister. Ted's father wouldn't have called it beaky, long perhaps. And such things could skip a generation, his records proved it. The main thing was, Dad continued, that it worked as a nose; she could breathe perfectly well, which was more than he could say for everyone under his roof.

And finally (he was not finished; Dad seldom was), what about her contempt for that personification of conventional propriety, 'Mrs Grundy'? For the tyranny of 'Grundyism'?*

This would require more explanation. She had never really thought about it before. Ory wondered, when challenged, if she had 'inherited' this character trait from her stepmother, Henrietta Escreet? The Escreet family were connected with the philanthropist Charles Booth, whose revelations about the state of the urban poor in Britain had had a profound effect on the Victorian consciousness. It had soon become clear that her stepmother and her stepmother's sister, Mrs Leighton-Hopkins, had made it a point of principle to get as close to 'disrespectable' people as they possibly could. Whilst her sister was working in the Battersea slums, Henrietta had persuaded Oriana's father to come out of the public school system to be Head of the British Seamen's Orphan Boy's Home in Brixham, Devon.

Ory was only 17 when her father remarried and moved them all to live a salty life amongst the Devon fisherfolk. She suspected that her early life meant that she had grown up to be conventional in some ways, but surviving the rougher edges of the orphanage meant, as she put it later, 'Mrs Grundy's hair must stand on end at some of the things I do.'[10] The Soupers equated contempt for Grundyism with moral courage

---

* Mrs Grundy was a personification of the tyranny of conventional propriety.

and she had been taught to judge her actions by the resulting angle of Mrs Grundy's hair. It was as simple as that. Was that nature or nurture?

Ory found that Ted's family, though scientists, were as religious as hers, but at least only Jim was thinking of reversing his collar. The oldest, Bernard, was a professional soldier. Ted had five sisters, the most able of whom had been educated at Cheltenham Ladies' College, set up in 1853 by Dads' friend, Miss Beale. (The fifth sister, Elsie, had learning difficulties, described by Dad as backward.[11]) Miss Beale's express purpose had been to provide 'a sound education for girls' but to what end? When it came to university, even those educated Wilson girls had been obliged, for financial reasons, to defer to their brothers. The girls had been praised for this act as a shining example of Christian self-sacrifice. (For Ory and Constance it was just 'Life'.) Nellie Wilson, the most academic, had had aspirations to go to university but had become a nurse instead.

As spring turned to summer in 1898, Ted should have been pursuing the fruits of his sister's self-sacrifice as a medical student at St George Hospital in London, but he was not. He was at home pursuing a form of self-education: bed-birding and increasingly, as he grew stronger, chair-birding. From his bedroom window at Westal he could see town birds sitting in the mulberry tree, but he longed to see the Kestrel's Playground, a magical place up on the scarp slope above Cheltenham where raptors spiralled in the updrafts.

Finally, Ted's health seemed to improve and he left Westal for a 2-mile carriage ride up to the Crippetts, the farm his mother rented on the hill above the town. The square bay windows let in big skies and the distant hills of Wales. It had the desired effect and Ted was soon allowed out on short walks accompanied by Miss Souper, who had come chiefly, of course, to see his sisters.

The beech woods poured off the scarp, clinging with their rock-gnarled roots to the steep limestone slopes. Ory and Polly, Ted's favourite sister, accompanied him. The thing was to sit as still as a tree stump until the birds forgot you were there. Ted sketched. He couldn't bear to be with restless people who chivvied him on. Perfect travelling companions sketched.

Ory did not need to be told twice. She sketched but kept none of her pictures. Although she was a 'useful' draughtsman, she felt her efforts lacked significance beside Ted's extraordinary talent, and besides, she had her own theories about artists. There were artistic, creative types and there were practical types. One couldn't expect an artist to, for example, dig a vegetable garden. It just wasn't part of the job description. At the other end of the spectrum, anyone could see that she was a practical type. The Wilson motto '*Res non Verba*' suited her well. Ory's sketching was just a practical way of recording facts, an *aide memoire*.

Miss Souper was never 'Oriana', Mr Wilson never 'Ted', and Polly was a conscientious chaperone. But what about the risk of contagion? More than his disease, Ory found Ted's enthusiasm was contagious. He was never morbid about his illness but calm, stoical and extraordinarily, as it seemed, joyful. Ory flattered him with questions; her own foreshortened schooling had left her self-conscious about the gaps in her knowledge, but she impressed him with her memory.

The pigeons in the granary behind the main house preened each other, billed and cooed. Miss Souper and Mr Wilson 'sitting like ... old stump[s]' watching for raptors.[12] There was something about birds of prey that appealed to Ted. Their superior grace, suppleness and swiftness. In later life, a friend compared Ory to an 'eagle'.[13] Ory was somehow superior, graceful and detached. She was different, she was uncompromising, she was independent.

And nature was uncompromising. Only the fittest survived. Evolution was hard-wired into God's creation and that meant that what humans perceived as cruelty, or heartlessness, lived alongside beauty. Ted had a pet sparrowhawk that had been killed by a pet eagle owl. Birds' sorrows were keen, but short-lived. It was not sad, it was not cruel, it just 'was'. 'All my religious ideas are founded on the principle of evolution driven to its logical conclusion,' Ted told Ory.[14] A tubercular invalid, he had already accepted what his 'logical conclusion' could well be.

As author of *The ABC Poultry Book*, Ted's mother Mary Agnes confessed that her weakness was for chickens, particularly her prize-winning Plymouth Rock.[15] She was a member of the Whishaw family of powerful Anglo–Russian trader-pioneers. One of her brothers had recently gone to live in New Zealand. Genteel Cheltenham was barely challenging enough for Mary Agnes, but at the Crippetts she could channel her settler skills. Ted, contemptuous of domestic birds, hated her raucous

Plymouth Rock cockerel and often threatened to strangle it. His relationship with his mother, perhaps because of the cockerel, was sometimes strained.

But Ted's father and mother were kind to Ory, not just because of their connection through her aunt, Mrs Leighton-Hopkins, the 'Mrs Warden'. From Dr Wilson's perspective, Ory had proved herself an instinctive nurse. From Mrs Wilson's, she seemed to make her, perhaps dying, son happy.

Ory and Ted were 'consciously detached' when he left Cheltenham on doctor's orders for the pure high-altitude air of Norway. If Norway didn't work, it would be the sanatorium in Davos, Switzerland. Ory threw herself into her work at Suffolk Hall and impressed the James' sisters with the recent surge in her enthusiasm for natural science. She was in her element, she loved the boys in her care and one day, perhaps, she would have some of her own.

Through Ted's letters to Polly from Norway, Ory knew that he was still glorying in nature, albeit at a higher latitude and that he was practising his ascetic self-control by drawing mosquitoes, before, during and after they feasted on his arm. But the part of his letters that was most revealing was his contempt for domesticity: 'no one is ever waited on at any meal, and things are not kept hot for one. It is Liberty Hall to the ground. I never realised such freedom.'[16]

Courage by Post

1899–1900

*In which Ory becomes Ted's penfriend. Through her letters she reveals her soul
and he responds. When challenged he denies any romantic intention,
but suddenly changes his mind.*

It was no use thinking of a future with Ted. He was a man who might
not have a future, and even if he did, not one that included settling
down. Ory tried to approach the friendship differently but, in another
striking coincidence, she happened to be back at Suffolk Hall as Ted
returned from Norway in mid-August, well before the start of the academic year. All was well until October 1899, when he developed a fever
and was prescribed a winter's treatment at the sanatorium in Davos.
Ironically, as it turned out, Ted hated snow: 'Awful, awful, I cannot abide
the snow.'[1] The treatment for tuberculosis was gauged according to
the patient's temperature. Those with no temperature were allowed to
smoke. Ted had a temperature and the craving for tobacco made him
want to 'bite everyone and run away!'[2] Thinking about Miss Souper distracted him and somewhere between the Crippetts Wood and the Swiss
Sanatorium, Miss Souper skipped rapidly through familiarity of address
to Oriana, then Ory, and finally simply 'O'. Before Ted left, they had
agreed to write.

Ory briefly returned home to Dorset to help her family move house
to Hilton, Cambridge, where the Reverend Souper had finally been
given a living. With musty packing boxes from Brixham all around her,
Ory sat at the desk in the spare bedroom of her new home, an elegant
Georgian vicarage. She filled her pen carefully, smoothed out a paper on

the leather writing surface and looked out over the wide, flat common that was Hilton Green. A stream ran in front of the house and the hollow golden stems of the common reeds along the far edge rattled softly in the breeze. With the sash window open, she could hear running water. The stream had a little bridge over it, with the garden gate opening out onto the Green. That bridge would be a picturesque place to write a love letter.

Ory stayed at her desk and placed the nib of the pen on the paper. She knew that she could be her best self when writing: people often complimented her on it, she always 'turn[ed] out trumps' in a letter.[3] She was far chattier at a distance. Her letters are breathless. Her written words, often three or four joined together by swooping crossed t's strung across the page. For an outwardly reserved, impeccably dressed, self-possessed young lady, they were surprisingly gushing. Ory's likes and dislikes were pronounced, but when that critical tendency appeared in letters, there was a chance it could be recognised, screwed up and binned. Her passions on paper could, however, run high; sometimes she would, 'fairly boil inside'.[4]

At these times, Ted sent words of calm: 'the only things worth being disappointed in or worrying about are in ourselves, not externals.'[5] For non-Christians, frustrations were a nuisance; for Christians, they were a test from God. The main thing was that it was always 'better to say nothing than to condemn, to laugh with than to criticise, and so much the happier.' Ory bit her lip – most of the time. When her temper got the better of her and she hurt someone's feelings, she gave herself lines reciting the title of a poem by Mary Ann Pietzker that she kept in bold lettering on her mantelpiece: 'Is it Kind? Is it True? Is it Necessary?'[6]

In Davos, however, Dr Huggard was not so confident about a cure. '… got very breathless', wrote Ted, 'had to sit and gasp, my head felt like bursting with the pulsation in it; pulse 168 per minute … For some hours also pleuritic pain in the left lung.' When his sputum was grey, he almost despaired: 'But I got a letter from O, so my left lung may go and bury itself.' By spring, however, the ban on his smoking had been lifted and he now 'Smoked all day!'; 'The joy of tobacco, and life – and ill-health, and how far above them Death, the door to Love and Eternity!'[7]

And as the awful snow began to loosen its grip, he heard a great spotted woodpecker rattling in a fir wood.

Life continued to improve until he came home in May 1900, still on strict orders to live a sedentary life. Ted scoffed to Ory, 'I think it's better to wear a thing when it's good and new, patching the odd corners as they wear out, instead of putting it away carefully year after year until the moths get in, and you find it's no good when at last you think you will wear it.'[8] If Ted had been healthy and the 'settling type', Ory might almost have mistaken that for a proposal? Was it?

'It is much to be wished that Ted had undertaken the treatise that he had promised his mother on Acute Love,' wrote his father in his handwritten memoir of Ted, '… for assuredly the vagaries and contrarieties might have been illustrated in his own person. Ory Souper was at the Crippetts and Platonic friendship had evidently arrived at breaking point …'[9] With his father's blessing, Ted's mother wrote to their son asking his intentions. His reply in the light of future events was remarkable.

Ted wanted adventure not domesticity. He wanted independence not obligation. And above all, he wished that everyone would stop 'fashing' about his damned future and leave him alone: 'I am not engaged to Ory or anyone else nor do I ever intend to be …' He protested that she was just like a sister, like Polly. '[Ory] is a good letter writer and we have written fairly regularly to each other for about a year … now I must leave you to think of the folly of Platonic friendships and the misery they invariably lead to.'[10]

Fortunately Ted was trying to be a doctor not a lawyer. He had convinced no one, least of all himself. But what his mother suggested was ridiculous. He had no occupation or income, both of which were a Victorian prerequisite to even be in a position to propose. He could not 'keep' a wife and could not even muster the health necessary to complete his medical studies. He did not take up the Davos doctor's suggestion that he focus on his painting and become a pathological draughtsman, but returned to Norway to spend the summer there.

Ted hunted rare northern birds from a mountain hut and wrote his theories about 'love' to Ory. He loved everything that God had given life. Even stones. 'There was only *less* life in a stone than in a bud …'[11] Ory may have wondered where she came into the 'stone to bud' theory.

He had said he loved her, but only as much as a stone? Ted knew how to give a girl a compliment!

And had he mentioned that he loved birds? Before he returned to England, Ted meant to get a buzzard chick from an eyrie he had spotted clinging to a vertical cliff. Buzzards were at the top of the food chain, superior, graceful, wild and true; they were 'different', just like Ory.[12]

Ory was back at the Crippetts for supper shortly after Ted's return. The panelled dining room smelled of silver polish and boiled pork, and was lit by the setting sun streaming through the open bay window that looked out towards Wales.

Dad stroked his grey patrician's beard and waited to say grace. At that moment, he was waiting for Ted, who propped his crutches against the wooden panelling and hopped back to stand behind his chair. Ted was typically cheerful about his latest war wound. He had no right to be anything but. It was self-inflicted. He had cut his ankle climbing the cliff to get the buzzard chick and the wound had become infected. But it was worth it. Ted loved the buzzard. It was his pride and joy, tethered, at this moment, to a falconer's perch just outside the window.

There was silence and Dad began to recite the grace, 'for what we are about to receive …' but was interrupted by a wild keening cry. He paused and waited until they could hear the ticking of the grandfather clock in the hall. As he finished, the Plymouth Rock cockerel crowed. Ory had refereed in the James' School playground – was that 'one all'?

Ted pulled out Ory's chair and seated her, before swivelling around his and lowering himself into his seat with his hands. The buzz of conversation rose. Just as Ted was about to pass Ory the shredded cabbage, there was a brown whirlwind of flapping feathers. The crash of glass. A pulled tablecloth. The tinkling of broken china.

The buzzard had got free from its perch, streaked into the room and, breaking to land on the table, skidded on a plate of sliced tomatoes.[13] It was now shaking its wings loosely and surveying the damage with reptilian disinterest.

Ted was delighted. The buzzard had thwarted the stultifying formality of a Victorian meal time. He coaxed the bird towards him whilst reaching into his pocket for the falconer's jessies. Ory watched as the bird relaxed and, as the Wilson family tried to restore order on the table, the bird fell asleep on Ted's lap.

Ted returned to his medical training at St George's Hospital in London in early October (and the buzzard found its way to the London Zoo). But almost immediately, he developed a temperature, compelling him to return to Cheltenham. He had gone down to London 'careless' of his health as usual, but something had changed.

So '… in spite of Ted's very positive assurance to his mother,' wrote Dad, '… it was with no great surprise but with the utmost pleasure that we heard from Ted on Oct 19th that he and Ory found they were just suited to one another.'[14] Perhaps it was simply that Ted had been caught short without a birthday present. Ory was 26 on 19 October 1900.

'Nothing is more extraordinary,' confessed Ted at last, 'than the feeling one has of loving people at first sight, and without a word being spoken. *You* know what I mean.'[15]

After three years of patient waiting, Ory, who had fallen in love at first sight with a healthy medical student with ambitions to go to 'Africa probably', had now aligned her future to a recovering tubercular invalid with uncertain prospects – and yet she could not have been any happier.

4

Birding

1900

In which Ted tries to complete his medical studies so that he can get a job that will enable him to marry. His knowledge of birds leads to a place in the British Ornithological Society – Ted and Ory start the century in ludicrously high spirits.

There was no time for mooning about. The immediate issue was enabling Ted to get his degree and become a doctor. He had two months in which to make good the ground he had lost in eighteen. Was it possible? The German Philosopher Friedrich Nietzsche had just died in August. Ted was happy to embrace his philosophy: 'That which does not kill you makes you stronger.' But he was an invalid, not an *Übermensch* (superman) and there were limits.

Together Ted and Ory set off to find digs in Stanmore, Middlesex. 'No country to be sneezed at …' Ted coughed and Ory agreed. The rooms were rooms, adequate as a base from which to venture out to Stanmore Common to spot 'owls, coot, moorhen, herons, gulls, a tern and even jays, kestrels, sparrow-hawks, nut-hatches, tree creepers and three woodpeckers'.[1] Stanmore Common was a 'bird-haunted' paradise. Ory had by now been thoroughly infected by Ted's passion for ornithology, and was beginning to be able to distinguish between calls, a skill called 'earbirding'. She was learning to be able to count the notes, to work out which notes were repeated, to write down nonsense words, onomatopoeia. With her musical ear she could sketch the sound, a line up if the pitch went up, and down, if it then went down. It was curiously satisfying.

Ory left Ted with his revision and returned to Cheltenham. Suddenly he felt the impact of his engagement. Even in early October, before he had proposed, 'I cared as little about getting well as I cared about being ill, and that wasn't much … Now things are different …'[2] He could be careless about himself but it would be selfish now that he had Ory to consider. From 80 miles away, Ory sent love and motivation, exchanging 'birds spotted' by post.

Ted began to research his thesis, 'Yellow Atrophy of the Liver', and devoted his spare time to drawing as the safest course for a livelihood to support himself and Ory until his health should allow him to take up hospital appointments. Dr Rolleston, who had first diagnosed his tuberculosis, gave him an introduction to *The Lancet* for pathological drawings. As light relief from yellowing livers, Ted also began illustrating *Land and Water*, commissioned by the editor, and his friend, C. E. Walker. Through these connections, he met Dr Philip Sclater, Secretary of the Zoological Society, who would become a pivotal influence in his life. He was already familiar with Sclater's personal collection of 9,000 birds, which had been transferred to the British Museum, and had drawn several of them. Sclater was so impressed that he offered Ted every facility for drawing and studying in the library of the Zoological Society and, despite the forty-year age gap, they became firm friends. Ted's pictures – swallows above the roof tops of Battersea, kestrels over the Crippetts, Great Northern Divers from the rocks of Norway and Alpine Jays of Switzerland – were really more acts of worship than art for its own sake. Ted didn't think they would bear comparison with the masters and he did not want to taint them with commercialism by selling them. It would be like selling a prayer! The fact was that he loved birds, really loved them, and wanted to capture the essence of that love in paint.

He sent in a selection of watercolours and sketches to the British Ornithologists' Union (BOU) for their examination: buzzards and wrens, a nest of pale blue eggs and a selection of details of everything from wing shape to toe configuration and feather barbs. As a rule, he tried to paint birds in motion rather than the static posed pictures based on stuffed animals that were the norm. They were a hit and Ted was immediately proposed and seconded as a member. As an ornithologist, he had arrived. Ory was delighted for him.

In December 1900, Ted went up to Cambridge to sit his finals, his brain bursting with hastily crammed facts. Between exams, Ted stayed for the first time with his prospective in-laws, the Soupers. 'Not many people know their fiancée for three years,' wrote Ted afterwards, 'and get engaged many months before they present themselves to their relations-in-law for approval.'[3]

The Reverend later confided to his daughter that he felt Ted was a 'peacemaker'. It was a careful compliment because Ted was obviously on best behaviour, his Wilson temper well in check. Ted stayed at Hilton for Christmas. With all the Soupers gathered under one roof, there was plenty of opportunity to exercise his talent for diffusing a 'lively' family situation.

Later Ory told Ted what her father had said. 'I want to tell you what an immense help that little remark of your Father's has been to me,' Ted wrote, 'You told me your Father had said I was a "peacemaker". What made him think so I can't guess, but I determined I would try to be one, for I had never thought about the matter before ...'[4] Did Ory sense that underneath her father's observation was the fact that a 'peacemaker' would be the perfect foil for his 'temperamentally critical' daughter? Later a friend observed that, without Ted's ameliorating influence, Ory lacked 'the balance of her husband's wider, wiser tolerance'.[5]

On Christmas Eve at Hilton, icicles hung, glistening from the eaves. The men and women were taking turns through the verses of 'Good King Wenceslas' before they tramped in single file through the snow to the flint-built St Mary Magdalene for the umpteenth time that day. Ted was beginning to realise that the Souper girls churched, but they had also decorated the house with shiny holly and fir, and the scent of dark green pine, candle wax and log fires filled the air. Ted retired to his room to finish his Christmas letter: 'This is a home letter for you all, ALL at Westal, married or single, maiden ladies or aunts, insects or Buzzard Eagles,' Ted wrote in ludicrously high spirits. 'Anyone who is keen on Christmas presents may choose anything they like up to fifteen or twenty shillings, but O. and I are both blowed if we will pay for them because we neither of us have any money to spare.'

If, however, anyone felt like sending them money he would spend it on 'Clifford Allbutt's six volumes, on a microscope, on a case for hypodermic injection, and …', through the door he could hear Ory's strong clear voice as she and Constance launched into the descanted last verses of 'Come all ye faithful', ' … and any small sum that may be left over on some furniture for our house, because we must have a good piano.'[6]

5

Bolt from the Blue

1900–01

In which Ory is obliged to write a prenuptial letter saying that Ted's decision to go on Scott's Antarctic expedition is mutual. Ted feels that this is a reasonable request, but how much choice does she have?

Neither Ted nor Ory had ever known anything but the widow Queen. Prince Albert had died in 1861 and by the time Ory was born, mourning had become the chief concern of Victoria's existence. Ory was only just engaged, and being widowed was the very last thing on her mind until, suddenly, she found herself staring it in the face.

It had begun with a letter described (again by Dad) as 'a bolt from the blue'.[1] Who would have thought that, by joining the BOU, Ted would be putting himself forward for Junior Surgeon and Vertebrate Zoologist for the forthcoming British National Antarctic Expedition?

What would Antarctica have meant to Ory? The blank patches on the school globe where it was held on its axis. What was there? Did magnetic fields result, as some thought, in an icy maw – an axis point exerting a physical attraction? Or was it a scantily clad lady hovering, impervious to cold, like a Siren above a field of snow? The most famous icy adventures had been led by John Franklin in a fatal attempt to find a navigable Northwest Passage over America in the 1840s. Franklin's widow, Jane, who died the year after Ory was born, had spent the rest of her life trying to find their bodies in an effort to dispel rumours of cannibalism. But that was the Northern Hemisphere, almost familiar territory in comparison with the South.

Whatever Ory's South Pole was, it was dangerous. No one disputed that. No wonder Dad had called it 'a bolt from the blue'. From songbirds to the South Pole in one leap? It hardly made sense. The connection was Dr Philip Slater. When Ted protested that he felt unqualified, Sclater replied, 'I am on the Committee that makes the appointments, and my opinion is that you would be a suitable person for the post.'[2]

This 'bolt' struck Ory's pigeon hole in the school post room in early June. But the news that buzzed around the classrooms at Suffolk Hall was that that General Roberts, had just accepted the surrender of Pretoria, the capital of the South African Republic. Finally, the end of the second Anglo-Boer War was surely in sight.

Ory tried to digest the implications of Ted's news in an atmosphere of relief and celebration. Even at Westal there were the beginnings of tentative festivity. Ted's older brother Bernard, who had been fighting in South Africa, would soon be home safe.

At Stanmore, Ted was more circumspect. He had not responded to the government call for volunteers. It was not his lungs. For all his celebration of avian predators, of birds that could inflict mortal wounds on their unsuspecting prey from a clear blue sky, Ted confided that he 'would sooner shoot myself than anyone else by a long, long way. I simply could not do it.'[3]

Ory, surrounded by the jingoistic sons of Empire and the public school brigade, was nursing Ted's anti-war principles. General Sir Redvers Buller, the *Cheltenham Examiner* reported, had withdrawn his troops early in order to prevent men like Bernard becoming isolated in an exposed bridgehead across the Tugela River. Buller was nicknamed 'Sir Reverse'. To those in the drawing room, reversals and retreats were deemed unacceptable. How did Ory feel about this? Was it always better to 'do or die'? Or were there situations when it was better to prevent men like Bernard becoming cannon fodder in the manner of Tennyson's 'The Charge of the Light Brigade'? In a phrase that came up often in the press at the time, which was better, a 'Dead lion, or live donkey?' It was a question that would come up again in what Antarctic adventurer Ernest Shackleton would later call 'White Warfare' – polar exploration, that battle without guns.

On 7 June 1900, Ted left Stanmore for Cheltenham to discuss his options with Ory. If he took the two-year contract he had been offered at St George's Hospital in Hyde Park, he could 'keep' Ory financially if he didn't become 'soot-sodden'. The Antarctic expedition also offered a salary. He could 'keep' Ory a world away if he didn't become snow-sodden. Soot or snow? For a while it looked like one or the other.

Ted had the better education, but intellectually Ory could hold her own. However, when they discussed love, Ted brought up the 'selfishness' of love. Ted wanted a love that did not involve 'jealous exclusion'. 'Human nature is jealous and selfish, and it's just this that we have to keep well in hand ...'[4] But Ted guiltily reminded himself that 'What is right for one may still be wrong for another ...' What was right for Ted might be wrong for Ory.

In order to ensure that the discussion had been concluded, Ted asked Ory to write him a letter to which they could both refer, to remember that the decision to apply for the post on the Antarctic expedition had been mutual.

What was her legal position? Under English Law the role of the wife was as a 'feme covert' so that, upon marriage, the husband and wife became one person. The Married Women's Property Act was passed in England when Ory was eight but for Victorian upper middle classes, the concept of female empowerment lagged behind the law. In the 'Solemnization of Matrimony' in the Church of England's Common Prayer, Ted as 'the man', would promise to love, comfort, honour and keep her, whilst Ory 'the woman', would promise 'obey him and serve him'. We know that Ted took this literally. In marrying him, Ory would 'give herself away to me'.[5]

As for living apart from one's husband, 'grass widows' were two-a-penny at that time in Cheltenham. The term was slang from the British Raj for wives sent away during the hot summer to the cooler (and greener) hill stations while their husbands remained on duty in the plains. If they married, Ory would become Ted's 'grass widow' and she would be in good company.

The letter only exists as a reference in Dad's handwritten memoir of Ted.[6] If it was ever in Ory's possession, she made quite sure it is no longer available for analysis.[7]

We know that, as Ted saw it, he hadn't sought out the Antarctic expedition, it had sought him, ergo it was God's will. Would Ted have been able to marry a girl who would thwart him and God in a single refusal? He might have gone anyway explaining his detachment from Ory as another form of self-sacrifice demanded by God.

As Ted saw it, God's guidance was 'like being taken by the scruff of the neck by an invisible angel'[8] and pointed in the right direction. One was expected to put one's hand to the plough: 'He does not like us to look back after putting out hands to the plough, He often takes the plough away as soon as he knows we mean to carry through.'[9] Ory might have wished that angel would hurry up and whisk that plough right out of sight. What they were dealing with was the primacy of the male decision to explore, of which female endurance was the consequence. But although it confirmed the different destinies of men and women, they could unite on the ground of mutual sympathy.

After Ory had signed that letter, Ted wrote in gratitude describing her removing all the thorns from his path: 'My maid, my maid, you picked them all off for me.' He wanted to marry her because of the feeling she gave him 'more than anyone else on earth, I mean the quick understanding your love gives you, you read me … you understand what I mean.'[10]

Signing the 'mutual decision' contract cannot have been easy for Ory. We can speculate that it may just have been the hardest thing she had ever been asked to do. We know, although she did not at this point, that it would not be the hardest thing she ever had to do. Or that an accumulation of such moments would be her fate.

But then, in another twist, Ted landed the job of Junior House Surgeon at Cheltenham General, starting on 20 September; perhaps there would be a third way between the soot and the snow. Ory was so relieved, she even wondered about leaving her job at the James' school and joining him as a nurse. 'I so long that you may come to work in the wards of a big Hospital,' Ted had written during their early acquaintance. 'Women know by instinct how to nurse … you are so very quick to grasp what is wanted & how it should be done.'[11] The Wilsons weren't keen. Ted's sister, Nellie, had died whilst nursing a typhoid patient, after all. Risk was tricky. It was a male prerogative, except for childbirth, of course.

After a blissful August, Ted found his House job at Cheltenham General hard and stressful. Soon he was back in the sickroom. This time it was not his lungs. He had pricked his finger during a post-mortem, resulting in blood poisoning and an abscess in the axilla. Ory could dress wounds but Ted required morphia injections day and night to manage what he admitted was the worst week of illness and pain he had ever had to endure.

On 22 November, three months later, Ted was still determined to go down to London to see Captain Robert Falcon Scott. Scott, a 32-year-old Royal Naval officer, had recently been appointed by the President of the Royal Geographic Society, Sir Clements Markham, to lead the British Antarctic Expedition. Ted could only wave Ory goodbye with his good hand, the other was still in a sling. Despite the sling, he told Ory that in London, Scott had offered him the appointment if his health continued to be satisfactory. There was still that 'if'.

Ted was in a state of suspended animation. On the one hand he was 'if possible even more hopelessly in love than before' – he had to come away from Cheltenham sometimes to get perspective and 'pick myself up'.[12] On the other hand, he thanked God that, 'Ory and I have seen and marvelled at so much of obvious guidance even against our wills in our life that we neither of us have the least fear of the outcome of the future.'[13]

In January 1901, 'much against my own and everyone else's will' Ted caught the 7.20 a.m. train for London.[14] His fiancée did not accompany him. Ory voted with her feet, providing an insight into her stand on 'will'. For this part of the story Ted took his stalwart sister, Polly. Together they descended, into a pea-souper of a London smog where the street lamps were lit even in the middle of the day. Shortly after the interview with Scott, Ted was put on the expedition pay roll. The money was welcome, although it made the possibility of separation more real. For the first time Ted was financially independent. He and Ory were in a position to get married.

On 22 January 1901, the 81-year-old Queen Victoria died. She was in her bedroom at Osborne House. Dr James Reid, her personal physician, had noticed that her speech had become slightly slurred and the left-hand side of her face had begun to sag. In the room as she died was her son, who would succeed her as King Edward VII, and her grandson,

Kaiser Wilhelm II who, thirteen years later, would lead German forces against Britain in the First World War.

Mary Agnes, Ted's mother, ordered yards of black mourning crepe from the Cheltenham haberdashery. She went down to the Isle of Wight to watch the old Queen's funeral procession, whilst her husband could not get inside the doors of the service at Gloucester Cathedral, 'so great was the crush in every avenue'.[15]

Over the question of her son's marriage, Mary Agnes made her position clear. In looks and dress and in the characteristic that her husband noted [in that infamous *Family Faculties* book] as 'downright and difficult to tire', she was almost indistinguishable from the late Queen.[16] Right at that moment, she must have appeared to Ory to be equally formidable.

Ted's mother was strongly against marrying before the expedition. This son of hers had nearly died of tuberculosis. She was extremely worried that Ted's health might suffer by 'adding to the burden of his responsibilities'.[17] By 'responsibilities' she meant children. Waiting was, as Ory should know, considered to be a wholesome occupation for any couple. It was what any sensible girl in her position (and in their right mind) would do.

Ory's uncle was in the Indian Army, and most of her charges at the James' were military. She knew the rules.[18] A subaltern may not marry, captains might marry, majors should marry and lieutenant-colonels must marry. Once a man married he was thought to become soft and incapacitated as a man of action because of the conflicting claims on his energies and sense of duty. Married to a healthy young woman, General Sir William Bellairs suggested, 'you cannot reasonably expect to have fewer babies to provide for than one in every second year …' But Ted was not a soldier and he left the decision about whether to marry before or after the expedition up to his fiancée rather than his mother.

Ory was no longer 'the vicar's eldest daughter' beholden to her elders and betters. She was an independent, salaried woman. She had tried to give the matter serious thought yet the rational part of her brain didn't seem to be working (what was a 'right mind' after all?) Whatever her future mother-in-law thought – in Ory's heart she had no doubt. She would rather be a widow than a spinster (even perhaps a 'single-handed mother'). She braced herself for the event of a 'non-return', but she couldn't really imagine the possibility. They agreed to delay setting a date until after a final decision on the Antarctic team had been reached.

Ted again went down to London. He was passed 'fit'. As he left the interview, his conscience smote him and he went back in and confessed to his tubercular-scarred lungs. But Scott had made his decision and told Ted he could come on his own risk. Ted made his decision. 'If the climate suits me,' he said later (to everyone but Ory) 'I shall come back more fit for work than ever, whereas if it doesn't, I think there is no fear of me coming back at all.'[19]

Ted left Scott, walked around the corner to the telegram office and sent a message to Ory. The telegram arrived by bicycle boy at the Hilton Vicarage within hours.

Ory sat at her Singer sewing machine. It was an old friend: reliable, useful and undemanding. Its comforting whirr was like soothing music in an upside-down world. She opened her mother's old sewing box and inhaled its old lace. She could hear the birds on Hilton Green as they sang about their business-as-usual, oblivious to the turmoil of the human heart. She chose strong white thread and spooled it onto the bobbin and then replaced it in its case under the foot. Familiar automatic movements. Something to do with her hands. Carefully she licked the end of the thread and rotated the hand wheel towards her until the needle rose. She took up the smooth pieces of white satin and pinned them vertically along the near edge. As she rocked the treadle with her foot, the threads passed through the material, one from the needle in the north, one from the bobbin in the south, slip-stitching a path through.

6

A Summer Wedding

1901

In which Ted and Ory marry and then try to fit a whole marriage, highs and lows, into the two weeks before the Discovery *sets sail for Antarctica. Ory, waving her hanky, promises to be cheerful and Ted knows she will try.*

It was 16 July 1901, and a high blue sky arched over the flat Cambridgeshire fens. The church bells peeled out across the village green, as the wheels of Ory's open landau crunched to a halt on the gravelled track that led to the lychgate of St Mary Magdalene. Every one of her father's parishioners seemed to be lining the path to the handsome flint church and a man in a brown suit scribbled in a reporter's pad. Ted was already newsworthy, touched, even if only in theory, by the great mystery of the Unknown. The knight off to erase the 'taint of ignorance' from the map at the bottom of the globe.

The knight and his lady had been together all morning (blow the Mrs Grundys, who said they shouldn't see each other before the ceremony) arranging the tables on the lawn. Ory knew she should enjoy herself. She tried to fix the moment: the damp cool air of the church, the heady scent of orange blossom from her headdress and the strong white notes of the trumpet lilies in her bouquet would stay with her forever. Constance and Polly, both dressed in full-length white dresses (each with a thin black ribbon as a nod to the late Queen), straightened Ory's white satin train.

Ory was extremely thin (she had been obliged to drink Maltine, 'a dreadful concoction', to build herself up for the day)[1] but she had sewed the dress to fit like a second skin. Her brother Adrian struck up on the organ and, as she glided up the aisle on her father's arm, she put the congregation in mind of a swan. Both Ory and Ted were in their finest plumage. Their courtship was complete, in a few moments they would be bonded for life. Their migration would be staggered. In just over a fortnight, Ted would be gone.

Ted's father watched from the groom's side of the church. 'They were very quietly happy. The service and singing were most impressive. Special psalms having been chanted, the address was given by Canon Escreet, Rector of Woolwich.'[2] Ory's step-uncle, Mr Leighton-Hopkins, who had first introduced them in Battersea, officiated. Ted felt there was 'plenty of music and a general feeling of happiness all round'.[3]

Mr and Mrs Edward Adrian Wilson walked out of the church over rose petals strewn by the village children. It was the only rose-petalled path Ted was ever likely to walk and, even now, they had arrived at it crunching over a drift of dead bees on the tiled floor.[4] (They hadn't been there when they'd decorated the church – where on earth had they come from?)

Before the guests returned to the vicarage for the wedding breakfast, the principal players stood stock still for photographs. It was the beginning of an awfully big adventure for all of them. This photograph would be the record of 'before' – would there be an 'after'? They were stern, serious and brave.

Ory, standing beside her new husband, looks severe. She had not entered into this marriage lightly, but as the traditional church service dictated: 'reverently, discreetly, advisedly, soberly' and on her knees. She was utterly exhausted. Dark sleepless circles around her eyes might have been spectacles. And even though Ted's photographic face was not a window into his elated soul, he later wrote that he was 'as happy as it is given for mortals to be on this earth'. He had his 'maid', he had his 'adventure', his maid 'approved' his adventure (he still had her letter of consent to prove it), it really couldn't get better.[5]

At 4 p.m. Ory changed out of her swan suit and she and Ted left for the train to Pinner. They arrived at 10 p.m. 'It would be absurd to try to write down the joy of this short time together,' wrote Ted, trying to write it down. They had to nest, create new life perhaps and try to live an entire marriage in a fortnight, just in case. Like a long marriage, there were highs and lows. To start with, there was Ted's mistress, the *Discovery*. Even the first day was a trial. It was spent aboard the expedition ship, lying at Blackwall in East London. It was almost an Edwardian marriage in which three was a couple. Ory had a bad headache, but Ted introduced her to every one of the scientific staff and their wives and mothers and was delighted to find that she was 'fully appreciated'.

But by Monday 22 July, things were improving. Ory's head had cleared, she rallied and it was her, rather than Ted, who acted as *Discovery* tour guide for twenty of her relations. They missed the train to Pinner and luxuriated in 'an extravagant dinner' at the Euston Hotel. '... home rather late'.

On 23 July, Ted's 29th birthday, they called on Captain Scott's mother, Hannah, in Chelsea, and Ory met his sisters for the first time. The Scott sisters had been obliged to sew for a living and it embarrassed them. (Their father had died leaving debts that their modestly salaried naval brother, Robert, would take years to pay off.) The Scotts had stooped to 'trade' of necessity but, for Ory, sewing clothes was just what one did. Ory had begun embroidering the Wilson motto onto Ted's sledge pennant. Which stitch suited letters best, did they think? And how should she finish off round the swallow-tailed edge. Blanket stitch or cord? Finally, on Tuesday 30 July, Ted's 'mistress' left the East India Docks, 'Cameras going off in all directions.' Ted had been given special permission to slip away and so went home to Pinner.

With the licence of marriage, their relationship was overflowing. In an effort to try to capture it forever, they took a cab to Thomson's, a photographer. Ted knew of one in Pimlico. The cabbie thought Bond Street. Like 'a pigheaded ass', Ted insisted. The cabbie had been right, damn it. They had no time for this! Ted lost his temper. That was the gritty side of married life. And as they arrived, flustered at the door of Thomson's Bond Street, so was the need to pretend that everything was – just fine.

Did Mr and Mrs Wilson want a background? A *trompe l'oeil* landscape, a drawing room? Ted and Ory saw a plain black piece of canvas draped over a screen at the back of the studio. Could they have that? Just that?

Then they had to choose a pose. One seated, one standing? One seated, one leaning over ...? Ted and Ory stood beside each other. They wanted the least artifice possible. To the photographer, it seemed almost scandalously plain. A potted fern?

They stared into the camera. The man disappeared behind his black photographer's shroud and they sat rigid whilst he counted down. There was a sudden pop and then a slow hiss as the magnesium flash filled the room with a blinding light. Had Ory blinked? She thought she had. Ted's pupils had contracted to pin pricks but he made himself keep his eyes open. Again? But it was impossible. Who could keep their eyes open with that going on!

They emerged blinking into the daylight. The thing was done. Captured. One marriage. Would the photographer give them all the photographs, even the ones where Ory closed her eyes? Those iceberg eyes were her signature feature, but Ory was beyond caring. They were running out of time, even the duds were evidence.

And a marriage wasn't complete without tears. On Saturday 3 August, they had to pack up Pinner. 'It was very, very difficult to pretend to be cheerful … Alas, there was a sound of weeping and woe.' They both wondered whether they had 'had the very cream of this life's happiness'. Ted, a man with an almost unhealthy obsession with heaven, even wondered if he had had the cream of happiness '… of the next life too'.

Their last night together would be spent in the Grosvenor Hotel, Southsea, looking over the Solent. Ted was finishing a report on seals for the Natural History Museum and Ory sat with him making a fair copy. From shortly after breakfast on Monday 5 August, everything changed.

As Ory waited for a cab at the Grosvenor, Ted, on board the *Discovery*, was shaking King Edward VII's hand. He'd come on board with the Queen and Princesses. Ted was amused to see the King struggle as he reached around his portly figure into his coat pocket for the Victorian Order of the Fourth Class for Captain Scott.

Ted spent the night in his cabin. It was, he noted, his first 'alone'. Ory was also practising 'alone' at the Grosvenor, but by the next morning she was back on board, and with her sister, Constance. The *Discovery* weighed anchor and set off to the west. Ory and Ted sailed together all morning until the ship reached Yarmouth, where 'we had to say good bye for several years'.

Ory had given Ted a pair of Zeiss binoculars and through them he could spot his mate clearly in her grey skirt and black hat, waving her hanky. She had promised him to be cheerful and he knew that she would try. She was a woman of her word.

'And so we at last were really off, and I on board, and Ory on land, left for three years. Dear old maid, may God keep us for one another, and we shall be ever more happy then.' To himself, Ted wondered whether Ory would be the one 'taken'. She was 'the very breath of [my] exist-ence ...' and in his experience, such precious things were often the most vulnerable.[6]

7

Marriage by Mail

1900–01

In which Ory starts her 'marriage by post' going 'on honeymoon' with her sister, where she gets dangerously ill. Living at Westal without Ted is hard. She tries to be a dutiful daughter-in-law, but is thankful when she leaves for New Zealand.

Two young women in full-length dresses and leather walking shoes sit on the grassy bank. Ory props her red canvas-covered Baedeker guide on her knees, closes her eyes and breathes pine-scented air. Before he left, Ted planned a substitute Alpine 'honeymoon' for Ory in order to 'try to forget me' and it was a lovely idea.[1]

At first Ory thought that her lack of energy was due to the altitude. She was exhausted by the slightest thing. Even a slow amble made her ribs ache and her head pound. Her cough had started as a nuisance tickle but now it had developed into a chesty affair and she found herself sounding remarkably like Ted. Perhaps the mental strain of last few months had taken its toll on her physically. Constance took her to the doctor, who diagnosed pneumonia.

The sisters left the surgery each in their private world. Pneumonia was the disease that had 'taken' their mother. She, Ory argued, had been weakened by childbirth. Was Ory pregnant? Was the process or even the inferred process of begetting children something these motherless sisters could discuss? The important thing was, could Ory overcome the infection? (Penicillin was twenty-seven years off.) The 'breath of existence'.[2] Had Ted tempted fate? Had he been right to worry about the real danger of her surviving his adventure?

Five years younger than Ory, Constance was only 8 when their mother died and her relationship with Ory was more mother–daughter than that of sisterly equals. They looked very similar, although Ory had softer features. But Constance, less formidable, was the sister more readily warmed to. Where Ory was self-assured, capable and no-nonsense, Constance was sensitive, naturally self-deprecating and gentle. She 'suffered with her nerves' and it showed. This new situation, with Ory as the more vulnerable half of the pair, was unfamiliar. Eventually, with Constance as a patient nurse, Switzerland effected its cure and the sisters returned home.

'Perhaps the greatest joy at Madeira to everyone,' wrote Ted on 14 August, 'certainly for me, was the mail. I had more than anyone, I think, and letters that made me intensely happy.' Getting 'mail' was bizarrely competitive. Ted was the current favourite. (No mention of pneumonia.) 'Dear Ory, I knew you would turn out trumps …'[3]

Ory wrote letters addressed to the ports along his route. Ted had, meanwhile, written to her and the ship carrying them 'crossed in the post'. News had to be pieced together in retrospect like a puzzle, and some pieces didn't fit. The newspapers covering the expedition misreported, but their telegrammed news often arrived before Ted's letters could set the record straight. In addition, the postal system was expensive and corrupt. Letters were paid for by the recipient, rather than the sender, and were charged according to distance travelled and the number of sheets used. Ory had already posted letters to Madeira, the *Discovery's* first port of call, but they posted their Swiss 'journal letters' from England to Cape Town. As a result of the Boer War, mails were sent there weekly and took only two weeks to arrive.

Even the act of writing was comforting for Ory. Letters were a way of releasing the imaginary conversations she had with Ted in her head. Ted kept all the letters he received, they made him 'intensely happy'.[4] Much later, when they came into Ory's possession, she burned them. Her early life as a 'grass widow' is inferred from the extracts of Ted's letters she allowed his biographer to immortalise. Ted's letters to Polly, however, survived and from them we can feel Ted's longing even now. 'I love her as I have never loved anyone, and she loves me as she has never loved anyone and it is an awful thing this separation …'[5]

Ory began her life as a hybrid, half wife, half matron. She and Ted had decided that although she would live in the rooms prepared for them at Westal, she would continue at the James' school until the end of the academic year. It was not only the independence Ory wanted, it was a reason to be out of the house. It was only for a year after all and she would be up and down to Hilton in the holidays. She had already booked her passage to New Zealand to be there for Ted's return the following spring.

Ted's parents tried to make Ory feel at home. They joked about their prodigal son. Mary Agnes organised a photograph of Ted's 'special wife' to send him. The image she sought was a painterly Victorian tableau, full of symbols of fidelity and waiting. Captioned 'Alone Once More', the picture is composed as a remembrance portrait, suggestive of the fact that Mary Agnes regarded her son's departure as a kind of death. Ory's submission to this sentimental Victorianism reveals a determination to play the dutiful daughter-in-law. But it was not easy. Her expression is direct, but she looks tense and tired, with frown lines and shadows under her eyes.

Mary Agnes had been opening letters addressed to Mrs E. Wilson for many years (her husband was Edward Thomas Wilson, her son, Edward Adrian). Letters addressed in her son's writing were, she assumed, for her. In a letter to his mother, Ted tried to iron out any jealousies between the women of Westal: 'I think you won't altogether mind that nearly everything I write and draw and do now goes first to Ory,' he wrote to his mother. 'Put yourself in my place honestly and I think you will see that it is the right thing for me to do. You must be very grateful to her because she has made all this time so much happier and easier for me whom you all love … Tho' I act the prodigal.'[6] To avoid having to wrestle the post off her mother-in-law, Ory asked to be addressed as Mrs Ted Wilson.

From Ted's letters, Ory realised that he was becoming firm friends with Ernest Shackleton, who had already become 'Shackles'. Shackles had arranged shade for his new red-haired, fair-skinned doctor friend to write and sketch in. 'I think,' wrote her husband, 'that Shackleton has so far done more hard work than anyone on board.'[7] Shackleton, a 27-year-old Merchant Navy officer, had worked alongside Cedric Longstaff, the son of the *Discovery* expedition's greatest benefactor, Llewellyn Longstaff.

Shackleton's obvious enthusiasm for the expedition convinced Longstaff senior to request a position for him on the *Discovery*.

In the same postbag as Ted's first letters to Ory was a letter from Shackleton to the father of a society lady, a Miss Emily Dorman. The timing was deliberate. Shackleton hoped that Charles Dorman had seen the expedition's royal send-off in the newspapers and been impressed. Shackleton was just a merchant seaman but he was ambitious and determined to marry up.

Emily Dorman was not sufficiently 'official' to have been on the *Discovery* as it sailed east down the Solent. She had not even been at East India Docks when Shackleton had semaphored goodbye to his sisters with flags. Now as Ted and Shackleton's letters sailed north from Madeira to their loved ones, the men themselves sailed south.

On 13 September they put in at South Trinidad, an island that had never before been scientifically explored. To Ted's delight, it was 'alive with birds that knew no fear'.[8] Ted heard a new call, 'a most delightful noise between the drumming of a snipe and the bubbling note of a cuckoo, arranged rather like the spring song of the common sandpiper.' It was a petrel he had never seen before. He shot one and prepared it as a specimen for the British Museum. Its plumage changes made its identity difficult to determine but it was taken back in a report for the Royal Geographical Society and provisionally named *Aestralata wilsoni*.[9]

On 3 October, when the *Discovery* arrived at Cape Town, South Africa, there was an undignified dash for the postbag. Mail had gone astray, long-expected letters were missing. 'I was lucky for I had about ten,' wrote Ted in his diary that night, 'but then mine's a special sort of wife.'[10]

Even though Ory was on the other side of the world, she was more intimately connected with him, with Ted's innermost thoughts, than those with whom he shared every waking moment. While Ory strove to curb her critical temperament at Westal and think before she committed words to paper, Ted wrestled with the irksome discipline of the British Navy. 'God knows it is just about as much as I can stand at times, and there is absolutely no escape. I have never had my temper so tried as it is every day now, but I don't intend to give way … It's a hard school down here.'[11] When the ship reached Lyttelton, New Zealand, at midnight on

28 November, Shackleton set off to wake the postmaster. No one questioned his impatience. (If he survived the adventure, Emily, her father Charles Dorman assured him, could be his.)

When the *Discovery* arrived in New Zealand, the English newspapers were full of reports that the boat leaked. Photographs showed it being dry docked with gallons of water pouring out of the hull. At Westal they worried that Ted might drown before he ever reached Antarctica. The newspapers, Ted warned Ory, were written with an eye to sensational headlines and without concern for peoples' feelings, and it disgusted him. She should be warned that when in Antarctica it might take a year to correct a misunderstanding.

The day before the *Discovery* left for the South, the Eastern Extension Telegraph Co. allowed final farewell messages to be sent home free of charge. On Christmas Eve 1901, whilst the Wilson family gathered at Westal, Ted sailed south from Port Chalmers bound for the Antarctic ice. The Wilsons had been married for five-and-a-half months, only three weeks of which they had spent together. Now they would not hear from each other until the expedition relief ship, the *Morning,* sailed south in a year's time. There would be no more letters. The long silence had begun.

The Voyage Out

1902–03

In which Ory and Constance begin their adventure. Ory is fixed on the idea of a reunion in the spring and has set herself to that mark. They travel with emigrants and quickly adapt to a life reminiscent of a floating boarding school.

There was still the lingering sense of farewell as the white cliffs of Dover slipped into the distance. Many of the people on deck looked wistfully backwards. But Ory had done her farewelling. She was finally heading in the right direction, doing something active and practical about closing the distance between her and Ted rather than just treading water at Westal and refereeing in the Suffolk Hall playground.

Constance came too. She had passed the Queen's Scholarship to teacher training college and obtained a post at a mission school in New Zealand's North Island. Woodford, their brother, was already out there teaching at a school in Marton. In fact, half the Souper siblings would be in the Southern Hemisphere within a couple of months, but they would be visitors. Most of the ship's passengers had bought a one-way ticket. The New Zealand government had been advertising the potential of emigration to 'God's Own Country', with what seemed to Ory, looking around the deck of the liner, to be conspicuous success.

Both Woodford and Ted's New Zealand cousins, the Whishaws, had warned her about the journey. Everything would depend upon 'what kind of a sailor she was'. At 12 p.m., the officers checked their position on the globe using a sextant. The sun's midday position told them the number of miles they had steamed in twenty-four hours. A daily sweepstake was held on the distance and the nearest guess gained a prize.[1]

Ory knew that the scale along the bottom of the isochronic school map measured distance in days. Six weeks of sea sickness would be suffering indeed, but Ory found to her delight that she was not sick, but a good sailor. In fact, she was in her element.

Even the architecture suited her. It was 'useful' rather than showy, functional rather than 'affected' and Ory felt curiously at home. She realised that perhaps travelling between places – being busy just sitting still – suited her restless nature and her compulsion to fill Rudyard Kipling's 'unforgiving minute' more than settling, after all.

For Ory and Constance, who had been born in boarding schools, living in a ship was familiar, like living in a floating school, but without being on matron duty. The sleeping arrangements were not luxurious; in both first and second class, a two-berth cabin had two bunk beds with a ladder. A basin area could be curtained off. There was central catering, the top table presided over by the captain-headmaster. The ship's life settled into a routine of starched white tablecloths, shining cutlery and 'Grape Nuts' for breakfast. Cups of beef tea were served at 11 o'clock each day.

The deck was an undulating playing field, swabbed each morning, rather than mowed. There were sports afternoons, often deck quoits where players took turns to throw rope hoops over targets on the deck. Ory had always loved school games and was relieved to see that quoits was not as spiteful as croquet, a game she'd never liked. Callisthenic body weight exercise classes were popular. Unusually these exercises (designed by Catherine Beecher in the mid-nineteenth century) were designed for women as well as men. They used the principle of resistance training to develop physical fitness. After exercises, they washed in sea water that refused to lather up.

If the ship was a boarding school, the kit list was comprehensive. Some people even had kit houses in the hold. Emigrant families might start in tents, A-frames or boarding houses. As soon as they could acquire 'a piece' (of land) they would set up their diamond-pane-windowed cottage and try to replicate Boulton & Paul's catalogue suggestion of hollyhocks and afternoon tea.

A Norwich-based manufacturing company, Boulton & Paul, had cornered the British Empire market. They left catalogues on board ships for passengers to send last-minute orders back from ports on the voyage out. The index of their catalogue began with Arboretum Shelter and continued via Ballrooms, Carriage Washing Sheds, Cottages, Dove Cotes, Farm Buildings, Grand Stands, Houses for Bears and Kangaroos to Tennis Pavilions, Umbrella Stands and Unclimbable Hurdles, and finally, the ubiquitous Verandahs. Carriage was paid to most railway stations in England, from which a place in the hold of a ship could be booked. The size of the B&P one had ordered was the measure of one's ambition. Taking a prefabricated piece of England as part of your luggage was just, well, common sense.

Ory, for once, had not been entirely practical. She had sky blue cotton frocks for the tropics and the old grey skirt she'd worn seeing Ted off. She planned to wear it when she first saw him to allay his fears that she would be unrecognisably 'fashionable' in some dreadful Edwardian 'swan corset' – her bosom thrust forward, her bustled behind, back – by the time he returned. She had also packed her wedding dress as well as a white chiffon tea gown. As a *Discovery* expedition wife, Ory imagined she might be asked 'out to tea' and the Edwardian 'teagie' was required for keeping up fashionable appearances. Put that way, it was almost practical. Part of the explorer's wife kit list. At any rate, she had come prepared!

Like a boarding school, life was lived in public, but sometimes when Ory wanted privacy, she retired to their cabin and read, whilst Constance took up her needlework. Ory had always been keen on theatre and she had seen photographs of Ted as Henry Thornton, dressed up in Regency costume, wig and all, for a family production of W.S. Gilbert's burlesque romantic drama *Engaged*. He still quoted it occasionally when feeling inappropriate: 'Marriage is a very risky thing; it's like Chancery, once in it you can't get out of it, and the costs are enormous.' Amongst Ory's books to read on the voyage was another play, *The Ticket of Leave*, by Watts Phillips, which had sold out in London for several seasons. The men had taken it to the Antarctic to entertain themselves through the long winter and as Ory read parts out to Constance from the bottom bunk, they giggled at the absurd farce. They wondered which of the *Discovery* men would be playing the ladies? Shackleton was in charge of costumes – there were rumours of frocks and fans. In the script, it suggested that the character called 'Emily' wear a pink bonnet. It was fun to picture Shackleton in a pink bonnet, or Scott, or even Ted. The script's terminology was a secret code. Aboard ship, Ory and Constance were, according to Watts Philips, 'gradely lasses', but they mixed with people of different classes from 'China ware' to 'Earthen ware', and enjoyed it.[2]

Sometimes Ory felt as if she was confined to the school grounds. Always a dawn riser, she took a brisk daily constitutional walk around the empty deck. The sun rose earlier and earlier, and it was important to adjust to the fact that New Zealand would be twelve hours behind the UK. The weather made sea swells so regular that you could be all day walking up or down hill on the deck. Ory's new binoculars seemed to snatch birds right out of the sky. If a bird flew past she tried to fix its flight path, its 'jizz', with pencil strokes in her sketch pad. Ted was already familiar with the signature movement made by a pointed winged tern, for example. It meant that he could spot birds on the edge of his vision. But for Ory gulls were still gulls. The thing was to draw them; it forced one to observe more closely. In the Southern Ocean, albatrosses floated on waves of air, just above mast level.

Sometimes, the 'gradely lasses' were given permission for a temporary weekend's leave. In every port, the sisters made the most of the thirty-six hour turnaround for adventures. They pounded up and down hills, and packed in as much sight-seeing as they could. Ted had stopped in Madeira, but commercial liners stopped at Tenerife, in the Canary Islands, Cape Town, South Africa and Hobart, Tasmania – all marvellously exotic for Ory and Constance, whose first experience of travel had been Switzerland the year before.

As they crossed the Equator they toasted the King, Edward VII. What would have happened if the King had succumbed to his appendicitis last June? The Antarctics would have come back to a different monarch – George V. It had been a very near thing. How much would have happened in the world by the time Ted came back? The Aswan Dam had been finished and Cuba had gained independence from Spain. But perhaps the things that Ted would find most interesting were the first *Tyrannosaurus rex* fossil (just unearthed in Montana) and the publication of Beatrix Potter's *The Tale of Peter Rabbit* (amateur artists could indeed make a 'living' from nature drawings).

It was February 1903 and late summer in New Zealand by the time the ship reached Auckland. Their first impression was not, as they had anticipated, of the landscape but of the overwhelming warmth of their reception. New Zealanders had none of the restraint that characterised the Old World. Ory wondered at the difference. Architecturally, the landscape was Little England, like a Boulton & Paul pop-up catalogue, but the scenery was not. The luxuriant bush, volcanic springs and spectacular mountains took their breath away. Ory and Constance saw their brother, Woodford, and Ted's cousins, the Whishaws, in North Island. By March they crossed the Cook Strait to South Island and continued down by the new train to the east coast capital of Christchurch.

Constance and Ory had been billeted with the expedition agents, Mr and Mrs Kinsey, who had two houses that would become important bases for the sisters. The Kinseys' main home, 'Warrimoo', was on Papanui Road, in the centre of town. They also had a summer house 'Te Hau Ote Atua' (Breath of Heaven) in Clifton perched on the slopes near Lyttelton Harbour, the port to which the *Discovery* would return.

It was Captain Scott who had enrolled Joseph Kinsey as the expedition agent. Kinsey was just fifty when Ory first met him, about the same age as her father but unlike Francis Souper, he wore a jaunty trilby and a boating blazer. Kinsey had taught at Dulwich College, in South East London for eight years before resigning and emigrating to New Zealand with his wife and daughter May in 1880. He settled in Christchurch and set up successful shipping agency 'Kinsey & Co.'

May Kinsey was Ory's age, she wore bicycle bloomers and rode astride her horse. She was a robust lady with robust opinions and wondered what the sisters from the Old World thought of the Suffragist movement? In New Zealand, women had had the vote since 1893; they had even had a woman Mayor, Elizabeth Yates, in Onehunga. What did they think of that? Ory's female friendships were carefully chosen and enduring, and she particularly warmed to New Zealand women with their independence, vitality and humour. Enfranchised or not, May was caught up in the romance of Ory's 'wife-of' status when, on 25 March 1903, they got the call that a ship had been sighted to the south-west. Could it be Ted's ice-ship, the *Discovery*? Ory had waited over a year and a half; now she might see her husband again in a few hours!

'A Glamour of Romance'

1903

In which Ory is told that she has another year to wait. At first she and Shackleton are the glamorous Discovery *couple, but she has Ted's diaries and private letters. She is the only one who knows the real story of 'Furthest South'.*

The man standing before Ory was not her husband. He was shorter and wore his hair like a banker, rather than a sailor, carefully slicked down either side of a central parting. She knew him from the early days of her marriage when she'd acted as a tour guide on the *Discovery* when it was in the London docks. She also knew him from her husband's letters. This was Ernest Shackleton, 'Shackles', the hard-working man who had been thoughtful about creating shade in Madeira. But why was he here? And where was her husband?

It was difficult to speak on the crowded dockside – sailors, porters, reporters all jostled for position. What was going on? Why had the *Morning*, the relief ship, returned without the *Discovery*? This wasn't part of the plan.

Shackleton had a tendancy to talk at people. As soon as he got within talking distance of Ory, he told her that her husband was well but that he had stayed south. Shackleton had been invalided home with scurvy but he seemed to have already made a complete recovery. The essential fact he wished to communicate to everyone was that, together with Scott and Ory's husband (who had been nicknamed 'Bill' from the Wil of Wilson) they had achieved a significant polar record, a 'first'. They had sledged to latitude 87 degrees 17 minutes – 'Furthest South'.

The postbag was key. Whatever Shackleton said, or, perhaps more importantly, didn't say, she would find out the truth from her husband in those letters. It was not only Ted who had written to her. The fact that Captain Scott had anticipated the depth of Ory's disappointment, better than he had Shackleton's, would have a lasting impact on all their lives.

'It isn't a kindness but a pleasure to write about your husband, therefore I do it again,' wrote Scott, 'I know he will tell you of our Southern trip, and my comments will be understood.'[1] Ory was Ted's outlet. Scott knew he would tell her everything.

Ory focused on Ted: 'We have had some trying times,' wrote Scott to Ory, '… and if such come my way again I hope I may have such a man as your husband by me … I have scarcely a doubt about the capability of us all to stand another winter, and I am quite sure your husband will … I feel confident he will get home safe and in better health than when he started, and I trust it may comfort you in your disappointment to know how well he is and how we all esteem him.'[2]

Ory tried to take heart from this, but she sensed that it had been a close shave. For the time being her knight had survived his quest. It would be selfish and ungrateful of her to despair. She tried to master her disappointment as Ted's boss had instructed her to and, returning to her adopted home with the Kinseys, began reading Ted's diary.

Ory soon learned Ted's private opinion of Shackles. When Scott declared his team selection for the Southern Journey, Ted had written: 'I feel more equal to it than I feel for Shackleton; for some reason I don't think he is fitted for the job. The Captain is strong and hard as a bulldog, but Shackleton hasn't the legs that the job wants …'[3]

As Ory skimmed the familiar pencil script, she learned that Shackleton had never reached the furthest point as he claimed, but been left 'invalid' on a sledge whilst the other two went on for a mile or two. On the return journey, Shackleton's health deteriorated still further. He was spitting blood. At one point he coughed out part of the lining of his throat. All of them were touched by scurvy, but Shackleton's symptoms were acute. By the end he could only shuffle alongside whilst Ted and Scott hauled the sledge home.[4] Ted was very careful about what he wrote in his diary, mindful of prying eyes and posterity, but he needed an outlet and perhaps in private letters he hinted at what had really happened between the three of them on that southern journey.

When, years later, the story was published, Ory neither supported nor denied it. Ted certainly told one of the team that during the Southern Journey he and Shackleton had been packing their sledges after breakfast one morning when Scott shouted, 'Come here you BFs [Bloody Fools].' Ted asked, 'Were you speaking to me?' 'No, Bill', said Scott. 'Then it must have been me,' said Shackleton. When he received no answer, Shackleton told his boss that he was '… the worst BF of the lot, and every time you dare to speak to me like that you will get it back.' Insubordination was a punishable crime in the Navy. Ted confided in Ory. She knew that if such truths got out, it would be disastrous not only for Shackleton, but for Scott and the whole expedition. Was that why the suspiciously healthy-looking Shackleton had been sent home?[5]

Buried in Ted's company, in his diary and letters, Ory tried to fit the jigsaw of slightings and latitudes together into a single truth, but it made her an antisocial guest. She had no sooner finished opening the post brought back with the *Morning*, than more arrived. Invitations, stacks of them. It was almost a competition. Entertaining Mrs Edward Wilson inferred status, it was a social coup. The New Zealand Government even issued free travel passes for Ory and Constance to tour their country.

Extracts from her earliest surviving letters date from this time and reveal Ory in outwardly good spirits. On 24 April she wrote to Ted's brother, Jim. 'There is nothing like being married to a "Discovery" man, there is quite a glamour of romance over one & I am having a splendid time.'[6]

Joseph Kinsey was responsible for organising Shackleton's passage home, but in the meantime it was Ory and Ernest Shackleton rather than Ory and her husband who were the expedition 'couple'. Did Shackleton wonder how much she knew – the hard words of insubordination, the fact that he had never technically reached that furthest point? Ory buttoned up her high collar and, fixing a genteel smile, took Shackleton's arm. They were the guests of honour at Christchurch's smartest garden parties, Ory in her white tea dress, Shackleton in his civvies, a dark suit and an almost apologetic smile. There was no denying that they made a handsome pair.

Middleton was the home of Sir Clements Markham's sister, Lady Bowen. As mastermind of the expedition, Markham, and therefore Lady Bowen, felt responsible for Ory. Photographs of wide-brimmed hats, lace tablecloths, silver tea pots and cake stands, immaculately dressed children, tennis racquets and china tea cups reveal a bastion of English aristocracy, New Zealand's 'royalty'. Ory and the invalid Shackleton were now moving in elevated social circles.

Shackleton sent news to Sir Clements at the Royal Geographic Society. The expedition should not be looked at as a failure, he said. Three of them, Scott, Ted and Shackleton, had reached 'Furthest South'. As an Irish man with a flare for story telling, Ory sensed that Shackleton was now in his element. Having been sent home because of weakness, he was now in a position of power. He and Ory were the expedition's public relations representatives. Ory had to look glamorous, plucky and proud. Shackleton had to look weather-beaten, square-jawed and worldly. They might have been cast for the roles.

Shackleton did not talk much about Scott. Instead, he told Ory that he was engaged to be married and showed her a photograph of Emily Dorman, eight years his senior. Ory was not surprised; true to his generation, the object of desire for the average Edwardian hot-blooded male was a mature, well-bred matron. Emily was a writer. Shackleton showed Ory a book she had co-authored, *The Corona of Royalty* by Laura Bennet and Emily Dorman. The embossed hardback history of the coronations of British Kings was prosy, abounding in fruity Victorianisms: 'the thrill of grief', the 'sombre moment'. Shackleton and Emily would get married, Shackleton hoped, in the spring of 1904, after the *Discovery* returned.

Love was, it seemed to Ory, in the air. She had recently met Lt Edward Evans, confusingly named 'Teddy', who had been seconded from the Royal Navy to be second officer of the expedition relief ship the *Morning*. (She supposed it wouldn't confuse anyone in the *Discovery*, who apparently knew Ted as 'Bill'.) Teddy Evans was a breezy fellow. He had met Ted. Admired him. Scott too. Good show. Ory got the impression Teddy would have liked to swap places with her Ted. Did she wish he had?

Teddy was caught up in the euphoria in Christchurch and he didn't want to go home. Besides, Hilda Russell, the beautiful daughter of a prominent Christchurch lawyer and Member of Parliament, had just caught his eye. Teddy asked for a transfer to HMS *Phoebe*, stationed nearby, whilst the *Morning* was refitted.

Ted, in the Antarctic midsummer, was also surrounded by entertainment that seemed to require formal clothing. 'Now and again one hears a penguin cry out in the stillness near at hand or far away and then perhaps he appears in his dress tail coat and white waistcoat suddenly upon an ice floe from the water.' Ted was painting frantically trying to capture it all for Ory, 'the whole fairy-like scene as the golden glaring sun in the south just touches the horizon and begins again to gradually rise without having really set at all.'[7]

Sometimes Ory fought shy of the tea gown crowd. Lily Bowen's cousin, Margaret, was a real breath of fresh air. She was a vicar's daughter like Ory and, like Ory, had grown up in a school. Margaret's mother, Annette, had been born near Ory's home in Hilton, Cambridgeshire, and when her husband, the Reverend Croasdaile Bowen, died, leaving her with four children to support, Annette set up the most successful school in Christchurch. Ory was impressed. This was not the self-indulgent Queen Victorian way of mourning, but the Capable Independent Woman. When Ory's thoughts strayed widow-wards, she reminded herself that her husband was alive and feted. She forced herself to be cheery: 'I have promised [Ted] to keep cheery,' she wrote, 'and I mean to till the very end.'[8]

'In Labore Honorem'

1904

In which Ory's loneliness overwhelms her and she tries to return home.
Her siblings working in North Island scoop her up. An idle life does not suit
her and she makes sure she is gainfully employed whilst awaiting Ted's return.

It was getting colder; June to August was the New Zealand winter. Ory
had acquitted herself in her filmy tea gown, but now it was time to
wrap up warm and tour the country. 'Waste not want not (W.N.W.N).'
The sisters were determined to use the free travel passes to experience
as many 'must-sees' as they could. They saw snow-capped mountains,
frozen lakes, chilly caves, icy waterfalls and even a few sulphurous old
geysers, but Constance was due to start work at the mission job in Patea
in North Island and soon Ory was on her own.

Her forced cheer was challenged in the summer of 1903, when the
Daily Mail published a damning report, copied in the New Zealand
papers. Despite Shackleton's claim of 'Furthest South', the Admiralty
had not given Scott permission to stay in Antarctica for another year and
organised for the *Terra Nova* to sail south with the *Morning* to force Scott
back, if necessary, without his ship. Was this insubordination on a grand
scale? Without Ted's words of reassurance, Ory felt exposed, and she had
a series of heavy colds that went to her chest.

Ory tried to focus on her ornithology. She was determined to know
more about New Zealand birds than Ted to impress him when he came
back. With her Zeiss binoculars slung around her neck, she braced herself
and, explorer-like, braved the bush. She tracked down the hunched-
back Kiwi, the parrot-like green Kea and its red and yellow equivalent,

the Kaka. In South Island, the moorhen lookalikes, the Takahe, Weka and Kokako. Along deserted coastlines she found the black-billed gull, Hutton's shearwater and even her fellow wanderer, the albatross, but she found the coastal steamers unbearably lonely.

Alone in her cabin she went back over the many letters praising Ted, most of them she had by heart. Her favourite was from meteorologist Charles Royds: 'Your old husband is one of the best and I missed him awfully during the long journey south …' Ory knew what he meant.[1] Albert Armitage (the only Merchant Navy man other than Shackleton) had a wife and child he had yet to meet but he was insulted by Scott's offer of an early passage home with Shackleton the previous year and 'absolutely refused' it.

What did Ory make of this? Ory knew why Scott might have made that offer, as it concerned something that Armitage, still in the Antarctic, did not yet know: Mrs Armitage, 'a hell of a woman',[2] had been involved in a 'boarding house scandal'. It had caused public outrage at the time and led to the police courts. It was clear that explorers' wives needed to be paragons of virtue if their husband's reputation was to be worth the snow it was written on.

Ory preferred private to public where paragonship was required. The woods had always been a place she could find solace and, once the lonely coastal steamer docked, Ory headed back into the bush. Native bush was 'very lovely, but nothing comes up to our English woods, specially the bluebell one at Crippetts … it seems to me when you have seen one lot of bush you have seen it all.'[3] Travel-weary, Ory '… got into a state when I couldn't write to anyone or thought I couldn't, it was only because of the idle life I was leading – so depressing it was!' Ory had reached break-ing point. She booked a boat to return home for Christmas. She boarded the ship but then 'escaped at Wellington'. Looking back, she realised she had been 'an absolute idiot, but have turned over a new leaf and am going to be happy and well'.

'Idle life' did not suit Ory. If she was going to be happy and healthy, she must do something. Constance and Woodford tried to help. Ory travelled to North Island. Church work at the mission in Patea with Constance, or matron at Huntley School in Marton with Woodford – which would it be? Huntley's moto was *In labore honorem*: 'Honour through hard work.'[4] Ory chose Huntley and slotted seamlessly into a frontier version of her role as lady-matron-teach. By the time Woodford left teaching to become a student at clerical college in Auckland, she was rediscovering her equilibrium. Work, hard work, Ory realised, was the best distraction. When the term ended, she decided to follow another lead, this time a possible family 'connection', a Miss Ethel Wilson who owned a tea shop a short distance away in Palmerston North. How hard could it be to make tea?

'I was told that Miss Wilson was one of the nicest girls in NZ and she certainly was.' Ory was on a mission to prove that English girls were capable of washing dishes because, 'it always rather astonishes a New Zealander to find that an English girl can do anything in the domestic line. But it was hard work.' Ory found the work refreshingly hard. Old photographs reveal pressed white tablecloths before a screened kitchen area. Ory gravitated towards the 'back of house', though her *Discovery*-wife celebrity drew curious customers. It amused her to think that within a few months she had gone from tea gown to apron. Joking in the kitchen with Ethel, whom she nicknamed 'the Connection', she rustled up 'tea for two, one fish – three chops'.

Initially Ory had been suspicious about the idea of associating with shopkeepers, of mixing with 'trade', but she found another soulmate in the serene and supportive Anne Hardy. Anne's father ran Hardy's Store, 'a real colonial store' in Rakaia, South Island, and was an MP for Selwyn. Ory learned that 'one gets used to mixing up with anyone here as long as they are good people – and one learns a mighty lot.'

She knew that Ted's brother, Jim, was becoming interested in the plight of the worker, and had offered her view on the question of class: 'I can never tell,' she wrote from New Zealand, '... which is a gentleman or a workman – the workmen are all so well off.'[5] Partly as a result of Ory's observations, Jim was made aware of the possibility of a different attitude to the worker, a position that would later, in his hands, become intensely political.

Ory gave Jim specific details of average worker salaries in New Zealand and noted a difference in attitude: gardeners had to be petitioned to come and servants were expensive and rare. It inspired Ory to see how a household could manage without servants and she was interested in the housewife's weekly routine – many of the women put their clocks forward thirty minutes to give themselves more daylight to do their chores.[6]

Towards the end of the year's wait, Ory was feeling optimistic. She had mastered her disappointment; acquitted herself well in society, in the schoolroom and the tearoom; and made plans for Ted's return. She had met fascinating people: amongst them the Royal Navy-connected Dennistouns of Peel Forest who owned one of the most beautiful homesteads in Canterbury. There was no denying, it had been a very difficult time, but Ory's preconceptions about society, servants, class and feminism had been challenged and evolved. Would Ted notice the change?

In a long letter to his medical student friend, John Fraser, Ory mentioned that she did not know what Ted wanted to do when he came back. Perhaps he'd be lured by the 'war in the east', or perhaps, the next 'expedition north'. 'War in the east' referred to the Russo–Japanese war of 1904–05, which would change the balance of power in Asia, setting the stage for the First World War. The next 'expedition north' referred to the Northwest Passage, that elusive link between the Atlantic and Pacific Oceans. As Ory wrote this letter, desperate for a 'peep into the immediate future', a little-known Norwegian explorer called Roald Amundsen was successfully navigating the passage. It would not be his only 'first'.

These were the kind of thoughts Ory worked to distract herself from, but she was working voluntarily. Constance was working out of necessity, having no husband to support her and, 'had a bad nervous breakdown from overwork … what horrible things nerves are', Ory wrote to John Fraser, 'but I suppose we couldn't get on without them.[7] Constance's mental health was becoming a reoccurring difficulty. The family took it seriously and their favourite Aunt Connie 'came out from England by the *Turakina* for the sake of my sister's health …' (Ory did not mention the fact that Aunt Connie had the added incentive of being close at hand if Ted did not return.)

John Fraser had asked after Ory: 'I am very fit and well thank you,' she told him. 'Lost a stone in weight and got scraggy and thin but have put it all on again even without taking Maltine or any other nasty concoction.' For Constance's sake, however, Aunt Connie took a house in Sumner, 'and we go up to the top of some hills as often as we can to watch for the ships.' Although the quiet place soothed Constance's nerves, it was difficult for Ory to get news: 'as there is no telephone in the house and I am only so afraid everyone in Christchurch will be meeting "the Discovery" while I am still pounding over the hills down to the harbour.'

The day 15 April 1904 dawned clear and still. 'I had woken early and was dozing again, when I heard a rush upstairs and breathless shouting – "All three ships are coming in! They will be in in an hour!" You can imagine,' Ory wrote to those desperate for detail at Westal, 'how quickly we huddled on clothes and tore off on the road over the Port Hills to Lyttelton.'

> We did that walk of four miles in record time; but when we reached the top there was no sign of any of the ships. By a piece of great luck we found the Harbour Master, Capt. Clarke, who said he would take me out with him before any of the Harbour Board got down … The Pilot's daughters were there; they had gone early with the Pilot boat. I asked them whether they had any news of Ted, and imagine my joy when they said they had seen him on the bridge with Captain Scott … Presently the Mayor, Mr. Wigram, came up and said that he had been deputed to see that I was the first to be put on board the Discovery. When Ted at last appeared beaming, and I was helped on board, then indeed all was well.[8]

Ory, breathless, was wearing the same plain grey skirt that she had had on when she'd waved goodbye at Yarmouth, in August 1901, 'looking,' Ted was delighted to see, 'not a day older than when I left her and far more beautiful.' Ted could not stop smiling. 'This kind of meeting,' he observed, 'beats a wedding hollow.' Both of them were ecstatic: 'What a day it was, brilliant sunshine and as still as possible. What a day indeed! We both felt it.'[9]

11

Honeymoon Mark II

1904

In which Ted and Ory enjoy a passionate second honeymoon in New Zealand. Ory demonstrates her capabilities as field scientist and fellow explorer and gets decidedly tipsy at the Discovery Ball.

Although they had been married since August 1901, in the early hours and days of Ted's return, they had to remind each other how to operate as man and wife. Letters were, again, replaced by whispered intimacies. Ory was honest about her experiences and about the part the Kinseys had played. Ted realised that it had been 'a very difficult time for her' and that the Kinseys had been 'really and genuinely good and kind to my wife, and I shall never forget it'.[1]

Ted had so much to tell Ory. He told her about the icebergs, sculpted by storms and luminescent blue like her eyes, a 'perfect miracle of blue and green light'. He showed her a sketch of 'Cape Wilson', a rocky head-land on the western edge of the Ross Ice Shelf that they had discovered in December 1902 and Scott had named after him.

The first month was spent in much necessary work upon penguin and seal skins at the Canterbury Museum in central Christchurch, where the pair spent many happy hours. Ory organised and labelled the specimens, but she was observant and began to notice how skins should be prepared. Hours of ink, feathers and formaldehyde by day and scrubbing up for society functions by night. The public face of the expedition was important and, as the most prominent expedition couple, Dr and Mrs Edward Wilson were asked everywhere.

Teddy Evans had asked Hilda Russell to marry him. The Wilsons went to their wedding. Then Lily Bowen got married. They went to that, too. 'She will make a Society man of me,' Ted warned his brother, Bernard, 'for she makes friends wherever she goes …' The one wedding that they did not, of course, attend was Shackleton's to Emily Dorman on 4 April, also at Christ Church, but the original one in Westminster, London. 'Antarctic Explorer marries Society Lady' was copied in the New Zealand press. Shackleton was still the only *Discovery* man on the ground in London, translating events for the British press as the news telegrammed in. He had also come back in the allotted time, rather than Scott who had stayed, without permission, for an extra year. Sir Clements Markham hosted the Shackletons' wedding breakfast at his home in Eccleston Square.

Finally, on 29 April 1903, the Wilsons escaped to Wellington on the south coast of New Zealand's North Island. The Antarctic was Ted's familiar territory, but now Ory was in charge. She had planned a tour from end to end of North Island through the volcanic region. It was an unfamiliar position of power. 'Ory,' Ted observed humorously, 'had seen it all before,' but to Ted it was intoxicating: the tree ferns, especially, were astounding.[2] Ory was his guide. That beautiful curlew-like whistle was a Weka, that, a Tui. That tree was a Lawyer, that a Lacebark and over there a Lancewood, Titoki, Totara …

Ted spent two hours delivering on Ory's promise to speak to the boys at Huntley School in Marton, where both she and Woodford had worked. Ted had spent so much time in the Antarctic wondering where Ory was, what she would be doing at any given moment; now he was very 'glad to see the place'. From there they went to Wanganui, arriving in time to see the sunset light up Mount Ruapehu, which 'was perfectly lovely'.

As they entered the wildest, most luxuriant, bush and forest, it really seemed that Ory and Ted were sharing the same adventure; their otherness and togetherness emphasised by contrast with the Maori settlements. Ted was running out of superlatives. His writing became smaller and smaller as he frantically tried to record everything in his travel diary. As a naturalist starved of 'nature' in an icy wilderness, as a lover starved of physical contact, the days that passed were heart-achingly wonderful.

Ory sketched the carvings on the Maori whare, the meeting house, and watched two Maoris greeting each other with the Hongi by rubbing noses. Ted spotted a little girl practising a dance on a dirt track all on her lonesome. She spun the Maori stick point forwards and back against her upper arms to imitate a bird in flight.

They bathed by moonlight in pungent sulphur hot springs. Ory felt nervous in the female changing hut, but Ted reassured her. Balancing passion with adventure, Ted was again 'happier than it is given for anyone on this earth to be ...' Soon it was back to the more conventional 'nature studies'. Ory proved herself again an excellent and willing assistant, collecting flora and fauna for Ted to take home. She agreed with her husband that 'while one has health and activity and can stand roughing and travelling one should be collecting "copy" so to speak ... not settling down.'

With Ory's resilience in mind, as well as their shared concern that the wildlife was 'fast disappearing', Ted wrote to New Zealand politician and future Prime Minister, Sir Joseph Ward. Conservation was a little-used word. Perhaps Ted could make a career out of it? When the first Europeans arrived in 1772, there was still thick, dense forest cover. Settlers were given homesteads, but forfeited their land if they didn't clear enough bush. He wanted to produce an illustrated natural history book on the birds and beasts of New Zealand: 'In a century or less, all or most of this unique flora and fauna will be extinct – they are dying out before one's eyes.' In fact, Ted concluded, producing a book on the animals of the South Polar Region and another on those of New Zealand, 'Why, I should think my life had been worth living.'[3]

This was in spite of the fact that Ted knew there would be a loud call for doctors when they got the place properly laid out with railways and more and better hotels and cure-houses. He knew that he could keep Ory comfortably as a doctor, but he didn't want to be so limited. He acknowledged the demand for medical care yet, despite everything, argued for the necessity of conservation, still referred to with a small 'c' in 1904.

During her year as a perpetual guest, Ory had begun longing for a 'shack' of their own. Inspired by the work of Thompson Seaton in Canada, Ted wanted to live in the bush and write and illustrate wildlife books whilst he and Ory recorded the vanishing species as government scientists. But before they became hermits, Ory had a party to host.

For two days, Ory was in charge of creating 'never-to-be-forgotten'[4] decorations to match the occasion of the *Discovery*'s farewell ball. She felt the responsibility keenly. She borrowed some huge baskets, planted them with palms, ferns and lycopodium and then, throwing a rope over the rafters, hoicked them up until the ceiling was all but obscured. Ted was overwhelmed still by luxuriant plants, none of the Antarctics could get enough of them – by the end of the first day, Ory had recreated a lush New Zealand bush in a large hall near the docks in Lyttleton.

The next day found her balancing precariously on a stepladder whilst the musicians practiced their three-quarter time. Ory leant out towards the gas brackets to hang the embroidered sledge flags, the knight's pennants, Arthurian style. She was going for colour and impact rather than sticking to a single theme. Finally she shipped in the Antarctic. She got hold of one of the *Discovery*'s sledges and piled it high with rolled up sleeping bags. It was a sort of polar index: 'all the things used on a sledge journey, ski, snowshoes, etc' and for the final dramatic touch? 'two ... lay figures dressed in furs and a tent'. Not mannequins, actual men.

Was this a theatrical flourish, or a Victorian 'tableau vivant' or did she see it more as a pop-up Baedeker's guide to the Antarctic? For anyone wanting to go South, this would indeed have been a 'Useful Help', a 'How to', a sort of school kit list or even, in Ory's most recent parlance, a shop window. Whichever way she argued for its practicality, it is evidence of Ory's interest in the theatre, in dramatic arts.

In the early evening of 1 June, Ory returned to the room they had taken at the Coker Hotel to change out of her working clothes. Her wedding dress was laid out, ready. It was a transformation Ted had seen before but it never failed to impress. Could Ted remember how to waltz? He wasn't sure. There had been little call for it recently. Was it still 'left foot change; right foot change; box step, forward progressive, promenade'? Ory danced out of the hotel on Ted's arm but soon he would have to hand her over. This evening, Ory was hosting the *Discovery* guests with Scott. She was the expedition's First Lady.

Tradition dictated that a bride should wear her wedding dress at her first ball as a married woman. Ory had been married three years but, like the brand new Mrs Hilda Evans, was also in her wedding satins. Hilda confided to Ory that her honeymoon had been an expedition in itself and that she had nearly drowned crossing a river in full spate. For the moment, the women were graceful white swans with all the effort of paddling well hidden.

Mrs Wilson and Captain Scott welcomed guests for pre-dinner drinks on the deck of the *Discovery*. Ted stood to one side. He was enjoying being superfluous to requirements but he couldn't take his eyes off his wife: 'I could only stand in the crowd and admire her,' he wrote home, 'and wonder how the deuce such a girl came to give herself to me ... She behaved as though she had done that sort of thing all her life – and she looked so tall and graceful.'[5] When he thought back to the drawing room of that Mission in Battersea, he could not believe his eyes. Was she really his? She was incredible. Did he deserve her? She had always given the appearance of 'a great lady' and now she lent Scott gravitas, glamour and credibility as they ushered 350 of Christchurch's finest into the hall.[6]

Ory had been looking forward to this moment ever since she packed her swan suit into the trunk at Westal. Ted was home – New Zealand had really begun to feel that way. No one could speak highly enough of him. He was a hero, not just to her. Looking about her at her new friends, Ory realised that she had gained confidence, admirers and self-esteem. She could stand 'rough travelling', she could host a ball and, most importantly perhaps, she could now afford to relax and enjoy herself. She waltzed, she drank, she ate, she drank, she ate (one could only wear a wedding dress twice) and she laughed. She was never without a dancing partner. When had she ever become so fascinating?

She paid for it the next morning. Both the Wilsons had overindulged. At the time it had been rather delicious but they were not natural hedonists and now they were feeling decidedly seedy. Ory's feet ached from all that 'box step, forward progressive, etc' and her throat was sore from raising her voice over the musicians. But Ted was worse, he was feeling really bad. He could barely move, let alone pack all his things down below deck in his *Discovery* cabin as the ship moved with the waves in the harbour. It hardly surprised him now that Ory could. Was there anything she couldn't do? Could she perhaps fold up and stow herself away in one of those labelled specimen drawers?

Ory had promised Ethel Wilson an immediate account and, whilst Ted nursed his head, she sat down at his desk and and took out some Coker Hotel headed writing paper.

'My Dear Connection,' she wrote, 'I am just recovering after the never-to-be-forgotten "Discovery" ball. It was such a jolly one. Over 350 people came and everything went off splendidly.' While Ted 'went off' to the heads or the side of the boat, whichever was closer, Ory continued. 'We kept up the dancing till past 3 o'clock. I was fairly dead!' It was not just her and Ted: 'Constance had a gay time and so many partners that she had to divide some dances between two men!'[7]

The men on board pronounced the ball a runaway success. It had been the most sought after invitation of the Season and it had more than delivered on expectations. But despite this euphoria, Ted felt like death. He could not bear to say goodbye. He did not want to leave his wife, ever, let alone right now. He did not really want to go home at all. This could be home, this country at the bottom (or nearly the bottom) of the globe. It was all wrong. What could they do? Ory, at this moment the more resilient of the two, was practical. Ted had to go back to England with the *Discovery*. Besides, Ory had already booked her passage home and would be back before him. That was that. They could come back to New Zealand, she hoped they would, but for now, it must be goodbye. He must stiffen his lip and promise *her* to be cheery. After the Discovery left the dock, Ted tried to console himself in a letter to his brother Bernard:

> … it was simply horrible having to part again … Tomorrow we shall have been married three years and we shall have had thirteen weeks together – never mind – when we next meet we shall have had three wedding days together for each of these meetings is a little better than the first.[8]

Settling in the Suburbs

1904–05

In which the Wilsons set up a servant-free home in Bohemian Bushey. Ted is set on becoming an artist, illustrator and writer, instead of the doctor he had spent years training to be, but neither he nor Ory are commercially minded.

The *Discovery* men who stepped onto English soil at Southsea on 10 September 1904 were not the same men who had left. Like Edward Lear's 'Jumblies', they had returned taller from their icy 'Torrible Zone'. Ted, the feted explorer, certainly walked taller. 'Bill', as he was coming to think of himself, was still as in love with Ory, more if possible, but he was also more in love with himself. Affirmed by the praise that was heaped upon him, Ted aimed higher. He told Ory that he wanted his monograph on the emperor penguin to be 'a classic'.[1]

Ory, although she never acknowledged it to herself, was now the most famous explorer's wife in all Edwardian England. Scott was single, Shackleton was an 'invalid', Hilda Evans' husband had only been on the relief ship, the *Morning*, never the *Discovery*. Who could she look to for a role model? At one of the many men-only post-expedition celebrations (a Royal Geographic Society dinner at The Criterion), Ted met Admiral McClintock, famous for his association with Lady Jane Franklin.

Lady Franklin had married her husband as a passport to adventure. Before she met him she had never left England, but her trip to Van Diemen's Land (Tasmania) when he was Lieutenant Governor in the 1830s had given her a taste for travel. Her husband set off to discover the North West Passage, but mysteriously vanished in 1848. Lady Franklin froze out all detractors and swept any unwelcome details under her polar-bear-skin rug. She sponsored seven expeditions to find his remains, dismissing those that found evidence of cannibalism as vicious rumour-mongers. Before she died in 1875, she ensured her husband, and by association herself, a place in exploration history, composing the catchy epitaph 'They forged the last link with their lives.' Jane had set out as a vicarious adventurer but, in the search for the missing bodies, her expeditions discovered more Arctic territory between the Atlantic and Pacific Oceans than her husband ever did. When Ory married Ted, she had never left England, but her recent trip to New Zealand had also given her a taste for travel in general and the Antipodes in particular. Over dinner, McClintock might have wondered conversationally what Ted's wife would do if he were accused of cannibalism? Seven expeditions and a smattering of powerful prose would surely be the very least of it.

Scott was also talking about McClintock, but more about McClintock's writing than his late employer, Lady Franklin. The Admiral's account of his search for John Franklin, *The Voyage of the 'Fox' in the Arctic Seas*, published in 1859 by John Murray, had been a best-seller. Inspired by this, Scott began taking advance orders for what he hoped might be the *Discovery* equivalent, to be published in October 1905. He commissioned Ted as the illustrator and chose Smith. Elder & Co. for his publisher.

Smith Elder's director, Reginald Smith, was a man with a private income who could afford to make principled rather than commercial decisions about his books. His wife, Isabel, was the youngest daughter of George Murray Smith, who had commissioned the *Dictionary of National Biography*, and was therefore publishing aristocracy. Reginald joined the family firm in 1894. Even to Ory's critical eye, Isabel appeared to be a practically perfect woman – 'the only person in the world,' according to Ted's biographer, 'to whose judgement Oriana deferred'.[2] Isabel could recommend a literary companion for Ory in any given situation: Tennyson was Ory's friend *in extremis*, Elizabeth Gaskell, a vicar's wife, put her in mind of her mother. Isabel was tall and elegant like Ory, highly intelligent, with a deep sense of social responsibility but also modest. She quickly become Ory's 'closest and most constant friend'.

Scott was modest when it suited him. At the eleventh hour, Scott decided to replace the frontispiece photograph of the two-volume *Voyage of the Discovery* (an image featuring Ted, Shackleton and Scott as they set off for 'Furthest South') with a new sketch focusing instead on the *Discovery* itself. Ted found himself on the cutting-room floor with a new sketch to produce. 'I can get it done in thirty-six hours if I sit up all night to it.'[3]

Meanwhile the Wilsons, searching for somewhere to call 'home', settled on Bushey. It was 'a fresh air village' within easy commuting distance of soot-soaked London, and close to Polly, now Mrs Godfrey Rendall. Polly was Ted's favourite sister; she shared his strong spiritual beliefs and was a close friend of Ory's. Ted liked the idea that they could keep each other company while their husbands were up in town. Bushey had the reputation of being an artistic epicentre where paint-splattered Bohemians lived out their unconventional lives – the kind of place where Mrs Grundys were a rare and vanishing species. Ory rented a cottage called 'Tynecote' for them while Ted focused on an Antarctic exhibition of his work due to open in Bond Street, Mayfair.

On 7 November, crowds of people had to be turned away from the door of the Bruton Street Galleries. Neither Ted nor Ory were commercially minded. The RGS temporarily owned Ted's Antarctic pictures, but he'd agreed to produce copies for twenty to thirty guineas. The unscrupulous gallery owner (referred to thereafter by Ted's father as 'the sharper') took advantage. After the owner's large commission, there was very little money left for Ted. Art did not make Ory's husband rich but overworked. But work was good: 'I don't ever really want to have less to do,' Ted told his wife, 'I want to be able to feel and to know that you feel, when my end comes, that I couldn't have done more – and then I shall die quite happy, and I shall know that you will always be proud.'[4]

Despite this, Ted was set on becoming an artist, illustrator and writer instead of the doctor he had spent years training to be. As the wife of a doctor, Ory would have had both status and financial security, but art was preferable to Ted going to the 'war in the East' or on 'the next expedition North'! This way the Wilsons would be poor, which she was used to, but they would be together. Besides, Ted could have no peace of mind with servants around and Ory could have no peace without

Ted. Practising Ted's principles might be exhausting, but it was a price she was willing to pay. Besides, the Wilsons craved privacy after so much time lived in an Antarctic hut, or as a best-behaviour guest.

Not having servants was shockingly unconventional in Edwardian England, where the number of domestic staff defined social status. In the 'Beeton Bible', Mrs Beeton observed: 'There are few families of respectability, from the shopkeeper … to the nobleman … which do not contain … servants.' As with her father, Ory's husband's uncompromising nature made him a hard task master: if she ever paused for a second to flick through one of the books Isabel Smith had lent her, Ted urged her to question herself: 'Am I getting good enough out of this book to warrant my getting others to do my drudgery while I read it?'[5]

Letter writing was more a chore than a pleasure for Ory. It was her job to keep Ted's family up to date since, in the first months after the *Discovery* returned, he was too busy to see them, but letter writing was a luxury as far as Ted was concerned. 'Does the writing of this letter, the painting of this picture, the good of this walk or ride or conversation, warrant my using [servant's] time for it?'[6] Ted worked away in the studio at the end of the garden at Tynecote in Bushey. Ory resumed a familiar sibling–parent role as Coventry Patmore's 'Angel in the House'[7] creating what Ted proudly described as 'our cosy home'. 'I don't smoke and I don't drink, and I have to swear horribly to prevent myself from becoming a little angel and flying away,' he informed one of his aunts.

Ted had lived a saltier life aboard *Discovery*. He was not accustomed to house-angels. A gentle teasing was his solution: 'So you must forgive O.,' Ted continued to the aunt, 'if she shocks you when we next meet, because she will pick up such horrible expressions. Sometimes she says "Oh bother," and sometimes she says, "Well, never mind," but it's awful to hear her when she breaks things washing up – luckily not our own things – she seems very careful about all our own things.'[8]

Ory was not clumsy, quite the opposite. Perhaps it was this femininity that moved Ted to take on the heavy dirty parts of their daily routine: 'We are down at six every morning. O. does all the cooking and house-cleaning, and I do the kitchen-grate and light the fire and clean the flue.'

She adopted the New Zealand pioneer routine: Monday, 'Washday'; Tuesday was 'Ironing Day'; Wednesday was 'Cleaning Day' …

Ory was beginning to enjoy herself, embracing her rebellious servant-less life style. The kind of unconventional approach that would set that ol' Mrs Grundy's hair at a gratifyingly steep angle. The spotless piano-forte was their one nod to convention. Ory didn't need sheet music, as she was good at 'picking out a tune', but the piano was time squandering compared to the music of the sewing machine. 'I think it would knock anyone out of a fit of the blues,' wrote Ted as he sat beside Ory and her Singer, 'because it has got such a very busy buzz.'[9]

As Ted was producing another set of Antarctic prints for a pittance, a wasp flew into the Tynecote studio. It stung him on the temple. Ted suffered a serious anaphylactic reaction. Within minutes of being stung he could hardly breathe, he felt faint and confused. The nearest doctor was Ernest Shackleton's cousin. He administered a heart stimulant, saving Ted's life.[10] Ory had read Ted's sledging diaries of 1903. She knew that Ernest Shackleton had nearly died on the return journey and that Ted, the team doctor, had probably saved him. Now the equation had been resolved – a Shackleton had saved Ted. Although he improved slowly, Ted's tuberculosis-weakened chest took days to recover. Ory had known that Ted was in danger in the Antarctic, but she had been powerless to help. She had not thought to worry in suburbia.

Between swatting wasps and churning out watercolour reproductions, Ted and Ory went up to Cheltenham for a lecture at Ted's old school, Cheltenham College. Public speaking was not Ted's forte, and only Ory knew that at times he took a mild sedative to calm his nerves before a talk. Ted made further applications to New Zealand to work as a warden on one of the two island wildlife sanctuaries. No post was forthcoming. Ory had not been there to witness Ted's disappointment at failing to get to the South Pole. As the 'sharper'[11] took the lion's share of his gallery earnings and the post brought no reply from New Zealand, she witnessed Ted's unshakable confidence that 'it' was all part of God's great plan.

On 18 December, the *Discovery* crew went to Buckingham Palace to receive their Polar Medals, silver or bronze hexagons with King Edward VII on one side and an image of the sledging party on the other. Ory left her kitchen sink and accompanied Ted, who took a watercolour to present to the King. The ceremony provided an opportunity for the expedition wives to meet: Emily Shackleton fighting morning sickness, Hilda Evans delighted to see Ory's familiar face and Ory, her gloves firmly on lest the others notice her housemaid's hands. Their job, as usual, was to 'stand and wait' and the medal for that particular endurance achievement had yet to be minted.

Did they stand outside the Palace or go for tea at the Ritz? Wherever they moved, they were in the presence of *polarhuller*, a Danish term for the magical lure of the polar wastes that would draw an explorer back again and again to extreme latitudes. Were any of their husbands immune? Studiously avoiding the topic, they searched for neutral territory. They could not talk children (Ory and Hilda, though considerably younger than Emily, were obviously not yet pregnant). They could not talk servants (the Wilsons' unconventional stand raised eyebrows). They could not talk Royal Navy (Ernest Shackleton had failed to get a place in Teddy Evans' profession despite Sir Clements Markham's putting in a word). What could they talk about?

Perhaps they discussed the latest news from America? The Republican candidate, Theodore Roosevelt, had been elected in November. His wife, Edith, was the first President's wife to employ a full-time salaried social secretary. What did they think of that? Was 'wife-of' a role or a job? They might have discussed the King, presently handing out medals to their husbands. Edward VII's morals were in contrast to his mother's. Edward's wife, Alexandra, it was commonly known, was fond of his mistress, Alice Keppel, and tolerated the liaison. Role and job? None of the wives had yet met the King, but Emily was an expert on the coronation; she had written *The Corona of Royalty* after all. They could all remember the drama of the King's pre-coronation appendicitis operation. Ory was an expert on that operation, dissected in clinical detail at the time by Dad in the Westal drawing room. Hilda remembered prayers said at her home half a world away in a country that was a Colony aspiring to become a Dominion. Only a minority of New Zealanders even wanted greater independence from Britain. King Edward VII, at that moment handing out medals to their husbands, was very much 'their' King too.

After the ceremony, the Wilsons returned to their rented rooms in Bushey, the Evans to Royal Navy married quarters in Greenwich, and the Shackletons to their town house in Edinburgh.[12] A year later, in October 1905, when Scott's book came out, Shackleton was dismayed to find himself described as an 'invalid'. He was humiliated by phrases taken from Ted's diary: 'we cannot carry him' and 'the Captain and I can quite well manage everything alone'.[13] Shackleton's determination to prove himself 'valid' would have far-reaching consequences for Ory.

But that was still in the future. For the moment, as 1904 became 1905, the Wilsons were preoccupied with occupation. Ted had just been offered a job by his university friend, Gerald Barrett-Hamilton, illustrating the *History of British Mammals*. He began by 'bat-hunting' in an underground passage that had been excavated through a chalk hill near Henley. He found Daubenton's, Natterer's, whiskered and long-eared bats, 'hoicked them out of crannies. I brought 20 home to O.!'[14]

'O.' was so delighted with this that she immediately offered to cook supper in the kitchen whilst he took the specimens to his studio. But halfway through a soufflé, she heard her husband call for help. Was it a wasp? Ory flew out to the studio to find Ted standing stock still, staring at the end of a pencil.

Ted asked her to move slowly towards him and to take over holding the pencil in exactly the position he had it. Exactly that angle. Ory smoothed her apron and hoped she was up to the task. Carefully, she took the pencil between her thumb and forefinger and tried not to breathe. Ted ran to fetch a tube of spirits. Ory's soufflé deflated slowly on the sideboard whilst she stood, as instructed with the pencil. Ted was glad to see that she had her priorities straight. He placed the test tube under the pencil and tapped it smartly before putting in the stopper. The captured flea was 'no common flea, but a rare and precious species of its tribe.'[15]

Grousing

1905–07

In which Ory loses her beloved brother Woodford and moves north with Ted to Scotland. Ted is tasked with discovering why Lord Lovat's grouse moor is being decimated by disease. Shackleton announces his plans for the South Pole.

In November 1905, Ory received a telegram from Auckland. Her brother, Woodford, had been found with his neck broken at the bottom of a tree in the grounds of St John's College, Tamaki, where he was studying theology. As the second death from a fall in the Souper family (following the 11-year-old James), this must have seemed the most unbearable tragedy. He had been trying to climb every tree in the avenue that led to the College. There was no fast way of getting back round the world to Woodford's funeral. Ory's father and stepmother provided a centre for the family to gather in remembrance at Hilton. Ory, the sibling parent, had practically raised Woodford. He had become a great friend of Ted's but now God had chosen him and he had 'passed over'. Ted tried to console her and Ory tried to share Ted's unshakeable acceptance that '*l'homme propose et le Dieu dispose*'. She found solace with her remaining brothers, Edward and Adrian, who had also become curates. Noel was a farmer in Canada. Together with Constance, there were five Souper children left.

At the beginning of 1906 Ted took Ory 'for a couple of nights' to Woburn Abbey in Bedfordshire, seat of the Duke of Bedford. Here, Ted told John Fraser, his closest friend from medical school, '… we shall study zoology for a time.'[1] 'We' and 'study' was a new word association. Perhaps Ted was trying to comfort Ory, to distract her from the tragedy. Whatever his motive, he seems to have acknowledged that his wife was eminently capable of study, and so Ory became an unofficial zoology student with Ted as her mentor.

Herbrand Russell, the 11th Duke, was president of the Royal Zoological Association and had recently built up a critical mass of endangered Père David's deer. Mary, his wife, was a passionate ornithologist and a clear-headed suffragist – an inspiration for Ory, she was very brusque and did not 'suffer fools'. She kept a meticulous record of data on her husband's deer, noting births, deaths and purchases. Importantly, the Russells had contacts. Lord Lovat needed a field scientist on his estate in Scotland. His grouse moor was being decimated by disease and someone needed to get to the bottom of it. Would that suit the Wilsons? Mrs Wilson could assist her husband as Mary assisted hers.

Ted and Ory returned from Woburn to 'dead grouse pouring in by every post'. The sharp end of field observation, as Ory soon discovered, would obviously be conducted not on the Scottish Moor, but in the studio at the end of the garden. This was zoology in action. The Tynecote studio was transformed into a laboratory, with Ory, Ted's chief (and only) laboratory assistant.

Ory's domestic skill with needlework and baking was now applied to dissection and specimen preparation – housekeeping took second place. If a game bird arrived at her door, it was instantly dissected and a report given. Ory soon knew a healthy grouse from an unhealthy one and assured one sender that the brace he had sent were 'entirely free from disease'. The reply showed her how far she had come: 'they were intended for consumption, not for dissection!'[2]

In April 1906, the Wilsons took a house in Colinton, a suburb of Edinburgh, where the dead grouse were fresher from the moor. Ory was learning to balance the demands of a servantless lifestyle with her role as Ted's laboratory assistant. For Ory, hostessing was another chore, but she was obliged to entertain. Leaving her dissections in one room, she prepared dinner for the likes of Sir Thomas Gibson-Carmichael (whom she later encountered as Governor of Victoria) and his wife in another.

About 10 miles to the north, the Shackletons lived a comfortably servanted life in South Learmonth Gardens, Craigleith, nearer the centre of Edinburgh. The making of introductions was one of Emily Shackleton's particular pleasures. If the Shackletons ever invited the Wilsons to one of their fashionable bridge parties, no written record exists. The timing was bad. In April 1906, Emily was one month pregnant with her second child. She found pregnancy irksome, morning sickness crippling and worried lest she would become a burden to her husband.

The Wilsons had been married for five years, though only two of those had been spent together. They both came from large families and Ory must have wondered which of them was infertile and why. Was it that she was perpetually underweight or was it Ted's tuberculosis treatment? As far as Ted was concerned, '*Le Dieu dispose ...*' covered life as well as death.

Even so, they loved children. Stanley Gardiner, Ted's former professor from Caius, had visited Ted's exhibition at the Bruton Galleries. Gardiner had been particularly impressed by the expressive nature of his drawings of the 'young chicks of the Emperor Penguin' and wondered what could be more maternal than 'the mother seal with her week-old baby'. Ted talked repeatedly of a desire to 'settle down'. Having a family would justify that. 'I love boys,' Ory wrote later in life, 'and have always had so much to do with them.'[3] But however much they longed for children, Ory was still a wife devoted solely to her husband and his career rather than a mother, like Emily, with divided loyalties.

In the Shackleton household, Emily's absorption with her oldest son Raymond's childhood illness meant that Shackleton found it an effort to 'keep things going brightly'.[4] Instead he confided in his boss's wife, the childless Elspeth Beardmore. At William Beardmore & Co., Elspeth's husband's steel works in Glasgow where Shackleton worked, and from there, in Edinburgh, it was rumoured that Shackleton and Elspeth were having an affair.

To Ted and Ory, even from the fringes, Edinburgh appeared to be a 'drunken city', 'a horrid place to live', 'excessive vulgar', a place where dissolute behaviour was normal.[5] By the summer of 1906 they had moved north to the clean air and cleaner morals of Fort Augustus, where Ted had been loaned Glendoe, Lord Lovat's shooting lodge. It was a beautiful spot at the head of Loch Ness with St Benedict's Monastery nearby.

Despite their remoteness, Ted complained to his mother that, 'One of our worst troubles is being over entertained! It would suit many people very well …' but not them.[6] Moor owners were curious about Ted's Antarctic experience and Ory found herself plucked from the sublime informality of her kitchen suppers to formal dinners in draughty castles with kilted lairds. When they could politely refuse an invitation, they did, and as Ted skinned and sketched, Ory read to him – any novel of Dickens would do, but Ted could not be trusted to read one himself. If he opened a Dickens, he could never put it down.[7]

Ted told John Fraser that Ory 'as a wife, or as a companion every day in the year or as a friend – has made me completely indifferent to the companionship of others … she is all my friends put together … shake me out of my selfishness and contentment now and again'.[8]

Conversation centred around the paradox of Ted's pursuing a conventional career, finding a 'regular billet', a junior post in the Royal Scottish Museum of Natural History perhaps? He told Ory that one of the things that he'd like to investigate was Ernst Haeckel's hypothesis known by the catchy title Ontogeny Recapitulates Phylogeny (ORP), which proposed that the evolution of an animal could be observed through its embryonic development. Haeckel had produced a series of drawings of embryo development. Ted wondered whether bird feathers might be proved to have evolved from reptilian scales by documenting various stages of embryonic development of a primitive bird. At the time penguins were thought to be the most primitive and of them, the Emperor Penguin was the most primitive. Emperors meant the Antarctic.

For Ory, the first option would mean moving back to Edinburgh, the second would involve another long separation. The Antarctic was always a spectre in the background but Ted claimed to have no desire to go there just to 'conquer the South Pole'. If he could collect Emperor Penguins' eggs and prove Haeckel's hypothesis, it would, for Ted, be the scientific equivalent of the Pole. It would have to be done in the dead of winter, of course, since Emperor Penguins hatched in the Antarctic spring and no one had ever survived a journey in those temperatures. But although it would be hard, Ted did not feel it would be impossible. Whichever way he looked at it, the South Pole on its own was a romantic notion to which he refused to subscribe. For Ernest Shackleton romance – albeit icy romance – was an end in itself.

On 11 February 1907, days after the birth of his second child, a girl, Shackleton lit the touch paper, announcing his own plans for the South Pole. It was news to Ted. It was news to Ory. But above all, it was news to Emily.

14

Shackleton & Scott

1907

In which Shackleton tries to persuade Ted to join him on his latest quest for the Pole. Ted is asked to broker a pact between Scott and Shackleton. Encouraged by what he sees of the Wilson marriage, Scott proposes to the artist Kathleen Bruce.

Emily's reaction towards Shackleton's latest venture was generous. She had sensed his frustration working for William Beardmore and had her suspicions about his wife, Elspeth. Shackleton's first letter to Ted arrived on 12 February 1907. 'You know me well enough to know that we can work together,' he wrote to Ted, 'Come, Billy. Don't say No till we have had a talk. Don't say no at all.'[1]

In most accounts Ted says 'No'. But he did not say 'No' immediately.

It was Valentine's Day and he discussed it with Ory. 'I would give anything [to come] and my wife shares in all my feelings and she is just as disappointed as I am.'[2]

'This is almost as bitter a disappointment as when I left *Discovery*,' Shackleton telegrammed. When Shackleton had left the *Discovery*, he'd cried.[3]

Ted tried to mitigate Shackleton's new 'bitter disappointment' now by telling him that 'my own inclinations are all one way & my necessities are all the other ... I would dearly love to have a hand in your effort to bottle the Pole.'[4]

'And still worst for me,' wrote Ted, 'Will he [Scott] ask me to go with him. He has carefully avoided giving me the faintest hint on these points in his letter – Naturally enough.'[5]

Ory could only conclude that, if Ted was to go back to the Antarctic, his inclination would be to go with Shackleton, that bottling the Pole was important to him and that he dreaded the possibility of being asked by Scott. It was not the first time that Ted had, and would, reveal his contradictory tendencies – it smacked of denial in the same way that he had denied his intentions to marry her.

When Michael Wilson, Jim's son, took his fiancée Mary to visit Aunt Ory many years later, he said something, presumably romantic, about Mary, and Ory said, 'in rather a sharp voice: "Yes of course – but you know it's very different being married to somebody".' Michael concluded: 'and I felt there was probably deep experience and patience behind that remark and I think any woman who marries a Wilson has a pretty thorny path to tread.'[6]

On 15 March, Finland became the first European country to give women the vote. They were five years behind Australia and fourteen years behind New Zealand. Did Ory want more autonomy? Ted was at pains to explain to anyone who was interested that Ory was not holding him back. When he mentioned that 'necessities' held him back from going with Shackleton, he meant the grouse work, he did not mean her. Shackleton agreed that she was 'splendid to be glad for you to do this work if you could have done it …',[7] and wondered whether, in fact, Ory could take over the grouse work to liberate her husband for the Pole. It was a backhanded compliment of sorts. Ted put him straight: '… though my wife is only too willing to do all the secretarial work that I can possibly hand over,' Ted explained, 'the bulk of it is work that I can only do myself.'

As a last-ditch attempt, Shackleton offered to pay for both the Wilsons to come out to New Zealand. This was tempting. After the grouse work, Ted would need another job. He and Ory had proved themselves as a field science partnership. Despite the loud silence from Sir Joseph Ward over the issue of a job in conservation in New Zealand, they both still hankered after the mirage of that island 'shack'.

Ted had been sledging with Shackleton, but Ory knew him too from their discussions at Middleton, New Zealand, in 1903. Back then, Emily had been Shackleton's muse. Getting 'out of the rut' of the Merchant Navy in order to qualify for a society bride had kept him going through the worst moments in the Antarctic. But now, with two children under 2 – Raymond and newborn baby Cecily, also Cook, Nurse and the Maid-of-all-Work – Emily represented his responsibilities and it seemed the childless Elspeth had replaced Emily as Shackleton's 'muse'.

Ory realised that, apart from her husband who did everything for God, Shackleton was not unusual. Many knights rode into battle with their lady's colours. 'What drives a man through storm and snow over ice … into a world of cold misery?' asked North Polar explorer Frederick Cook. 'The real pivot upon which all his efforts are based is the desire to be rated well among his colleagues, and inseparably linked with this is the love of some feminine heart. Is not this also the inspiration of all the world?'[8]

Living up on the grouse moor gave Ory a taste of the pioneer life-style. Ted took her to watch the black grouse displaying on their lekking grounds. The male grouse fanning out his black tail and, ducking his head, to reveal his snow white rump feathers. Ory returned to base to keep the home fires burning, but Ted often stayed out all night. He observed his own clock, his own set of priorities and he did not want her to keep 'anything hot' for him.

In the long days of summer, as Ory continued with the grouse field work – dissection and notes – at home, Ted told her he did not want to waste any time sleeping. He was obsessed with the notion that life is not about rest and that 'here we have no abiding place'.[9] Perhaps it had got worse since he had been chatting to the Benedictine monks nearby. Their tight communal timetable – the horarium – was meant to ensure that the time given by God was not wasted. Without anyone but Ory to lend a sense of proportion, Ted indulged his asceticism. He was becoming more and more like a monk, except that monks chose not to marry.

Ted hoped the matter with Shackleton and the Antarctic was over and told him not to bother sending expensive telegrams, but soon both Scott and Shackleton approached Ted to act as mediator. Scott wanted Ted's opinion, '… because it is one that I consider conclusive in a question of honour,' and Shackleton, because 'it is the penalty of being considered capable in judgement.'[10] The Wilsons could not have been further from the politics of civilisation and yet it insisted on turning up in their

Highland wilderness. Ory must have felt that she was married to a modern Solomon. Ted suggested dividing the baby.

He told Shackleton that he should not cover territory already mapped by Scott, he should certainly not under any circumstances use Scott's old hut as a base, but find his own route south. In the eyes of his contemporaries, if he attempted to leapfrog Scott it would be seen as 'forestalling'. Forestalling was almost a crime. If he were to use his former leader's hard-won research to seize the prize of the South Pole, it would be as immoral as mutiny. And, as Ted pointed out, 'the gilt would be off the gingerbread.'[11]

The only downside to this conclusion, as Ory could see, was for Emily. As Ted put it, 'I am most sorry for your wife because of course any other base is much more an uncertainty.'[12] If Ory had ever wondered whether having children would be settling, the Shackleton situation must have given her one answer. If Ted was in Shackleton's place, would children have encouraged Ted to become a patriarch like his own father, refusing positions because 'I am a family man',[13] or would children have represented a runner's starting blocks, as they seemed to for Shackleton? Was it just losing Emily to motherhood that made Shackleton run for the ice? Certainly the Shackleton's idea of parenting was very different. Shackleton expected the instant obedience of the Navy, but when Emily later told the children to keep out of the waves in their Sunday best, Shackleton walked them right into the sea and they came back dripping.[14]

The grouse was still the main subject of conversation between the Wilsons, particularly because, whilst passing through Glasgow Central in May 1907, Ted's suitcase was stolen. It contained all the dissection statistics he and Ory had so painstakingly acquired. Luckily there were rough notes but much additional work would be needed before the loss could be even partially repaired.

From May to September, both Wilsons worked unceasingly. Visitors found them 'surrounded by a halo of grouse feathers and unravelled entrails'.[15] Laboratories were 'hastily improvised' in random Highland inns, or in the station hotel, with the result that they were 'not at all popular in station hotels'.[16] In one they had even forgotten a bag of slugs left on a windowsill! Ory kept pace with her husband, but when, in September, Reginald and Elspeth Smith invited them for a holiday at their shooting lodge at Cortarchy, near Kirriemuir in Angus, she accepted with alacrity. Isabel, always a breath of fresh air, would make a refreshing change from her feathered companions.

It was here, in September 1907, with their best friends around them, that Ted captured the most informal pictures of Ory. They provide evidence that Ory could smile and that her fine-featured face became animated when she did. In one photograph he captured a picnic in the heather. The Smiths and Wilsons are joined by another guest, a curiously tweeded Captain Scott. Ory and Isabel, while not 'lounging', look as relaxed as their corsets and full-skirted shooting clothes would allow. Both wear country flat hats supplemented, in Ory's practical case, by a mosquito net. From under it, Ory looks sideways at the bachelor adventurer.

Marriage with all its commitments was, in fact, very much on Scott's mind in the person of the 28-year-old Kathleen Bruce. Kathleen, also a vicar's daughter, was seven years younger than Ory and twelve years younger than Scott. She was strident, ebullient and artistic. She had been to the Slade and then studied in Paris under Rodin. She had not a penny to her name (much to the Scott sisters' disappointment) and although she was anti-suffrage, she felt she was her own exception to the rule that all women were silly and unworthy of the vote. Unused to female company, she talked directly – like a man. (George Bernard Shaw said his relationship with Kathleen was the nearest he ever came to a homosexual affair.)

In Kirriemuir, as Ory posed for the photo and regarded Scott from under the mosquito net, she had no idea that she was being assessed as representative wife and grass-widow. Ted told Scott that Ory was so 'suited' to him that she was '*all* my friends put together and all my relations'.[17]

On the basis of what he saw on that holiday in Kirriemuir, Scott asked Kathleen to marry him, driven to it, so he claimed, by the Wilsons' example of its felicity. More than that, Scott's Naval salary was modest, but Ory did not seem to require costly keeping: 'You're a glaring example of how happiness may be achieved without a large share of worldly gear ...'[18]

Ory was naturally thrifty and loved a bargain, but she and Ted both took great care over their appearance and hated anything that looked shoddy or cheap. As for servants, Ory would rather 'do' than 'delegate'. She knew some men whose wives had 'curious' domestic ideas above their station, but she had never been rich and budgeting was second nature. The practical side of life she could manage, although when it came to the trickier areas of abstract 'responsibilities' between husband and wife, she found it harder to find a way through. She remembered that Ted had originally dreaded the idea of being asked to accompany Scott, or at least that is what he said to Shackleton. What was his position now?

15

'𝒜 Bubble of Fresh Highland Air'

1908

In which news comes from Antarctica of Shackleton's 'fight'. Ory does not warm to Kathleen Scott, who is keen for her husband to go south and bag his prize. If Shackleton reaches the South Pole, surely the Antarctic will lose its attraction.

Ted was disgusted by misreporting in the newspapers, and so he and Ory were circumspect when, in March 1908, the *Daily Mail* headline 'Explorer's Fight' appeared even on the shelves of the Fort Augustus general store.[1] The article concerned Shackleton, who had dismissed Rupert England, captain of his expedition ship, the *Nimrod*, on grounds of mental health. The press fuelled suspicion that there was more to it, embellishing the story with rumours of a fist fight. But when later the Wilsons learned that Shackleton had reneged on the agreement Ted had brokered with Scott – that Shackleton had used Scott's McMurdo Sound base after all – Ted decided to break with his former friend.

If they 'broke' with Shackleton, would they also break with Emily? Was she also what Ted called a 'wrong 'un' by association? Ory remembered back to the time when the Admiralty sent the *Terra Nova* to force Scott back from the Antarctic. It was iniquitous being the visible face of the expedition without being in possession of all the facts. Two months before on 12 January, a long-distance radio message had been sent from the Eiffel Tower. It had travelled 500 miles. One day technology would allow explorers to speak directly to their wives but for the moment, Emily would have to wait weeks for her husband's version. It was May before Emily finally learned that the fist fight was just an 'argument' and that a shift in the ice had prevented Shackleton from landing where he had promised. Emily was ready to go public with her husband's defence but was dissuaded by the Royal Geographic Society committee. The news, they maintained, was old news and besides, an excuse for using Scott's base would be implied, when the public were not even aware that any excuse was needed.

Scott and Wilson and their 'wives' were not 'the public'. Kathleen reassured her new fiancé, Scott, that Shackleton would never reach the Pole anyway, he wasn't up to it, he would soon break down as he had on the sledge journey to 'Furthest South' in 1903. For Kathleen, Emily was an irrelevance. If a man's word could not be trusted, his status as an explorer and even as a gentleman was under threat. The man's status dictated the wife's. Events unfolding on the other side of the world had a direct impact on Emily's life in Edinburgh.

But the 'status' link could work the other way. Scott, who confessed that he was 'dreadfully sensitive to appearances',[2] realised that Ory could dress expensively without having 'a large share of worldly gear'.[3] Ory was a credit to her husband; Kathleen was, in James Lees Milne's opinion, the worst dressed woman he knew, with a sort of 'aggressive no-taste'.[4] For now, 'The serious consideration,' [Kathleen could be thick skinned, Scott had to spell it out] 'is that you must look as though there wasn't any poverty at all.'[5] Kathleen was learning that becoming an explorer's wife was not as simple as it seemed. She offered to dress in a corseted frock just to show him how appalling she would look.

The Wilsons felt for Emily. When the question of a wardroom present for the Scotts came up, Ted discussed the thorny problem of whether to put Shackleton's name to it. Was it Ory who decided that they should, purely for his wife's sake?

On 2 September 1908, Ory changed from her laboratory work clothes to her 'finery'. Ted's 'finery' was an old frock coat that made him feel 'exceptionally like a jaunty undertaker or shop walker'.[6] Together they headed through the streets of London to the Chapel Royal, Hampton Court, for the wedding of Captain Scott to Kathleen Bruce. At this stage they had spent very little time with Kathleen but sensed her ebullient optimism might be well suited to balance Scott's self-doubt and his occasional 'black blights'.

The Wilsons moved in a bubble of fresh Highland air: Ted's long, lean figure stalked. Ory, also tall and thin, moved, as a friend later observed, with a 'bird-like grace and liveliness ... an indescribable freshness and lightness'.[7] Preoccupied as he was, Scott noticed that the Wilsons stood out from the wedding crowd. It wasn't the first time they had been told this. John Fraser said it, too. Ted was at a loss: '... either we must be strikingly beautiful or else very ugly ... which was it do you think?'[8]

Had Ory tried to prepare herself for the possibility that if Shackleton did not get to the Pole, Scott might ask Ted to accompany him? 'The marriage [Scott's],' announced *The Times*, 'will make no difference to Capt. Scott's future plans with regard to Antarctic exploration.'[9] If Ory had wondered whether children would change Scott's plans, she did not have to wonder for long. All her life Kathleen had been searching for 'the father for my son'.[10] 'Capt. South Pole Scott', as she called him, was that man.[11] If he didn't get the Pole, what was he? She assured him that it was a little thing to be done. He must just go off and do it and leave no stone unturned. Plain old Captain Scott just didn't have the required ring.

Shortly after the wedding, Ted and Ory made an effort to get to know Kathleen; after all, Ted was Scott's best friend. Passing through London, Ted wondered if they might stay the night at the Scotts' home in Buckingham Palace Road. Scott was at sea and it would be a good opportunity.

One thing must have been obvious from the moment the Wilsons' warm winter coats were taken from them by the couple who 'did' for the Scotts. Kathleen was not a home maker. The Scotts' modest London terraced house was basic; she spent more time in her art studio. Cook was in charge of dinner. Over supper Kathleen concluded that Ory wasn't much use.[12] Ory, ignorant of this assessment, did not explain that 'Useful' was, in fact, her middle name.

Kathleen decided that Ory was not pretty but 'drab' (she really didn't like women) though Ted was 'a good-looking ... fellow' (fellows were another thing).[13] Kathleen assumed that Ory was as conventional as she appeared. Ory assumed that Kathleen was as Bohemian as she appeared. Both of them were wrong. Kathleen was outwardly unconventional but inwardly puritanical. She had led a Bohemian life in Paris but guarded her 'masterful virginity' until marriage.[14] Ory was, however, something of a rebel. She scorned social conventional and was not one of the simpering wifelettes whom Kathleen despised.[15]

Kathleen imagined that all women wanted to talk about was home decoration, servants and fashion. She flattered men by talking their language until, generally, they fell in love with her. Ted was a scientist; Ory was a sideshow. She had tried hard to get the evening just right but she had no experience of being a conventional hostess. She had no experience of normal family life. Her mother had died from childbirth-related problems shortly after her arrival and she had been passed between relatives before being put in a convent orphanage. Now in her first real 'home', Kathleen and her husband's friends tried to find a common ground, but it was difficult. 'We both disregarded the others' sense of humour,' she wrote to Scott later – the Wilsons' school boy larky, against Kathleen's London art-scene gay, it was never going to work.[16] After dinner, the Wilsons were shown to the guest bedroom. Kathleen liked to sleep outside in a hammock, but might have curtailed this eccentricity for appearances' sake.

Ted's thank you note to Scott is a study in tact. Ted often advised Ory to look always for something that is lovely and of good report. The loveliest thing Ted could find to report was Kathleen's enthusiasm for the role of hostess: 'We were simply delighted by [Kathleen's] kindness and abundant hospitality and welcome.'[17] Ory could not imagine a time when they would ever become friends. If Shackleton reached the Pole, perhaps they wouldn't have to.

16

Donkey or Lion?

1909

In which Shackleton has turned back from the Pole, making Ted's departure with Scott now increasingly inevitable. Ory wonders whether he really has to go. Ted cannot bear to think that Ory 'would fail' to support him in his duty to Scott.

Early in 1909 Emily received a coded message from Shackleton by telegram. Later a long article, telegrammed from across the world, appeared in the national newspapers. Shackleton had reached a new 'Furthest South' but he had not bagged the Pole. Scott immediately wrote to Ted. 'If I should go South again you know there is no one in the world I would sooner have with me than you, though I should perfectly understand the ties which might make it impossible.' At some point Ted must have talked to Ory. It was history repeating itself, except that unlike in 1901, she was not required to sign a prenup; as Ted's wife, her agreement was assumed.[1]

'A live donkey is better than a dead lion isn't it[?]'

'Yes darling,' Emily replied, 'as far as I am concerned.'[2]

It was a genuine question from Shackleton. Was it better? Would she rather be the widow of a dead lion? And Emily's reply is also qualified. A live donkey was better for *her*, but she couldn't speak for the general public. It was Sir Reverse from the Boer War, but Shackleton's comment misquoted, as Ory knew, from *Ecclesiastes 9:4*. Which would Ted choose?

When Shackleton and Emily finally emerged and took the train to Charing Cross, London, the crowds that had come to greet them at the station unharnessed the horses from their carriage and pulled it themselves in the manner of a classical hero of ancient Rome. Shackleton, 'dog' or 'donkey', was immediately lionised. The hero of the moment perhaps but not for the Wilsons. After the Savage Club reception given by Scott, Ted wrote to Shackleton: 'I wish to God you had done any mortal thing in the whole world rather than break the promise [not to use Scott's Discovery base] you had made.'[3]

By November 1909, Sir Ernest Shackleton appeared in the King's birthday honours list. It was the knighthood Scott had missed through outstaying his Admiralty-allotted time in the Antarctic in 1903. Emily became Lady Shackleton. Ory was a staunch royalist, but did the King really have so little idea of that most Edwardian crime of 'forestalling'? She realised that she existed in a bubble, an exclusive club where only a few people had any idea of the real truth.

It was in Fort Augustus that Ted and Ory first heard news wired from America that would set an unhelpful template for Scott v. Shackleton. Dr Fredrick Cook returned from the Arctic claiming to have reached the North Pole on 22 April 1908, but it took him a year to get home with the news. Ory and Ted read the newspaper reports. While the South Pole lies on a continental land mass, the North Pole is located in the middle of the frozen shifting sea ice of the Arctic Ocean. Where was Cook's proof?

Ted had just been asked to be godfather to his medical friend John Fraser's son and hoped baby Hugh would be happy that his godfather '… was fired in the South by the same enthusiasm that fired Dr Cook in the North! – let us hope with better regard of the conventionalities and Truth'.[4] Ory knew that she would never have to wonder whether Ted had done what he said he had.

Shortly after Cook's announcement, his former leader on previous Arctic expeditions, Captain Robert Peary, returned from his trip to the Arctic claiming to have reached the North Pole on 6 April 1909. Who could be sure who'd got there first? Josephine Peary was certain that Cook couldn't have beaten her husband to it and told the press. Cook was the surgeon on Robert Peary's Arctic expedition of 1891–92. Peary had dedicated a lifetime to nailing the Stars and Stripes to the North Pole. Cook's claim was a northern hemisphere version of 'forestalling'. The 'D.O.P.' (darned old Pole) as Josephine referred to it, was her husband's by rights. In the euphoria of relief at his safe return, her unguarded comments, quoted in the *New York Herald*, say the unsayable:

> … You don't know what it means to me. Twenty-three years he has been working for this, and during all this time I have just existed, that's all. Hardly a year of real happiness during all that time have I had because of the worry and anxiety and fear. But it is all over now. No one knows how much my husband has suffered or sacrificed to reach the pole. Many times he has risked his life. The best years of his life have been spent in that frozen country, far removed from every comfort and from everything … no one can appreciate how happy it makes me.[5]

Was Jo voicing what every other explorer's wife had felt but never said? Did Ory do more than 'just exist' when Ted was in the Antarctic? Could she be happy despite the worry, anxiety and fear? Ted had acknowledged that he knew that she had found waiting for him during the *Discovery* expedition 'a very difficult time'. Josephine Peary had worried not only about the physical dangers in the Arctic, but now about the fact that people questioned her husband's veracity, that most precious commodity, his 'word'.

When the Peary family came to London in the Spring of 1910 for the North Pole medal ceremony the claim was still not entirely settled. Shackleton had been photographed in America with Peary, but who was lending whom credibility? Ory agreed that Ted should consult Peary on dogs and depot laying. There was no doubt that Robert Peary was an expert in both. Did Ted agree that Ory should consult Josephine on waiting? There was no doubt that Josephine Peary was the expert there.

Ory had probably read her autobiography, *My Arctic Journal: A Year among Ice-Fields and Eskimos*, which sold out in Britain at this time. On that occasion in 1891–92, Josephine had accompanied her husband and given birth to her first child. Marie Peary was the first white child to be born within the Arctic circle and the Innuit called her 'Snowbaby' on account of her extraordinarily white skin. Latterly, Josephine had stayed at home with their growing family and become 'the one who waits'.

In his preface to his wife's bestseller, Peary drew attention not to Josephine's prowess as an explorer but to her wifely 'self-sacrifice' and her desire to 'be by my side'.[6] And Josephine corroborated. She was at pains to emphasise that, apart from the odd unavoidable burst of 'pluck' in a crisis, she was replicating the 'ennui' of the civilised drawing room, on ice. Despite this, the received opinion in England was that an American woman who accompanied her husband was somehow 'pushing'.

Lord Curzon would have put it more bluntly. So would most of the people Ory knew. It was more about class. In a classless society like America, one couldn't expect proper feminine behaviour. But even there, in the early years, women were not allowed to attend American National Geographic lectures wherein photographic images of bare-breasted native maidens were the only females allowed. Civilised maidens, fully clad, were not scientific and therefore, self-evidently, another thing entirely.

When later Ory was jokingly signed in the *Terra Nova* log book as a member of the crew, Ted was at pains to explain it away. It was not his idea and he did not want anyone to misinterpret it as 'pushing'. Ory was in no doubt about how her husband would react if she asked to 'come too'. Coming down to New Zealand was fine, but beyond? There were to be no maidens, bare-breasted or otherwise, in the Antarctic. A man dressed up as a woman for entertainment (a character in, for example, *The Ticket of Leave* play) was the only kind of woman Ted could imagine down there in that bastion of male territory.

On 5 May 1910, the Albert Hall was packed. Kathleen Scott had been commissioned by the Royal Geographic Society to sculpt Peary's profile onto a special gold medal. As Peary took his medal, he noticed that, although he had been introduced as the conqueror of the North Pole, the edge of the medal was inscribed simply: 'Robert Edwin Peary, 1910, Presented by the Royal Geographical Society, for Arctic Exploration 1886–1909.' The RGS (or was it Kathleen?) was obviously not absolutely sure he had actually got there. Peary, perhaps struggling to come to terms with this betrayal, held the medal up before the audience but suddenly, it slipped from its box and fell with a clang to the floor, disappearing between the floorboards of the platform.[7]

Was Ory there? Did she see the medal fall through the floor? Did she witness the awkward attempts to retrieve it and the nervous laughter that rippled through the Hall? Perhaps the part that most interested her was that Robert Peary was at pains to point out that his wife Josephine was not 'pushing'. She may have published her *Journal*, but she 'shrank from publicity' and her version of their time in the Arctic was 'a plain and simple narrative'.

Although Josephine had not accompanied him on all of his expeditions, her presence, on the last one to the North Pole, had been evoked. Josephine is the nameless 'wife' to whom Robert Peary's book *The North Pole: Its Discovery in 1909* is dedicated: the cook who made the candy the men opened at Christmas, the seamstress of the US flag Peary wore 'wrapped about his body' throughout the trek and the addressee of the postcard he wrote when he reaches the North Pole. This, murmured his approving audience, was more like it. The classical muse. It was the first time that the now teenage Snowbaby, Marie Peary, had heard an audience call out 'Hear, hear'. She was confused. Were the English hard of hearing?

The day after the ceremony, King Edward VII died. 'We knew that he had been too ill to attend Dad's lecture,' recalled Marie Peary, 'but we did not realise it was so serious.'[8] The Pearys continued their European North Pole victory tour to Berlin. Josephine, second-generation Prussian, was bilingual and what she heard was unsettling, but Marie was thrilled at the soldiers goose-stepping past their hotel.

Ory may have read news reports about trouble brewing on the Continent. On 20 May nine sovereigns attended Edward VII's funeral, including his nephew, Kaiser Wilhelm II, Emperor of Germany and King of Prussia. The newspapers noted that Reverend Henry Scott Holland, Canon of St Paul's Cathedral, delivered a sermon, entitled 'Life Unbroken', but often referred to by its first line, 'Death is nothing at all.'

Ted couldn't have agreed more. 'Death' was just a means to an end, not an end in itself, as Queen Victoria's attitude to mourning etiquette seemed to imply. Even calling it 'death' was misleading, it was just 'passing over' – to make the point, instead of calling life 'life' he began prefixing it with 'this': 'this life'. Ory knew that even Ted's parents had been amazed at the calmness with which he had drawn a pencil sketch of his little sister, Gwladys, on her death bed. Ted's attitude was like Ory's father's, but instead of reciting Job's 'maketh and taketh' version, Ted often seemed to be longing for 'this life' to be over, '… this is not our rest, and the sooner it's over the sooner to sleep.'

Both in their mid-thirties, Ted reckoned that he and Ory were 'about halfway' through Psalm 90's suggested allotment of 'threescore years and ten'. Only God knew for sure, 'we may one or both of us be much farther towards our rest than we can guess.'[9]

Frankly, he hoped he would go first because the thought of living without Ory made him 'inexpressibly sad'. It would be awful, like 'autumn days with their early-closing dark cold wet grey evenings, cheerless to a degree'.[10] Ted was getting sentimental. Ory realised that it was yet another of her husband's contradictions: to look forward to one's own death cheerfully but dread another's. How would Ory feel, Ted wondered, if he died first? Ted was a doctor (preventing dying) and a field scientist (preventing grouse dying) and Ory, his right arm, tried to be sufficiently useful to prevent both. At that very moment the ghillies were piling very dead grouse in drifts by the back door. Philosophy would have to wait.

The Wilsons were busier than they had ever been: 'my work is endless; it seems as if I could not possibly get through it all, and yet bit by bit it gets done.' Ory made sure it did. Ted, trying to finish the grouse commission report, had come to rely on her editorial skills. Now he charged her with 'two maps and copying out the Index'. Her copy checking was fastidious, her technical drawing skills excellent and she had a good eye for detail.

As Ory and Ted steam-trained their cross of benediction across Britain (Cambridge to Cheltenham to Scotland to London) Ory tried to create homes but it was difficult. Ted detested 'comforts'. 'I am getting more and more soft and dependent upon comforts, and this I hate,' he told her. 'I want to endure hardness and instead of that I enjoy hotel dinners and prefer hot water to cold and so on – all bad signs and something must be done to stop it.'[11]

Ory had simple tastes but she was not a masochist and found occasional luxuries uplifting. She framed an aphorism by the American Quaker poet John Greenleaf Whittier, that she carried around with her as protection against the more extreme elements of Ted's asceticism:

If thou of fortune be bereft,
and in thy store there be but left
two loaves, sell one, and with the
dole, buy hyacinths to feed thy soul.[12]

Between Christmas and the *Terra Nova* departure in midsummer, the Wilsons worked without ceasing:

> We have had work to get all done, but thanks to O. who has worked like a solid brick as she is, it has been done. I couldn't have done it without her. On the contrary she has had very heavy packing to do in London in very great heat, without me to help her. She then got ready and packed up all my clothes for the whole voyage as well as for the ports of call and the Antarctic. I left all to her and she managed it all wonderfully. Then when I came home I had to work late every night, and she would not be sent to bed until I was near to coming also. We were both tired out and dreadfully short of sleep, but I remember these last days with her as days of the most perfect companionship I have ever known.[13]

Much later, Ory allowed Ted's biographer to include this whole quote. It was the best description anyone had ever written of her role as a 'UH'. It gives us an insight into her stance on the suffrage question. For her, helping Ted, being Ted's 'solid brick' of a wife, was an end itself. Ory let the pro and anti arguments slug it out elsewhere and busied herself with practicalities. Ted knew how hard she had worked and thanked her in a letter to an unknown recipient. His biographer knew it and published the letter for all to see. For the moment, Ory's usefulness was exclusively focused on Ted. She was working with her man in 'perfect companionship' but still, at 35, she had perhaps not quite given up on the possibility of babies.

Kathleen Scott had given birth to Peter Markham eight months before, on 14 September 1909, just a year after her marriage. He was named 'Peter Markham' after his godfather J.M. Barrie's famous character Peter Pan and Sir Clements Markham. Ted had assumed that his friend John Fraser's boy would be called 'John' – if he and Ory had

had a son, he would be called 'Edward' to continue a patrician family tradition established in 1772. A girl would not have been Oriana, however, but probably 'Constance' after Ory's only sister, maternal aunt and great aunt. Both Ted and Ory loved being godparents and took the role seriously. If the godchild's parents died, they would adopt the child. If Ted did not return from the expedition, Ory might still become a single parent.

Hugh Fraser and their nephew, Peter Randall, were the only children Ted wanted '¼ plate square pictures' of in the Antarctic. With some prescience and not a little levity, he saw them as his legacy – he wanted to see them 'before I go South and am seen myself no more'.[14]

Ted could be flippant about 'non-return'. Ory couldn't. Shortly before Ted's departure, Ory requested a portrait and, because it would be a 'comfort to my "grass widow"', Ted agreed to it. With the portrait artist, Alford Usher Soord,[15] whom they had got to know through Herkomer in Bushey, Ted could discuss the unmentionable. Using a version of his 'slang' gallows humour that would not have amused Ory, Ted wrote to Soord following his portrait sittings: 'Funny if I go all the way to the South Pole to drop into a crevasse.' Soord has Ted seated and leaning back, hands in pockets with a smile on his face, a picture of relaxed nonchalance – 'That will give you something to think about. What good? And why so far to so small a purpose? Still funnier if I am allowed back again, don't you think?'[16]

When Ory expressed her concerns for his safety and perhaps her ability to endure another long separation with an uncertain outcome, 'I cannot,' Ted responded emphatically, 'I cannot bring myself to think that you would fail.'

Ted told her that it would be failure if he 'had to be afraid on [Ory's] account' and it would be failure if he had to 'desert Scott if he goes ...'[17] As the *Family Faculties* book attested, Ted could get angry when roused. The thing that really got his 'monkey up' was 'difficulties being put in the way of his proper work'. Although it would have done no good for either of them to have made this explicit, Ted felt his polar stuff was proper work and it was Ory's unwritten duty to not become a difficulty in his way.[18] The situation was iniquitous. He was impossible to argue with. It was familiar territory. As his nephew, Michael Wilson, concluded, it was indeed 'a thorny path' being married to a Wilson. Ory's outward expression of anger was icy, rather than hot. She could freeze most opponents into submission 'at 20 paces', but she could not freeze Ted.

After an argument, Ted tried to make it up to Ory. He assured her that, 'For real happiness our marriage would be hard to beat, and our married life hard to improve upon.' Everyone had disagreements and he felt sure that as they got older their lives would quiet down and 'God will grant us to be gentler, less ready to take offence, less likely to give it ...' He tried to reassure her that whether he lived or died 'whatever happened I know I should come back to you ...' Dead or alive she would be married to Ted. If Ted died he would be permanently with her. Through tempestuous discussion, he was gaining insight into his own character and eventually, at a loss to justify himself, he laid his latest contradiction at her feet: 'It looks almost as though in real love anything short of death is insufficient; and yet, though death for one's best and truest love is the highest thing of all, it is to be avoided by every means ...'[19]

Ted concluded the decision for both of them in the same way that he had elicited her consent for the *Discovery* but this time without requiring a contract. With studied chivalry he summarised: 'Anyhow you will do your duty, my brave kind lady, and your "kind sir" will do his ...'[20]

17

'The Right Wife'

1910

*In which Ory accompanies Ted to New Zealand. After reaching the Cape, they
escape for a third honeymoon. Well away from the increasingly acrimonious*
Terra Nova *politics, they lie in bed together watching bright orange weaver birds.*

The sun was still high in the sky when, at 5 p.m. on 1 June 1910, the
Terra Nova steamed out of the heat and bilge waters of West India Docks
into the muddy Thames. Ory was as much in her element as she could
ever be without Ted by her side. For three hours, she had effectively
been, the crew jokingly said, the Officer of the Watch. She had stayed
on board stowing medical supplies and scientific instruments into
Ted's cabin, but occasionally she came up on deck and basked in the
summer sun. She watched the banks slipping away on either side, Surrey
Quays, Greenwich, Woolwich. For once, she was not the one waving
on the bank. She was the one on board. At 8 p.m., the ship docked at
Greenhithe and Ory disembarked.

'Ory was on board but not I,' Ted wrote (he was whaling in the
Southern Orkneys). '... Ory's initials may be seen in the *Terra Nova's*
log as one of the Officers on Watch,' he continued. Either someone on
board thought her capable or it was that same someone's idea of a joke.
Ted, however, did not see the funny side. 'I did not put [Ory's initials]
there or suggest it, but they are there.'[1] Ted knew from his *Discovery*
experience that his journal, and any other written records, would
become part of the expedition's chronicle. To that effect he had cau-
tioned both Scott and Shackleton to mind their sledging diaries. The
resulting silence is loud. Their records, diaries and letters reveal strikingly

little about the workings of the human heart. 'The voice of authority on the processes of mental sublimation had as yet echoed only faintly from Vienna,' wrote Reginald Pound ' … and the expedition's first-hand chroniclers were also bound by sanctions that both respected and feared the private mind.'[2] These were not sanctions imposed by Ted but, ironically, by a democratic freedom of the press. It was a freedom exercised without responsibility for 'Truth', and it disgusted Ted. Ory as an aspiring Officer was one thing, a little thing maybe, but Ted did not want her to lay herself open to misunderstanding. They might discuss private thoughts, but Ory must understand that anything written down might be taken as evidence 'again'.

Perhaps it was also the Josephine Peary effect. What would have happened if the *Terra Nova*'s one and only female Officer of the Watch had refused to give up her place? It was relatively quick to get to the Arctic. The Antarctic was the other end of the world, adding months of separation either end of an expedition. How could one shorten the distances? The morning after Ory's 'Watch', Charles Stewart Rolls was working on the answer. Together with Henry Royce, he had bought a Wright Model A aircraft with 35-horsepower engine and seating for two. He took off from Dover, crossed the English Channel, turned around over Sangatte and was back again in ninety minutes. Ory was travelling to New Zealand to see Ted off but she had no intenion of attempting the journey by flying machine. The desperate handkerchief waving of newly-weds in 1901 was less desperate on 14 June 1910 as Ory watched the *Terra Nova* steam out of Cardiff under Lieutenant Teddy Evans, Scott's Second in Command: '… O. and I looked forward,' wrote Ted, 'instead of back'.[3]

On 16 July 1910, the Scotts stepped out of the Waterloo boat train, still smarting from Shackleton's disingenuous public 'three cheers for Captain and Mrs Scott' at the station. His wife, now Lady Shackleton, had not been at Waterloo. Ory knew that Emily was pregnant again and was also aware of rumours that Shackleton had 'an actress', a Mrs Rosalind Chetwynd, in London.

Scott and the three *Terra Nova* wives – Ory Wilson, Hilda Evans and Kathleen Scott – foregathered at Southampton docks and boarded the iron screw steam ship, the SS *Saxon*. Looking up as they walked up the gangplank, they noticed aircraft flying 20 miles to the west. Charles Rolls had died in an accident four days earlier when the tail of the Wright flyer broke off during a flying display.

Ory loved to watch avian flying skills but was putting man in the sky natural? Was putting a man at the Pole natural? Was it just exploration for exploration's sake, an end in itself, or did it, as she had always believed, have a higher purpose? Ory, Hilda and Kathleen settled into their separate cabins with knitting, books and seasickness cures. They were linked by circumstances rather than by choice and it would be six weeks to the Cape.

Kathleen and Scott had a shared cabin. Kathleen planned to be pregnant again before Scott left for the Antarctic. When she and her husband discussed 'the sex question', Scott decided that it was 'the women, I believe, who keep it in so foremost a place'. Of course, agreed Kathleen, 'It's their life whether they will or no. They can't get rid of it however intellectual or well educated they are.'[4]

It was modern to talk about sex academically, especially with reference to eugenics. Leonard Darwin, son of Charles and Chairman of the British Eugenics Society, was an acquaintance and President of the Royal Geographic Society. The Wilsons also talked genetic inheritance, mostly with ironic reference to the *Family Faculties* book for which Ted's dad had recently won a prize.

Which characteristics did one inherit and which did one try to avoid? Scott was worried that he might have inherited indolence from his indolent father. Kathleen assured him that he had not, that he was a 'lion' and together with her artistic skill and optimism, they had created a little 'Hercules': Peter, whom Kathleen had forced herself to leave behind in London. In Kathleen's opinion, it was men with the right hereditary characteristics, Nietzschian 'Supermen', like her husband, who could do things like fly, go to the Pole. Women were a contributing conduit, or at least that was what they were supposed to be. Both Hilda and Ory had failed in that purpose and were therefore 'not much use', and as Kathleen watched England recede into the distance, she couldn't help wishing that her husband had chosen the wives as well as he had chosen the men, 'better still, have none'.[5]

Life since the *Morning* had not lived up to expectations for Hilda. After five childless years in naval married quarters in Greenwich, Teddy's 'baby' was an expedition he planned to lead to the South Pole. He had raised considerable funds but Sir Clements Markham persuaded him to throw in his lot with Scott (including funds already raised) in exchange for a position as second in command. Hilda wondered whether he had done the right thing. Now, aboard the SS *Saxon*, Hilda was nominally second in command to Captain Kathleen, where the implication was that the wife took her husband's rank. But Hilda was from New Zealand, she was heading home and with every mile her confidence increased.

Ory was determined not to be involved in the competitive atmos- phere building between the lead wives. Ted hoped that as Scott's only companion on the previous voyage he would have a good position, and Ory was the only previous *Discovery* wife. She shared Ted's 'good posi- tion' but was outside rank; she was not a naval wife but nor was she just a 'housewife'.

The *Terra Nova* was an all-male affair but each man had in fact secreted a 'housewife', in the form of a travel sewing kit, in his luggage. Ory knew that Ted, a surgeon, was good at patching but she was the better dressmaker. As they steamed south, Ory could absent herself from the Captain's table with the excuse that she was creating a super 'Souper' line, the last word in next year's polar attire. And 'splendid article[s]' Ted found them, 'including … a very thick woollen vest, a thin woollen shirt, a knitted cummerbund reaching from chest to hips with canvas shoul- der straps to keep it from slipping down.'[6] It was fashioned with love as armour against the forces of ice.

After six weeks at sea, Scott and the wives reached the Cape on 2 August. The *Terra Nova* was nowhere to be seen. Scott and Kathleen left for a fundraising trip to Pretoria. Ory and Hilda waited in Simon's Town, a Cape colonial town near white sandy beaches and calm shallow water interspersed between boulders of Cape granite. As waiting went, it was beautiful. They were between worlds, Ory's to the north and Hilda's to the south. Ory had always warmed to New Zealanders and over the fortnight that they were there, she found Hilda was 'exceedingly nice and a very pleasant companion …'[7]

On 15 August, the *Terra Nova* blew in on a heavy gale from the north- west. Hilda and Ory went out to meet it. The Wilsons dined with the Evanses at the British Hotel. The wives were accustomed to female conversation, but the men were too tired to curb their salty talk for the ladies. Everything was prefixed by 'damned' and the *Cape Times* reporters who came to the hotel would not leave without their double reunion story. Ted carelessly noted that Teddy Evans had beaten Scott's England-to-Cape time by a day.

For the first time, the men of the *Terra Nova* had a chance to get to know the chief wives. To Henry 'Birdie' Bowers, Ory seemed 'coldly genuine to a fault, impatient of nonsense & without a particle of frivolity', a 'woman of strong will & fertile brain', 'thoroughly good' and 'the right wife for Wilson'. Mrs Evans was a 'womanly woman', she was beautiful and charming and '... almost everything a wife should be.'[8] Five days later, the Scotts arrived back. Kathleen Scott was another thing altogether. '... somehow I don't like Mrs Scott ... Nobody likes her on the expedition,' wrote Bowers, '... and the painful silence when she arrives is the only jarring note of the whole thing.'[9]

Ted Wilson told Scott that Teddy Evans had made an excellent captain. Scott thought that all aboard the *Terra Nova* were very pleased with themselves and announced a dramatic change of plan. He would take over command of the ship from Teddy Evans for the rest of the voyage and Ted Wilson would be put on fundraising duty, travelling by liner to Australia with the wives. Everyone was amazed. Bowers observed that, 'Unfortunately [Mrs Evans'] excellent qualities have laid her open to very much jealousy ...' Kathleen was happy to sacrifice time with her husband if it meant keeping Hilda and Ory's husbands in their place. 'Captain South Pole Scott', as she called him, must captain his ship and, moreover, must be in the depot laying parties to the Pole to ensure that no one made a dash for glory without him. Bowers felt that this was 'the last straw that broke the camel's back ... [and] Mrs E's pluck after her most trying of times must nearly have given way.'[10] He was convinced that Kathleen was behind it all, that she was trying to demote the popular Mrs Evans through Teddy.[11] Tensions were high. Could what Bowers referred to as the 'feminine point of view' jeopardise the whole expedition?

The Wilsons had a fortnight before SS *Corinthic* sailed for Australia, and planned a trip to see the whaling operation in Saldanha Bay. In Hopefield, Ted got them a room in a funny old Dutch inn. One of the other guests took such 'a fancy to Ory that he bought her a lovely bunch of very rare scented lily', and Ted was reminded that his 'wife look[ed] pretty well sometimes to other eyes than mine ...'[12]

Ory and Ted set out in a Cape cart driven by a Kaffir boy. Ted was in his 'discomfort' zone and only noticed that it was sunny. Ory focused on her admirer's lilies rather than the lurching cart and saw a 'gem' of a Sunbird's nest in a 'lemon scented' bush. She put the hen off and in it were 'two delicate little bluish eggs with brown spots'. Perhaps those eggs could prove Haeckel's ORP theory? Was it really necessary for Ted to attempt to collect eggs from the Emperor Penguin's breeding colony in the Antarctic? Ted thought the Sunbirds weren't primitive enough. Penguins were, he believed, half bird, half fish. The Sunbird was a southern sophisticate.

They were welcomed into the Saldanha Bay Company Hotel by Mrs Hart, a 'nice, clean, neatly dressed English woman'.[13] Ory could take almost any amount of adventure as long as there was somewhere 'clean' to retire to, and on their bed there were the most beautiful embroidered pillow cases. They were rowed out to the whaling station. It was not a gentle row, 'but a long business and 6 black boys had to come with us. There was a heavy swell' coming in from the South Atlantic which, together with the smell of the whaling station, made Ory feel sick. After enduring a tour she received 'a splodge of blubber on my skirt and on my gloves as a memento!'[14] But there were compensations.

After returning from the whaling station very quickly by rail they had dinner at 5 p.m. and then walked up into the hills amid a 'perfect wealth of flowers'. Ted was running out of superlatives. 'Scores of new and beautiful ferns and colours such as I have never seen or dreamed of in hot-houses or anywhere else; we were in a sort of enchanted land where the commonest things were all new and beautiful and one's foot crushed new beauties at every step.'[15] Ory sent pressed flowers in her diary letters home. She loved scented flowers, and they neutralised the sickly sweet smell of blubber that she couldn't quite scrub clean.

In the evening, a large black and white buzzard with a red-brown tail led them up a hillside. Ory and Ted sat side by side in the enchanted land and focused their binoculars on the eyrie, a column of granite about 40 feet high. It was incredible. As the sun began to set, two more buzzards appeared and the three birds circled above them until the sun sank into the ocean.

It was such a relief to be away from the politics of the *Terra Nova* and the Wilsons could finally relax. Political correctness was replaced by soul-baring intimacy. The whaling trip was turning into yet another honeymoon and the morning after, '… as we lay in bed we could watch a colony of orange coloured Weaver birds building their compact grass nests swinging at the end of long Gum tree branches. They were ridiculously funny in their chattering eagerness,' Ted observed, 'and the cocks were continually being scolded for bringing the wrong stuff for the nest, or for gadding from one nest to the other to visit friends.'[16]

Boat of Wives

1910

In which Ted escorts the wives to Australia and threatens to drown his charges in Port Melbourne. Fundraising becomes a necessity and tension between the wives is near breaking point. Who is really in charge of the expedition?

Ory was just one of a harem that Ted escorted up the gangplank of the SS *Corinthic* bound for Melbourne. For Ory, liners were a means to an end, but Ted saw them as floating idleness, trapped in a tin can with up to 1,000 souls. What could be worse?

Kathleen found her cabin and retired to it promptly with the sick bucket. Ory watched her go. She knew that Kathleen would prefer to have Ted to herself. The feeling was, at least, mutual. In her cabin Kathleen wrote about Ory's husband: 'I gather he thinks women aren't much use, and expect he is judging from long experience, so I bear him no malice.'[1]

'Mrs Scott was a bad sailor,' wrote Ted, '… and I saw little of her.' The Wilsons had given up trying with Kathleen. For the moment, she was a person to be endured and Ory regarded her with blue-eyed indifference. But Hilda Evans was a different story. Ory enlisted Hilda's help in an effort to shield Ted from the 'idle life' that always brought out the worst in him. Hilda was a willing accomplice. Ted found her 'exceedingly nice … as well as being always ready for active games all the voyage'. By the end of the trip Ted would bestow his biggest compliment upon her: 'On the whole I was very glad to get to know her so well, for she is a real brick …'[2]

'Active games' were all things that could be done in a whalebone corset: deck quoits, table tennis and deck golf, but they were no substitute for 'Furling the Top Gallant Sails' (a boisterous game which involved ripping each others' clothes off) aboard the *Terra Nova*. Hard as Ory and Hilda tried, Ted moaned about the 'impossibility of keeping as fit'. Things did not improve. 'It was a very cold wet journey,' wrote Ted, 'the crowd of Ocean birds was our chief interest all the way.' This was Ory's third journey across the world, and she prided herself on her ability to distinguish between gulls – increasingly Ted found himself out-twitched. In the 1890s up at the Crippetts he had been the expert; now he had competition. Rare occasions when he was '… glad to be able to identify for Ory' were noted down.[3]

She didn't want to score points off Ted and so, between sea-birding, Ory occupied herself with needlework and books. It calmed Ted to see her busy. Apsley Cherry-Garrard, Reginald and Isabel Smith's nephew, who was on the *Terra Nova*, had lent Ted a small leather-bound copy of Tennyson's *In Memoriam*. It was 'difficult reading'. Ted and Ory were religious and scientific but was it really possible to be both? In the poem, Tennyson tries to reconcile any conflict by claiming that the functions of nature – natural selection, individual development, and species' evolution – fall under God's jurisdiction. As Ted read, Ory concentrated on her needlework. She had bought some natural canvas, textile tape and a metal buckle to make Ted a belt purse for his sketchbook whilst sledging. She measured the sketchbook and cut around the canvas to fit. As she stitched the sides together, she realised that God and Nature had different ideas of an individual life's worth and Ted was voluntarily putting himself forward as the experiment. Tennyson also dealt with grief, asking God to 'forgive my grief for one removed' when he came to the understanding that heaven was a 'worthier' home for one of such 'noble type'.

As Ory sewed around the canvas belt loops she realised that the poem seemed to be a 'how to' in the event of Ted's 'non return' – sometimes it was a relief when he returned to the more prosaic issue of raising funds for the expedition, the task Scott had given him. Ted was not looking forward to having to beg the Australian government for £5,000, especially since 'the Government has already published its intention of giving no money at all to Scott's expedition.'[4] Ted suspected that the Australian geologist Dr Mawson might cause trouble. When the sketchbook pouch was finished Ory made Ted try it on and stitched two canvas belt loops to the back. Ted told her that Mawson, 'having failed to get appointed to our expedition on his own terms [as Head of Scientific Staff for which Ted's presence demonstrated there was no vacancy] he will no doubt have Shackleton to back him'. Ted was wary of committing thoughts to paper. He was the one who warned every-one to mind what they wrote. If questioned, the Wilsons would have held the party line and denied any difficulties between Shackleton and Scott, but Ted had become used to having Ory, his confidant, at hand on the liner and somehow their conversations flowed, uncensored, out of his journal pen.

Together with Kathleen and Hilda, Ted and Ory walked down the gangplank to Melbourne, Australia, and were immediately invited to Government House with Sir Richard and Lady Barron. Ory had a sar-torial moment. Her travelling suit was hardly 'Government House', but she was relieved to be told by Lady Barron that they could come 'just as we were'.

Being an ambassador's wife, albeit with a small 'a', was very like being a vicar's wife. Ory realised that she had been acting this role for years without knowing it. When they met the Governor of Victoria, Sir Thomas Gibson-Carmichael, and his wife, she remembered that she had already entertained them at Colinton in Edinburgh five years before. 'It was funny to meet them here as "Their Excellencies".'

This was the kind of idle life Ory could get used to. A life full of 'beauty and interest' and somewhere she could practise her effort-fully acquired new skill of saying 'nothing'. Ted was a bit shaky on his knowledge of children's books but he was trying to quote Joel Chandler Harris' *Brer Rabbit and the Tar Baby* when he advised Ory to make 'like Br'er Rabbit lie low and say nuthin' all the time and keep on saying nuthin''. It was a way of preventing critical comments popping out of her mouths, comments he knew she always regretted later.[5]

By now Ory could even tolerate people that talked 'rot' if they might be useful. She deliberately made the acquaintance of the 'enormously stout and apoplectic looking' Sir John and his wife, Margaret Forrest, who had done a great deal of exploring in Central Australia. She asked a few questions but otherwise said 'nuthin' and let the Forrests expound. At the very back of Ory's mind an idea began forming. If Lady Forrest could explore central waterless deserts, perhaps Oriana Wilson could too. Australia had its own *terra novas* – the unexplored territories inland from Port Darwin, for example.

On 12 October they heard that the *Terra Nova* had been sighted and, grabbing the mail bag, took the first train to Port Melbourne. They arrived at 5 p.m. in a deluge and Ted, Ory, Kathleen and Hilda sheltered in a petrol canning factory. They took turns with the Wilsons' binoculars, peering out to see if they could detect the profile of the *Terra Nova* in the bay. They were told it was 4 miles out. It was getting late, but Ted borrowed a motor launch and, loading the wives into it, ventured out to sea.

As night fell, Ted motored the soaking wives around likely ships in the bay but none was the *Terra Nova*. They returned to the factory once again. Three of the four of them would have left it at that, but Kathleen insisted on going on. The sea was getting rougher, they were all soaked and Ted tried to reason with her that it was 'now so late that I thought the chances of our getting on board were small as the sea was distinctly more dangerous for our crank little motor launch each time we went out.'[6] Kathleen wrote that he was 'furious and protested that the other women were cold and hungry, but I knew, that my man would expect me ... so [I] insisted, getting more and more unpopular.' Kathleen would not give up.[7]

Finally, at 9 p.m. the lighthouse people telephoned, 'so once more we set out,' wrote Ted, 'the wives with me and the mailbags'. The conditions were by now dangerous. 'It was pitch dark, and we were dancing about like a cork and rocking so quickly ...' Ory was sitting in the bottom of the 'beastly boat'. She was clinging to a seat in an effort not to be catapulted out into the 'bad' sea. She was soaked and shivering. Through the pitch dark she spied the black hulk of the *Terra Nova* with its lanterns swinging.

'It was for those on board, Capt Scott and Evans to say whether I should risk drowning their wives now,' Ted wrote, also by now ambivalent, '... so as they seemed in favour of it, I went in and they soon dropped down the side of the ship into our launch and I went on board with the mails.'[8]

Over their cups of cocoa that night, Ted told Ory that he was impressed. She had behaved 'like a brick all through our difficulties in the bay, but in the future I hope it may never fall to my lot to have more than one wife at a time to look after, at any rate in a motor launch, in a running sea at night time.'[9]

Ory had a finite resource of 'nuthin's and had used them all up in the 'beastly boat'. That same day Scott had received the now famous terse telegram from Norwegian explorer, Roald Amundsen who had set off to the Arctic and then secretly changed his plans: 'beg leave to inform you *Fram* [his ship] proceeding Antarctic'.[10] To a man, and woman, everyone connected to the *Terra Nova* expedition was studiously silent. Everyone that is except Ory. 'Scott had a cable from Scott Keltie to say that Amundsen was on his way to McMurdo Sound!' she wrote. 'It is really very mean of him.'[11]

Ted rejoined the *Terra Nova* and swept into Lyttelton, New Zealand, on 29 October. Ory had been joined again by her sister Constance and her New Zealand friend, Lily Bowen. Over tea at the Kinseys', Ted got his letters. It emerged that Clements Markham thought Amundsen a 'blackguard', though Captain Oates, a taciturn cavalry officer who had been hired to look after the ponies, didn't see it was underhand not to have given away his plans from the first; it was fine just 'to keep your mouth shut'.[12] Ory had heard that there was Japanese competition too: 'what will happen if [Scott] and the Japs arrive there I cannot imagine; it will be a bit worrying ...'[13] Ory continued as ambassador's wife when 'Ted had to interview the Prime Minister and many others'. Ory was proud that Ted's fundraising skills both in Australia and New Zealand had been performed with conspicuous success. Ted could play at ambassadorial roles, but Ory knew it was not where he felt most useful.

Ted was thinking more and more about being an ambassador, not for Scott or for the *Terra Nova*, in fact, not for man at all, but for God. Religion was the major subject for discussion when *Terra Nova* business relented. Ory wrote that she and Ted had enjoyed a very pleasant week at Bishopscourt. Frederic Wallis, Dean of Caius for the first four years that Ted was studying medicine, had been elevated to Bishop of Wellington since 1895. Ted used the 'pleasant week' at Bishopscourt to discuss post-*Terra Nova* career possibilities with his old dean. Ory left him to it – he knew that she had always believed that a scientific man like him could do a lot of good without becoming ordained.

The part of their visit that made Ory most proud was that: 'I found the other day that Ted was always called "Bill the Peacemaker" on the *Discovery*. On the T. Nova they call him Uncle Bill and me Aunt Oriana!' She didn't write 'Aunt Oriana the Peacemaker', but the suffix was, she hoped, perhaps implied.[14]

The Wilsons returned from their visit to high tension aboard the ship. Kathleen had by this time established herself as an insider and was frustrated that Ted Wilson persisted in treating her as 'an outsider as regards expedition affairs'.[15] Birdie Bowers wrote, 'There is no secret that she runs us all just now & what she says is done – through the Owner. Now nobody likes a schemer & she is one undoubtedly … We all feel that the sooner we are away the better.'[16]

Ory had practised diplomacy in South Africa, in Australia and here in New Zealand. But the final test of her fitness for the role of the diplomat's wife was just around the corner.

'The Influence of the Petticoat'

1910

In which the hour for departure grows closer, and near mutiny threatens the whole enterprise. Teddy Evans tries to resign over 'vague and wild grievances'. Ted is called to resolve the differences between Scott and Evans, with Ory's backing.

Harold Stemmer, the Kinseys' gardener, had been working hard since dawn, weeding beds and raking the gravel paths. Kinsey had commissioned the fashionable architect, Samuel Hurst Seager, to design the summer house above the steep coastal cliffs of Sumner, on the Banks Peninsula to the south east of Christchurch. 'Te Hau Ote Atua' was an octagon-turreted, verandah-skirted affair with a view to take the breath away: about as much Pacific Ocean as one could see at a time without being actually afloat. It was here that Kinsey entertained his visitors, such as Mark Twain, George Bernard Shaw, and this afternoon, the cream of Christchurch society would gather for afternoon tea.

That morning, the Bishop of Christchurch had come on board to bless the *Terra Nova* as it floated alongside Lyttleton quay. At the stern were gathered most of the officers, dressed for the last time for many months in gold-laced uniforms awaiting the arrival of the Bishop for the parting service. Frank Debenham, expedition geologist, described the scene that Ory witnessed from her place on the quayside: 'Someone among them suddenly says 'There's Bill,' and immediately a chorus of 'Come on, Uncle,' 'You're late Bill,' and 'Shake your long legs, Director,' draws attention to a tall, grave looking man coming through the crowd. The chorus and the answering smile revealed more than many words could do …'[1]

After the service, as the Bishop turned to leave, there was a loud splash. Petty Officer Taff Evans had toppled into the harbour. He was drunk. Taff had been to the Antarctic with Scott on the *Discovery* expedition but as soon as he was retrieved, dripping, from the harbour, he was dismissed. By that afternoon, there were 150 to 200 guests gathered in the garden of Te Hau. It was a sought-after invitation – the *Terra Nova* farewell tea party. The Wilsons, Scotts and Evans were the guests of honour. They stood under bunting strung from the 40 foot mast and greeted the other guests. The flags spelled a breezy 'g.o.o.d.b.y.e'. The garden was, as Captain Scott described it: 'wholly enchanting and such a view ... tends to feelings of inexpressible satisfaction with all thing.'[2] Although the garden acted as a salve to his embarrassment at Taff's little show, it ended in treacherous volcanic cliffs descending 50 feet vertically to the rocky shore. There was nothing but a long drop between them and the channel to the Brighton Spit.

The flags rippled in the wind like the ladies' long white dresses, their pretty hats firmly pinned. With white gloves the ladies picked the seafood eats off trays held by uniformed waitresses. The waiters had been told to keep their champagne glasses topped up. Up on the roof of Te Hau, the press photographer captured the scene for posterity.

On 26 November 1910, Ory and Ted took Hilda Evans onto the bridge of the SS *Marama*, from which the three of them watched the *Terra Nova* signalled back to Kinsey's flagged 'goodbye' as it sailed south to Port Chalmers, its final port before the Antarctic. The three of them stood marvelling at the crowded harbour, every ship decked with flags and the air filled with the sound of sirens, hooters and guns firing.

This could be enjoyed wholeheartedly by those for whom there was no emotional risk attached. Hilda used Teddy's phrase: 'They also serve who only stand and wait.' They both suspected it was too passive for Kathleen but Hilda found it comforting. It was the last line from 'When I Consider How My Light is Spent', Sonnet 19, by John Milton.

Ory knew that the Shackletons, and perhaps the Evans, borrowed catch phrases from poetry to help them in extremis. For Ted and Ory, the Bible was the script by which they lived their lives, but it wasn't very helpful on 'waiting'.[3] It just advocated patience. Lashings of patience. Sometimes it made Ory wild. 'Wild Patience' might be her epitaph.

The Wilsons had a last supper at Christchurch. It was an intimate feast at Warrimoo and afterwards they examined Kinsey's zoological and geological 'treasures'. It put Kinsey in mind of his last supper with the American author Mark Twain in 1895. Had he mentioned to the Wilsons that he had entertained Twain? Kinsey was fond of quoting his guest's 'after dinner' speech: 'if I carry on dissipating like this I shall be as extinct as your Great Moa.'[4] Ted wasn't given to speeches but he was given a Moa bone of his own. A rare treasure. Ory wished she'd seen a Moa. The females were the biggest birds that had ever lived – giant ostrich-like animals, six-foot-six at the back. If they hadn't become extinct, they'd have made an easier subject for the ORP theory than the Emperor Penguins Ted had set his heart on.

Which brought Kinsey onto Ted's birding trip. Kinsey had never been to the Antarctic, but a winter journey to the penguin colony? Really? Could a human, unprotected by the blubber of penguins, seals and whales for example, ever survive those temperatures? What would they get down to? Minus 40? Minus 60? More? Did they even have instruments capable of recording it? Conversations like these served to highlight the risk Ted was taking. For the scientifically minded, it was an academic experiment, but for Ory, Ted actually was the experiment.

Ted realised that he was never going to catch up with the thank you letters. Instead, he wrote about his hosts in his diary, confidant that Ory would rewrite the relevant passages to those mentioned after he had gone. Ted concluded that the Kinseys 'were dear good friends both to the Expedition and even more to us.'[5] Whilst the Scotts spent the night at Clifton, the Wilsons were driven to stay with the Bowens at Middleton.

As Ted wrote, Ory sat beside him writing, too. The panelled drawing room at Middleton was silent but for the scratching of pens on paper and the carriage clock on the mantelpiece. It was an active stillness, a companionable silence, peopled by the addressees of their imagination; those at Westal, at the Hilton Vicarage, by their family and closest friends.

They wrote upbeat letters, often pausing and scribbling a note on the other's page: Ted leaned over Ory and added cheery margin notes about looking forward to a family reunion in the summer of 1912. To John Fraser, Ted wrote that Ory was 'fit and well and is so much stronger for the trial than she was nine years ago'.[6]

On 28 November, Ory was up first 'and made my tea, Dear girl!' Unlike the Wilsons, Lady Bowen and Lily were not early risers, but they were 'actually up to see us off, which was a sad thing to remember,' wrote Ted, 'for I don't think the dear old lady was a bit happy over it'. Ory knew that when the time came, she must hide her feelings as she had in 1901. Her handkerchief was for waving only.

Waiting at Christchurch to board the train, the Wilsons and the Scotts were joined by the recently dismissed Petty Officer Evans. Ory did not see him get into the Scotts' carriage, perhaps because she was only aware of many 'kind friends' who had come to see them off. A 'sweet old lady, Mrs Anderson, came all the way from Pouawa to see my Ory off,' wrote Ted, 'and to give her some lovely flowers which were full of scent'.[7] For Ory it was an act of extreme kindness. Of all the confirmations of 'an immanent spirit of goodness' that she would encounter in her life, this simple act by a complete stranger, was the most astounding.[8]

The intimacy of their separate train carriage was interrupted at three of the four stops on the way south to Port Chalmers, where they were met by friends. 'At Rakaia, Anne Hardy waved to us from the Store which lies close to the Station.' Anne had given Ted a miniature New Zealand flag that she begged him to take to the Pole. The Wilsons had made many friends in New Zealand, but still Ory knew the country better than Ted. He was glad to see 'Peel Forest country where Ory will go for the first few days of her temporary widowhood to stay with the Dennistons [sic]'.[9] Ted had never been there, could not even spell it. Saying 'widowhood', albeit prefixed with 'temporary', was a way of disempowering fate. Ted had referred to Ory as the 'poor left behind one', his 'grass widow', and now a 'temporary widow'. He never referred to her as his 'ice widow', his 'Ice Burgher'. There were limits. It was 'carelessness' in line with his religion – a carelessness he increasingly did not feel. He never referred to himself as a 'temporary widower'. He was the active one, the one doing the widowing. Leaving her was his decision, but again he wondered, what if something happened to her when he was away?

The Wilsons' train reached Dunedin at 4 p.m. Petty Officer Evans emerged, jovial, from the Scotts' carriage. In lowered voices, outside the earshot of the unofficial reception committee, Ted was briefed on the current state of affairs. The official line was that the *Terra Nova*'s departure had been delayed at the request of the chairman of the Harbour Board so that an opportunity be given for a half-day holiday to allow the locals to give them a decent send-off.

The unofficial line was quite different. Scott had allowed himself to be talked round by Petty Officer Taff Evans. The expedition was being run on naval lines. Teddy was an officer, Scott's second in command, Taff was a rating. In Teddy Evans' opinion, Scott's decision to go against his advice undermined him, flouted naval discipline and showed rank favouritism which could prove dangerous when selecting teams in the Antarctic. Bowers saw things slightly differently. In a long letter home he wrote, 'In minor ways the influence of the petticoat raised that uneasy feeling ... the hand behind Capt S. could be seen in many minor ways not against anybody but at Mrs E through Teddy.' Bowers considered that Teddy had made the expedition possible through his fundraising, and now Kathleen was jealous of Hilda's popularity and the fact that the Evanses were in the ascendant. She worried that their increased influence on the *Terra Nova* might threaten her husband's position. Encouraged by Kathleen, Scott suddenly announced his intention of going on all the depot-laying journeys himself. The obvious implication was that he didn't trust Teddy not to make a break for the Pole and claim the glory. 'It was a slur on Evans' honesty to do that,' wrote Bowers. And it was the 'final straw in the heavy load that broke the camel's back & then the beast fell.'[10] Teddy announced privately to Bowers and others on the *Terra Nova* that he planned to resign unless clear boundaries were set. Many supported him.

There was a very real threat of mutiny. The only thing that Ted ever wrote about the situation was, 'Ory knows, and knew then, why.'[11] The information she 'knew then' would have discredited the expedition.

20

The Terra Nova Finally Sails South

NOVEMBER 1910

In which hours before the Terra Nova *is due to set sail, Ory, out of loyalty to Hilda, is implicated in a 'cat fight'. The situation calmed, Ory persuades Ted that there is a place for him on the expedition despite the petty politics.*

'Mrs. Scott and Mrs. Evans have had a magnificent battle,' Captain Oates wrote to his mother, 'they tell me it was a draw after 15 rounds. Mrs. Wilson flung herself into the fight after the 10th round and then there was more blood and hair flying about the hotel than you would see in a Chicago slaughter house in a month …'[1]

It was the late afternoon of 28 November 1910, in a Dunedin hotel on Princes Street. On one side was Kathleen Scott, on the other, Hilda Evans. Captain Oates hammed up his 'school boy' writing style to describe the incident as 'a battle' for his mother's entertainment. It is unlikely that Caroline Oates ever showed Ory the letter. Actually, Oates liked Ory, which was unusual because as the wardroom ditty went:

Who doesn't like female society?
I said Captain Oates
I prefer goats.

But Ory was an exception: 'Wilson is a first-rate chap, perhaps you remember him, he has a very nice wife.'[2] The very nice Mrs Wilson, challenging that prized title 'Aunt Ory the Peacemaker', had held out for 'ten rounds'. It was ten rounds longer than she would have done a decade before but it was ten rounds fewer than her husband would have wanted.

Kathleen blamed Hilda for 'working [Teddy] up into an insurrection'.[3] She disapproved of Hilda's tendency to wear her heart, or at least her fears, on her sleeve. Kathleen's extreme stoicism had infected her husband with a kind of careless courage: 'We may get through, we may not,' Scott said when quizzed on their chances of success. 'We may lose our lives. We may be wiped out. It is all a question that lies with providence and luck.'[4] Kathleen approved and assured Scott, in a note he took with him to the Pole, that she and Peter could manage without him, 'I want you to realize that it won't [crossed out] wouldn't be your physical life that would profit me and [Peter] most. If there is anything you think worth doing at the cost of your life – do it. We shall only be glad.'[5]

Teddy Evans realised how hard waiting was. Like Ted, he prayed to be spared for his wife's sake. Ory did not think it was cowardly to agree with Ted that 'though death for one's best and truest love is the highest thing of all, it is to be avoided by every means …' and asked the same of him.[6] Somewhere in this clash of attitudes to risk, somewhere on the scale of slightings and fears for the future, the gauntlet was thrown.

After three months with Hilda and Kathleen, Ory had managed to remain neutral, following her husband's advice. But to remain passive as she witnessed this particular battle would surely have compromised her loyalty to her friend Hilda. Oates claimed that Ory had 'flung herself into the fight', but Ory's perception of her involvement was different.

Ory had always had weakness for the 'lame duck'. Kathleen, by her own admission, disliked women in general. Her dislike, when verbalised, could be unkind. That Kathleen 'ran the show' on the *Terra Nova* was Scott's affair. Running the wives' show was not.

Perhaps Ory instinctively reached back to the time as a sibling parent when she had been obliged to adjudicate in family battles by applying: 'Kind, True, Necessary', the aphorism now collecting dust on her mantelpiece at home in Hilton. Defending Hilda would be 'Kind'. After 'ten rounds' with Kathleen, Ory's involvement was even 'Necessary'. Ory believed Hilda's honesty about her fears for her husband's safety to be 'True'.

Ory's first reaction after what is now referred to as the 'cat fight' would have been frustration at losing control. She had tried to broker peace but had she in fact let that 'tempestuous' streak get the better of her?

Ory was already dressed for dinner when Ted finally returned from his more successful peace-brokering mission four hours later. They were due to dine with May Moore, Kinsey's daughter. As he rushed around the unfamiliar hotel room, getting into the clothes Ory had laid out for him, she tried to assimilate the facts. Ted was really shaken. He had come to the *Terra Nova* as an act of God. Was it really just a cauldron of petty politics? Was there a place for him? He asked Ory outright: is 'there a place for me?'[7]

Ory knew that, to some extent, Ted had dreaded being asked by Scott. He had told Shackleton as much in 1907. Why had he dreaded it? Was it because he really felt he would be obliged, out of a sense of duty, to go? Where was his duty now? Ted trusted Ory's opinion, which is why he asked her again, was there actually a place for him?

The Wilsons were at the last stopping off point before the Antarctic, in the south of South Island. Tomorrow, they would part. It was back to God's plough again. Both Ted and Ory had their 'hands to the plough'. They knew that a reprieve had biblical precedents: 'he often takes the plough away as soon as He knows we mean to carry through …'[8] It was very like God to surprise them to send another 'bolt from the blue'. God did things just like this, right at the very last minute, the eleventh hour.

If Ted decided not to go, the expedition would be grounded. Scott would have been ridiculed for not being able to control his ship. Teddy Evans might have been punished for fomenting mutiny. Taff Evans would have faced disciplinary action in Portsmouth and probably been dis-rated. Everyone else might have gone home. Ted and Ory might have emigrated 'since they were there' and set up their conservation research, or gone down the vicaring route (Ory finally the vicar's wife?) or perhaps they'd have cut their losses and brought forward their plans to visit Japan, that nation of fine calligraphic artists Ted admired so.

Ory was practical. Ted asked her if there was a place for him. There was indeed. He had his cabin, she had stowed all his things in it after all. He had his position as Chief of Scientific Staff. He had his duty to Scott, that duty he had often told her about. And he was Uncle Bill the

Peacekeeper. He had peace to keep, a noble purpose whatever he might think of politics and pole bagging. For that matter they were late for dinner and then a ball.

In the back of her mind she must have realised that Ted was asking for her consent again. Her answer was like her signature upon that prenuptial contract a decade before. After ten years of marriage, he was asking her again. He looked her clear in the eyes – 'Was there a place for him?'

As they sat round the Moores' dining room table at Mornington, she tried to finesse 'say nothing when things go wrong ...' After supper the Wilsons were driven to a ball given by Mrs Edmond in honour of the expedition. The ball had a surreal atmosphere. The *Terra Nova* men had shed extraneous gear in Christchurch so that 'none of our people had dress clothes'. Ory, in her finery, danced with officers in 'tennis shirts, flannels or whites or any other clean garment they happened to have handy'. Ory moved between dance partners as etiquette dictated. Ted watched her, amazed, as he had watched her standing beside Scott at the post-*Discovery* ball. After two hours, the Wilsons retired gratefully out of the spotlight to their hotel.

As they lay there together on the unfamiliar bed, Ted's doubts took hold: 'I don't see another course open to me than to carry through the job I came here for ...'[9] Could she? Ory acted intuitively, soothingly. Whatever he thought of the men involved, his scientific reasons were inviolate. It was impossible, in those intense last hours, to answer objectively. Their 'perfect companionship' meant familiar rhetoric, each providing reassurance to the other. Ted assured her that she was 'my own love', that 'I love you for yourself' and that, 'You are all in all to me in this life and the next.' She reminded him that although she knew he didn't count his life particularly dear to himself, it was dear to her and she would like him back alive, thank you very much.[10] Ted's sentimentality was leavened by Ory's no-nonsense practicality. Amused, he recited his creed 'that *L'homme propse, mais le bon Dieu dispose*' – his conscience was clear that *l'homme* hasn't decided to do anything from first to last that he wasn't convinced would be approved by his infinitely better half'. As their last night drew to a close, they concluded that whatever the future held: 'even if it's worse than anything one can bring oneself to imagine, there is no more to be said or done than this.'[11]

As the dawn broke, Ory asked Ted to calculate the approximate length of her 'temporary widowhood' so that she could pace her 'long wait'. He could only estimate – two or three years, maybe even more. He told her not to be anxious if they didn't come back in 1912. They could, he assured her, live on indefinitely without any supplies at all, for with seals, penguins, skuas and a boat with whaling gear they could live on for years and years.

They dressed carefully and went down to breakfast with the Evanses, before leaving the hotel to call in at the Dunedin museum. They did some 'small shopping' and boarded the 1.17 p.m. train crowded with people who had been given a special half-day holiday to see them off at Port Chalmers. The Scotts and Second-in-Command Evans were on the same train. Relations were still strained. One moment 'we were happy and good', the next Kathleen reported that Teddy Evans' 'tantrums spoiled the day ... he told me a string of lies and hot air'.[12]

When the train reached Port Chalmers, Ory and Ted made their way through the crowd of mayors, chairmen, officers, officers' wives and well-wishers. Ory was wearing a broad-brimmed hat with a chiffon veil tied around and under her chin. She looked like a elegant lady at the seaside, no outward sign of stress. Together, the Wilsons walked up the gangplank of the *Terra Nova*. Someone, a photographer perhaps, made a joke. The Evanses and Wilsons turned and laughed, the shutter clicked, capturing their smiles, though Ted, tucked in behind Ory, is staying close. At 2.30 p.m. on 29 November 1910, the ship fired up its coal engines and moved slowly south out of the harbour. From the deck of Ted's ship, Ory saw the cheering crowds receding into the distance. The fleet of small be-flagged boats followed for a while sounding their hooters and sirens. Lieutenant Colonel Smyth's boat, the *Lady Roberts*, together with most of the other smaller craft, peeled off at the heads. One tug, the *Plucky*, continued with them out into the open sea.

'Ory was with us on board to the last,' wrote Ted, 'when she had to go off on a tug and there on the bridge I saw her disappear out of sight waving happily a goodbye that will be with me till the day I see her again in this world or the next. I think it will be in this world and sometime in 1912.'[13]

From the bridge of the *Plucky*, Ory waved at the diminishing figure of her husband on the *Terra Nova*'s bridge. She knew only that she must appear to be waving 'happily' as she had when she had waved off the *Discovery*. Back then Ted had been 'happy ... for my pride in her pluck and determination to be bright to the last.'[14] Ory managed to sustain the illusion until she was sure that Ted could no longer see her, creating the impression in Kathleen's mind that she was 'plucky and good'. Shortly afterwards, when Kathleen tried to muster them all for tea in the stern, she noticed that 'we all chatted gaily except Mrs Wilson who sat looking somewhat sphinx-like'.[15] As the *Plucky* docked back in Port Chalmers at about 6 p.m., the heavily overladen *Terra Nova* sailed south towards a terrible storm that had been brewing in the Antarctic Ocean. Without weather forecasts, neither Ted nor Ory knew anything of this as she stepped from the tug, marched up the stone quayside and carried on walking – straight out of the history books.

The Long Wait Begins

1911–12

In which the wives quickly disperse. Ory begins the long wait first in the privacy of Peel Forest and then in Britain. In the Antarctic, Ted builds a hut in her honour and goes on a deep winter trip to collect Emperor Penguins' eggs.

As Ory sheltered in the leafy calm of Peel Forest with the Dennistouns,[1] the *Terra Nova* sailed south into the mouth of the storm. Ted and his fellow men worked without ceasing. They were often submerged by giant waves curling down the deck. One dog was strangled by its own chain, two ponies were killed in their stall, 10 tonnes of coal slipped off the deck and with it, 65 gallons of petrol – and yet they were cheerful. The storm had exorcised the politics that had preceded departure, but even Scott admitted, 'It was touch and go.'[2]

Ory, without a crisis to help her and with none of that sense of camaraderie, put on her sturdy leather boots and walked. When the storm abated, Ted climbed the still swaying main mast to hide in the crow's nest.[3] 'It is not very warm in a bitter wind,' he wrote to Ory, 'but as private as can be, and therefore a very easy place to find you …'[4] Ory was looking for an easy place to find Ted amongst the birds weaving through air green and heavy with pine resin. She climbed the stony stream bed to the 46-foot-high waterfalls, noticing detail in nature to see if that is where solace lay. Hilda went home to her family in Christchurch. Kathleen left for Admiralty House in Sydney to wait for her P&O back to little Peter. All three wives realised that they were expected to behave as 'the good-mannered nice little wife' – only Kathleen chafed.[5] Scott had told her that she could do 'anything you like but don't get talked about'.[6] Ory would not be 'talked about' either. From Port Chalmers, even Ted's biographers don't 'talk … about' her since she is no longer a conduit to Ted.

On 3 February 1911, around the time that Kathleen and Ory arrived back separately to Dover, in the Antarctic, the British explorers discovered Amundsen's ship, anchored just down the coast ready to overwinter in the Bay of Whales. Borrowing his fellow countryman Fritjof Nansen's ice ship *Fram* without disclosing his intentions, he filled it with 120 sledging dogs bred from those he had used in the Arctic traversing of the Northwest Passage.

Kathleen's birthday was on 27 March and she threw a party for fifty-two guests to celebrate. Ory was not invited but sent birthday wishes from Westal. Before the last of Kathleen's guests left at 2 a.m., she received a telephone message from a news agency: 'Ship Sighted All Well'. She immediately informed Ory. The next day the cables themselves came from New Zealand. Guglielmo Marconi, the Italian electrical engineer who invented Marconi's telegraph system, had given them unlimited free use of Marconi grams before the *Terra Nova* left in 1911. Now they would come into their own.

At Westal in Cheltenham, Ory was avoiding answering the door. Outside Kathleen's door in London, she told the reporters that the expedition still needed money. Why didn't they make themselves useful and report that? Ory just said nothing, as she knew Ted would advise. Which ship had been sighted? Was it the *Terra Nova* captained back out of the ice by Lt Harry Pennell RN, to winter in New Zealand as they assumed? Slowly news filtered back that Amundsen's *Fram* had been sighted in the Bay of Whales, 60 miles nearer the Pole than the British expedition at Cape Evans on the McMurdo Sound. The Norwegians were on their starting blocks. As Ory and Kathleen tried to piece together the story, they tried to imagine how their men would have reacted. Ory hoped Ted would continue to think 'science first'. Kathleen joked that Scott would probably offer Amundsen a helping hand. It would be over a month until the mail boat reached England with their husbands' latest letters and journals.

Kathleen and Ory waited through the spring. Aviator Charles Rolls' parents commissioned Kathleen to sculpt a monument to their son. They invited her to come to their house to get his clothes. She came away with his coat, trousers, leggings and cap – the cap had blood stains on it. Rolls was a lion. He was dead. Kathleen would immortalise him. Ory buried herself in the lettuce-leafed beech woods above the Crippetts. In his scientific journals at Westal, Dad noted that, in May, New Zealand physicist Ernest Rutherford had discovered a dense positive and negatively charged centre in the middle of the atom. Ory took books from the Westal library. Many had been in her position before. John Donne's 'A Valediction Forbidding Mourning' described the Orys of the world as the 'fixed foot' of the compass and the Teds, the 'roving arm'.

> And though it in the centre sit,
> Yet when the other far doth roam,
> It leans and hearkens after it,

The summer of 1911 was the hottest on record and on 24 June, Midsummer's Day, the nature correspondent of *The Times* reported that, even in the deepest, most sheltered lanes, it was impossible to find green leaves.[7] Writing to Ted at the barley twist table in the shade of the mulberry in the Westal garden, Ory's hand slipped down the pen in the heat.

In the frozen Antarctic the temperatures were down to $-40°F$ – as cold as England was hot. Down south, the sun never rose. Up north, where the sun barely set, Ory imagined Ted sharing the Midwinter's Day treat she had given him, a parcel of sweets from Anne Hardy's Store in Rakaia. But would he be out collecting the penguin eggs from Cape Crozier? Who, she wondered, would he have chosen to accompany him?

Ted had chosen Apsley Cherry-Garrard and Henry 'Birdie' Bowers to accompany him. Cherry was landed gentry, Birdie grounded gentry. Both of them were stalwart. Ted felt the responsibility of keeping them all alive; this unprecedented journey was his idea after all, and it had made sense in theory.[8] On their wedding anniversary, Ted built a stone igloo about seven feet in diameter and roofed with canvas near the Emperor Penguin colony and christened it 'Oriana Hut'.[9] It wasn't a mountain range or a stretch of coastline but Ted felt Ory would approve.

Back in the northern hemisphere, Ory had many visits to make. Ted had urged her to visit Antarctic mothers: Mrs Caroline Oates in Essex, Mrs Emily Bowers in Scotland and Cherry-Garrard's mother at the family seat, Lamer Park in Berkshire. She hosted New Zealand visitors at Westal, in an effort to repay their generosity. The final report of the commission on grouse disease was due to be published by Smith Elder & Co. Ory, the only available expert, visited Reginald and Isabel's home in Green Street, London, in order to supervise last-minute edits.

Ted and Ory had agreed that he would not stay an extra year if 'home letters' brought by the relief ship recalled him. If the separation was too painful, if it made her ill, she must tell him. His boss intervened. On 1 October 1911, Scott wrote asking her permission to 'rob her' of her husband for another year:

> I don't forget that it is for the second time and that it must be a heavy tax on your patience but I hope it will be some comfort to you to know … I never saw him looking fitter than he does at this moment after the winter darkness and one of the hardest sledge journeys on record.

Scott had a 'sort of conviction that whatever happens your husband will come out sound & well'.[10]

It was a rhetorical letter. There was little chance that home letters would get to the Antarctic before they had to leave for the South Pole. Scott outlined his plans. Sixteen men would set out, using motor sledges, ponies and dogs for the Barrier stage of the journey, which would bring them to the Beardmore Glacier. At this point the dogs would return to base and the ponies would be shot for food. Thereafter, twelve men in three groups, using man-hauling, would ascend the glacier and begin the crossing of the polar plateau. Only one of these groups, the composition of which would be decided by Scott during the journey, would carry on to the Pole, while the supporting groups would return to base camp. Scott ordered that the dog teams set off again in early March 1912 to restock the depots and meet the returning polar party.

In the late autumn of 1911, Ory went up to London to attend occasional Antarctic lunches. Kathleen told her that she had bumped into Shackleton at a lecture given by Douglas Mawson. 'Shackles' told her

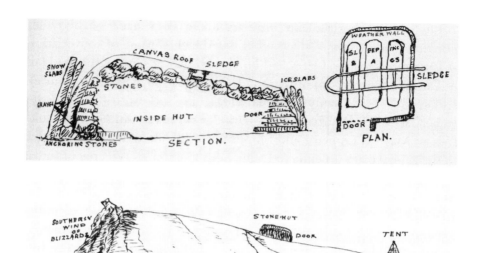

Ted's sketches of Oriana Hut (section) and location on Oriana Ridge at Cape Crozier in July 1911. (Copy of Ted's Journal, SPRI)

that Captain Scott was the most courageous man he'd ever met – she agreed. 'Yes,' she said, 'and he has moral courage too.' Was Ory courageous? She had high morals, certainly, but what about fibre? Kathleen saw her as a type defined by 'putting up with ... making the best of, the nonsense of Victorian feminine ideals'; it was a 'weakness' Kathleen 'didn't like and had no patience with'. And Ory, Kathleen noted disparagingly, was behaving to type, she was 'missing [Ted] badly' and had decided to go out to New Zealand in case the explorers returned after one year. Kathleen 'thought this would be awful'.[11]

For his part Ted wished that he could send a wireless message to say they were healthy. It would take a load off his mind and he was sure, a load from hers, but, he concluded, they must take things as they were. Writing on 31 October, Ted assured Ory that she had been right, there was a place for him, 'I was really wanted here after all, as you assured me I was and would be when we parted ... My next few notes will be in small envelopes from camps on the Barrier – God comfort you, my own dear wife.'[12] The next morning, he set out for the Pole. He hoped to see Ory's letters on his return.

On 1 November the extraordinary imperial spectacle of the Delhi Durbar scheduled for 12 December was the chief topic of conversation as Ory and Caroline Oates had lunch together at Gestingthorpe Hall in Essex. India was common ground. Caroline's son, Lawrence (Laurie), had served in the army in India. Ory's Uncle Rowcroft was in the Indian Army. The Durbar would mark the coronation of George V and Queen Mary as Emperor and Empress of India, along with the transfer of the capital from Calcutta to Delhi. Lord Curzon, ex-Viceroy of India, having resigned in 1905, had just replaced Leonard Darwin as President of the RGS. Would the Durbar ceremony secure India as the star in the British crown? If Ted and Oates reached the South Pole first, would it become a similar jewel? What would happen if the Antarctic was intrinsically valuable, with mineral reserves, gold perhaps. Or was it just the fact of producing men that would, as Oates had famously said, come to fight and not surrender? Caroline Oates did not need to remind Ory that her son had been awarded the Victoria Cross for that attitude during the Boer War. That was the stuff of Empire, the right stuff.

In the Antarctic, Ted thought of Ory and hoped that '… my old Ory [is] getting through the time without any sorrows or sickness or sadness of any sort. I always have the feeling before me that although I ought to be the most uncomfortable … it is you who are having all the more difficult part of uncertainty and doubt …'[13]

Soon it was December, and the Antarctic was everywhere, not just in Ory's mind but everywhere she looked, because Herbert Ponting's films of the *Terra Nova* had just been released by the Gaumont Company in London. Ponting had come back on the relief ship in the spring of 1911. His films were of the previous year and they created a sensation.

On 22 December in the 'real' Antarctic, at latitude 85 degrees, 20 minutes south, Scott sent back Cherry, Dr Edward Atkinson, glaciologist Silas Wright and Petty Officer Patrick Keohane. Ted was one of the remaining eight men who continued south.

Ory went down to London with Ted's family to see the films. There was 'the vessel [the *Terra Nova*] cutting her way through the pack ice, the huge ice cliffs of the barrier and the moonlit view of Mts Erebus and Terror … extremely beautiful', and, Ted's father continued, 'the Adélie Penguins on the ice were wonderfully realistic.'[14] Since they were in fact Adélie Penguins, what else would he have expected them to be? Moving pictures were such a novelty it was hard to digest. Ory, used to living with photograph-Ted, tried to adjust. This version of her husband was living in a different two-dimensional place – like real life but faster, flickering, glitching, repeatable and without colour or sound.

In the film, Ory could see Teddy Evans priming the stove as the men sat around the tent after a hard day's sledging. Scott seemed ebullient, rubbing his hands to warm them on the cooker flame, joking, often smiling. Birdie Bowers, and that beaky nose of his, moved quickly, efficiently. Ted's movements were jerkier but recognisably his. He took off his boots. He rubbed his bare feet, wiggled his toes. He adjusted his hat and the canvas belt she had made for him with the pouch for his sketch book. He looked so happy, so purposeful, the movements so practised, so familiar and yet it was a world full of 'dangers' that she did not share.[15]

On 3 January 1912, at latitude 87 degrees 32 minutes south, Scott made his decision on the composition of the polar party: five men (Scott, Wilson, Oates, Bowers and Petty Officer Edgar Evans) would go forward, while Teddy Evans, William Lashly and Tom Crean would return to Cape Evans. The decision to take five men forward involved recalculations of weights and rations, since everything had been based on a four-man team.

In London, Ory saw the film again and again. The bit that fascinated her was the end of the tent-pitching sequence where the four of them rolled out their sleeping bags and got into them like a row of sardines in a can. This was what Ory had tried to create with that live tableau at the *Discovery* Ball in 1904. Now the film allowed her get as close as she ever would to Ted's everyday life: the sledging, the camping – it was all there in flickering black and white. Ted had been gone a year but, for a moment, every time she watched, she felt he had been there, in the same room, walking and talking across the great white projection canvas. After Christmas, the Kinseys arranged Ory's passage back to New Zealand, leaving England on 21 January.

Kinsey was busy both with his shipping business and with his role as Scott's agent. The *Terra Nova*'s expedition had been substantially funded by an exclusive news deal. The Central News Agency (CNA) London gave Kinsey strict instructions that the telegram that would be given to him by Captain Scott on his return addressed 'Hereward, London', would be a coded message. Kinsey was to understand that if the news leaked prematurely, the CNA sponsorship offer would be withdrawn.

In the Antarctic, it was 6.30 p.m. on Wednesday, 17 January 1912. Ted and his companions camped on the South Pole in 23 degrees of frost, after hauling their sledge, 'the coldest march I ever remember'.[16] Close to their camp, Amundsen's Norwegian flag was already raised on the still point of the still turning world.

'Goodbye for the Present'

1912

In which Ory starts for the South. Ted begins the long slog back home. The thought of 'home letters' sustains him until he realises that he is never going to read them.

As Ted turned his back on the South Pole and began walking north, Ory turned south from Cheltenham heading for Plymouth. 'Our dear Ory sailed for New Zealand', noted Ted's father in his new diary on 21 January 1912.[1] The *Rotorua* was a large five-masted liner, named, encouragingly, after a place where Ory and Ted had 'honeymooned'. It was good, but it was not the best. A few miles up the coast in Southampton, the finishing touches were being made to Berth 44 in the White Star dock. It was being customised for a new class of giant transatlantic liner – RMS *Titanic* was due from the Belfast shipyard in just over a month's time.

As tugs pulled the *Rotorua* into the open sea, John Fraser and his wife waved from the quay. Second class was a departure for Ory, but with the expedition debt as it stood, anything else seemed immoral. She tried to settle down. Hers was a three-berth cabin. In first class they had plenty of large drawers and a hanging cupboard; in second class, nothing at all. She had tried to be anonymous but it was impossible – everyone knew who she was.

On the morning that Ory set out in the *Rotorua*, Ted was storm-bound in his tent – there was only just room for them to lie five across, with the men on the outside buffeted as the gale strained the canvas. When the blizzard cleared, the snow surface was 'really heavy'.[2] As he pulled, Ted tried to concentrate on the science, noting altitude, crystals in the air and whether the sastrugi, those parallel wave-like ridges on the hard snow, ran SSE or just S. But he was counting rations and glancing at his companions' frostbite. They had all suffered at the Pole. 'Evans has 4 or 5 of his finger tips badly blistered by the cold. Titus also his nose and cheeks ...' [3] They had cut it very fine, very fine indeed.

Three days after Ory had set sail, Amundsen returned safely to his ship, the *Fram*. The Norwegians had taken fifty-two Greenland huskies to the Pole and returned, on 25 January, with eleven. As Amundsen said later, it had been good sledging.

On the same day Ted, eight days' march north of the Pole, had bad snow glare. His eyeballs were on fire and, since he could not see well enough to ski, he marched on foot. That night he put drops of cocaine in his eyes but still couldn't sleep for the pain. 'We are all pretty hungry,' he admitted days later, 'could eat twice what we have, especially at lunch and breakfast.' [4] Oates' big toe was turning blue black, he hobbled as he walked. He asked Ted what he should do. 'Slog on,' came the reply, 'slog on.' [5] If the *Terra Nova* had come back down to the Antarctic from New Zealand in early January as planned, Ory's letters from October 1911 would already be at Cape Evans. Ted ached for those letters. On 29 January he wrote: '400 miles about to go before meeting the dogs with the ship's news.' [6]

Everywhere the *Rotorua* stopped, Ory sent letters back, 'ship's news', to Westal. The Bay of Biscay was stormy, but at Tenerife, where the ship bunkered fuel, she finally found sunshine and warmth. The tropics were hot and the second-class cabin airless. She spent as much time as she could on deck bird watching and occasionally people watching, particularly the promenaders in first class.

Franz Lehár's hit operetta *The Merry Widow* had spawned a craze for copying the Lucile-designed costume of the female lead, the widest brimmed hat one could balance (Constance had read of one of 18 inches), topped with filmy chiffon, feathers and even stuffed birds. Ory, sympathising with the newly formed Royal Society for the Protection of Birds (RSPB) and their mission to counter the trade in exotic plumage, felt such 'swagger' hats to be 'awful', but it was difficult to get that frothy signature tune out of her head.

Ory sailed on into February, peering between hat brims with her binoculars, on her way to Cape Town. In ornithological terms, of course, it was called sexual dimorphism. Why were humans the opposite? The Sunbirds of South Africa, for example: the males in their 'swagger' suits, dazzling iridescent plumage, the females camouflaged without even a striking pattern to distinguish it from the nest site. Sunbirds stirred old memories of Ted, of crossing the flower-studded veldt, of that whaling station and 'blubber on my skirt'.

On Sunday 4 February both Ory and Ted read Holy Communion in their prayer books. Scribbling with his sledging pencil, Ted noted that Petty Officer Evans 'is feeling the cold a lot always getting frost bitten … Titus' [Oates] toes are blackening and his nose and cheeks are dead yellow.' Evans' fingernails had all come off, so that the ends of his fingers were very raw and sore – Ted dressed them every other day with boric Vaseline.[7] On 8 February, despite everything, they 'geologised'. Ted found some 'splendid [rocks] in the short time, weathered coal with fossils, vegetable.'[8] He got some good things written up in his sketchbook.

On 15 February, the polar party had to reduce food rations again, 'only one biscuit tonight with a thin hoosh of pemmican. Tomorrow we have to make one day's food last for two.'[9] On 17 February, Evans collapsed. Scott was the first to reach him and was shocked at his appearance. Evans was on his knees with 'clothing disarranged, hands uncovered and frostbitten, and a wild look in his eyes'.[10] By the time they got him into the tent he was comatose. Ted, the doctor, noted that he 'died without recovering consciousness that night at about 10 p.m.'[11] Scott felt the responsibility. 'It is a terrible thing to lose a companion this way …' but more terrible still was that they had lost precious time. 'I wonder,' wrote Scott, 'what is in store for us …'[12]

Ory's ship sailed east into the Antarctic Ocean following the south coast of Australia. She was nearer to Ted, but not near enough. Perhaps it wasn't a question of proximity. Ory assumed that if she had been 'there' she would have known what he was thinking, but would she? 'My companions are unendingly cheerful … still confident of getting through – or pretend to be,' wrote Scott in his sleeping bag with Wilson and Bowers on either side, 'I don't know!'[13] Perhaps they were all pretending, though Scott, the confirmed agnostic, had started ending his diary entries, with 'Pray God …' 'Pray God the wind holds …' (11 Feb). 'Pray God we have fine weather.' (12 Feb). Just 'Pray God …'[14] On Tuesday, 27 February, around the time Ory's ship reached Hobart, Tasmania, Ted had stopped writing in his diary.

Ory visited the Hobart Botanical Gardens, which included sub-Antarctic specimens from Macquarie Island to the south. This part of the Australian State of Tasmania was where King Penguins were hunted for their oil, almost to extinction. Ory knew how deeply Ted despised it. It was just one of the many projects that she looked forward to working together with him on.

In the Antarctic, Titus Oates revealed the extent of his frostbite to his companions. Quite apart from his suffering, they all realised that any further delay might be fatal. Oates asked Ted if he 'had a chance'. Ted said he did not know. 'In point of fact', wrote Scott, 'he has none.'[15]

Amundsen's ship, the *Fram*, docked in Hobart shortly after Ory's had left for New Zealand. The next day, he cabled his success story to London's *Daily Chronicle*. On 6 March 1912, Kathleen Scott, still in England, was the first of the *Terra Nova*'s 'temporary widow[s]' to receive news, but it got scrambled in the telling. Posters shrieked 'Scott at the South Pole – Brilliant Victory'. Kathleen took the earpiece of her phone off the hook. 'I don't know if I have ever found my own company less entertaining,' she wrote. When Kathleen learned the truth, that it was Amundsen's victory, she found that 'My friends are afraid of me …'[16]

The news reached Ory en route to Wellington. She told herself that the South Pole was, and had always been, as Ted described it, the 'Sentimental Journey'. She remembered his arguing that when polar exploration became possible to any form of motor transport or flying machine, its attraction to most people would be finished. Ory knew the theory, but how had Ted reacted to the reality of the Norwegian flag? That was assuming he had been part of the polar party. Ory did not have enough facts and said 'nuthin'.

In the Antarctic on 14 March 1912, Titus Oates asked to be left in his sleeping bag. His companions refused. That night he slept through the night, hoping not to wake. When he did, it was blowing a blizzard. 'Should this be found,' Scott wrote, 'I want these facts recorded … He said, "I am just going outside and may be some time." He went out into the blizzard and we have not seen him since.'[17]

In New Zealand, Ory made her way from Wellington to Christchurch and to 'her' room at the Kinseys'. Hilda Evans, at her childhood home nearby, could fully empathise. In the face of friends who were 'afraid' of them after Amundsen's news, Ory and Hilda could show solidarity. Christchurch friends, the Burtons, noted that Mrs Evans was, like Ory, a regular churchgoer: a plucky woman, a worthy wife for an adventurous man. Ory focused on being a worthy wife for Ted, but Christchurch was just too busy. She decided to go south to Peel Forest. The Dennistouns had given her a standing invitation to go whenever she needed a home. She would hide in the wood and go birding.

On 21 March, Ted, Scott and Bowers pitched their tent. Scott had a badly frostbitten leg. Ted and Bowers were still fit enough to sledge and planned to try for the food depot 11 miles away the following morning. That evening a blizzard set in. Ted had not written his journal for almost a month but now he took out his pencil:

To my beloved wife
… Life has been a struggle for some weeks now on this return journey from the Pole … Today may be the last effort. Birdie and I are going to try and reach the depot 11 miles N. of us and return to this tent where Capt Scott is lying with a frozen foot.

We have been short oil and short food for so long and such low temperatures and bad weather that we are all done up. Evans and Oates are dead – our effort today is rather forlorn hope but I hope this will reach you … Don't be unhappy darling – all is for the best. We are playing a good part in a great scheme arranged by God him-self and all is well – I find absolutely no terror in the thought that this is my last day of life yet it almost certainly is. I am only sorry I couldn't have seen your loving letters and Mother's and Dad's and the Smith's and all the happy news I had hoped to see, but all these things are easily seen later I expect when we are with Christ which is far better.

God be with you … We will all meet after death and death has no terrors. God keep you in this disappointment. We have done what we thought was best …

Goodbye, for the present.[18]

Ted had planned to 'fall asleep in the snow' either on his way, or on the way back from One Ton Depot. There was a real chance that he and Bowers might have made it there, and probably back, with food for them all, but the blizzard continued to rage. He and Bowers had been fit enough for the task at the beginning but they were getting weaker. If they did try for the depot, Scott might die alone. Could they leave their leader? Some days later, Ted wrote again:

To my Most Beloved Wife:
I leave this life in absolute faith and happy belief that if God wishes you to wait long without me it will be to some good purpose …

… God knows I am sorry to be the cause of sorrow to anyone in the world, but everyone must die – and at every death there must be some sorrow … All the things I had hoped to do with you after this Expedition are as nothing now, but there are greater things for us to do in the world to come … My only regret is leaving you to struggle through your life alone … All is well dear.[19]

As the snow piled up around the tent in the Antarctic, Ory slipped out at first light into Peel Forest …

On 21 or 22 March, Ted died very quietly with his eyes open and his hands folded over his chest.

Scott was left. He zipped Ted's sleeping bag over his face and wrote to Ory:

I can do no more to comfort you than to tell you that he died as he lived a brave true man – the best of comrades and staunchest of friends. My whole heart goes out to you in pity.[20]

23

'Uncle Bill's Cabin' Takes Shape

1912

In which Ory, unaware of what has happened, hears that she must continue her wait. She is encouraged by Ted's report of the journey to Cape Crozier. Amundsen believes that anyone surviving those conditions can survive anything.

It was the beginning of April and a brisk autumn day when Joseph Kinsey buttoned his tweed coat and set out from their weekend house in Sumner. Ory and Constance her sister and travelling companion, loved 'Te Hau Ote Atua': '… such glorious views all round of sea & sand dunes & snow mountains'.[1] But no sooner had the front door shut, than 'a ring on the telephone came'.[2] Through the shrill persistent ringing, Ory and Mrs Kinsey looked at each other. Both of them loathed the instrument. The crackles made it difficult to hear, or worse, easy to mishear or to say something one regretted later. Bracing herself, Mrs Kinsey picked the Bakelite receiver off its metal cradle and held it to her ear. Minutes later Mr Kinsey returned, panting up the hill, with Ory close behind. Ory knew that she should have left the room to allow him to have a private conversation, but somehow she couldn't. 'I felt this must be something really about the ship & waited to see the expression on his face!'[3]

It was the Central News' special correspondent, ringing from Akaroa in the south of South Island, to say that the ship had been sighted and 'all is well'.[4] There was no detail. Later that morning 'another ring came'. This time Mrs Kinsey passed the earpiece straight to Ory:

… & I then heard that all the Expedition had not come back – that Mr Evans was on board. Dr Wilson was not … for a moment I had a shock as he put it in a way that I did not understand, so I asked if 'all was well' & he said yes & that Dr Wilson had remained South ...[5]

Determined not to wait for another heart stopping 'ring to come', she walked as fast as she could to Kinsey's office in town where she learned that Ted was in the final Southern party. 'It was an exciting day.'[6]

Ory knew that she had to say 'nuthin' to honour the news exclusive with the Central News, but she contacted Hilda Evans. Teddy had been invalided home with scurvy; Ory thought it must be a very 'bitter blow'.[7] Ory and Constance booked into a little hotel near Hilda's in Lyttleton and set their alarm clock for three o'clock in the morning. As the sun rose red in the sky, Hilda and Ory watched from the tug as Teddy Evans hobbled up to the bridge of the *Terra Nova*. He was bloated, he couldn't do up his jacket and couldn't stand for long without fainting.

After he had greeted Hilda, he told Ory that he'd last seen 'Uncle Bill' 148 miles from the South Pole on 4 January, one of the fittest of the final five-man party. He gave Ory Ted's journal from what he referred to as 'The Winter Journey'. Ted's birding trip to Cape Crozier was, Teddy Evans told Ory, a genuine 'world first'. No one had ever attempted an expedition during the polar winter at either end of the earth. There were three Emperor Penguin eggs carefully packed in the *Terra Nova*'s hold. The 'awful but wonderful' collection of those eggs, was, Ory knew, Ted's personal 'South Pole'.

As Lt Pennel steered the *Terra Nova* quietly back across the rose-tinted sea into harbour, Ory remembered the flotilla of 'fuss' that had accompanied their departure – now 'there was not a soul on the wharf' and 'all was well'.[8] As soon as she got back into Christchurch on the steam train, Ory sent a delighted telegram to Westal: 'Last News from South Pole Plateau Ted absolutely fit exceedingly happy Ory.'[9] Ted's relatives were relieved. On the following day, the *Cheltenham Echo* reported that their local hero Dr Edward Wilson was fit, happy and advancing.

Ory was taken aback when some of her New Zealand friends rang up to commiserate. 'I asked them if they had read the paper & they hadn't – so I told them that when they had done so – they would see why I was glad he had stayed South – that I was so very proud of his work & to think that he had been chosen to go on the final journey to the Pole

& that no one else in the world had ever done such a winter journey as those three men did …'[10] She was frosty and frankly 'quite annoyed' at their misreading of the situation. She did not need their sympathy; if anyone did it was Hilda.[11]

She wrote to Isabel and Reginald Smith in England. They would understand. *Entre nous*, she told them that according to Pennel, '"Uncle Bill" was the making of the Expedition – that in fact he was the Expedition!' and others agreed that he had 'held the expedition together in his peace making way.'[12] Ory could hardly contain herself – she was 'almost bursting with my pride in him'.[13]

Herbert Ponting, the official expedition photographer who had returned with the *Terra Nova*. He showed her the team photographs of Ted, Cherry and Birdie that he taken 'before' and 'after' The Winter Journey. Ory found them 'really quite painful to see'.[14] Ponting assured her they had recovered from their frostbite and that when Ted left for the South Pole, he 'weighed over 11 stone with nothing on!'[15] Ted, he told her, was made of 'piano wire' without an ounce of superfluous flesh on him.[16] Ory nodded. Clothed or naked, Ted was obviously thriving. Ory wondered wryly whether 'we shall have to live permanently down at the South Pole! The life seems to so absolutely suit him in every way.'[17]

Ory broke the seal that had been put on Ted's diary and opened it carefully. She flicked to the date of their wedding anniversary the year before. She remembered it well, she'd spent most of it on her knees in church, praying for his safe return. 'Fifth Sunday after Trinity,' she read, 'and an anniversary not easily forgotten.' Beside the date, there was a drawing, a sketched pencil diagram of a hut, and not only that, a section, a profile and a ground plan with three sleeping bags drawn in: '… and I called it Oriana Hut, and the ridge on which it is built Oriana Ridge'. Which is how Ory first learned that there was a stone hut and a rocky ridge next to the Emperor Penguin colony in Cape Crozier that was named for her.

'To the south we looked over the Barrier to White Island and the Bluff, and to the west we had the summit crater and all the slopes of Mount Terror,' wrote Ted standing at the entrance to Oriana Hut. 'Facing the door was the Knoll, a small extinct crater with the day light in the north at noon behind it. Ross Sea was completely frozen over as far as we could see in the moonlight.' Ory could close her eyes and look south over to White Island, west to Mount Terror and then turning, out across the frozen moonlit sea. 'It was a fine hut and would have made a top-hole living place in any other land.'[18]

The hut, it transpired, had not been a 'Useful Help' – it wasn't even snow proof. 'In some inexplicable way,' wrote Ted on the night of Saturday 22 July 1911, '… the snowdrift was finding its way through every crack and crevice of our stone hut notwithstanding the canvas cover and sides and snow and gravel packing. It came in in such quantities that we and all our gear were soon inches deep in it.'[19] Then, on 23 July, Ted's birthday, the roof blew clean away. It didn't sound like a very 'top hole living place' to Ory. Cherry and Birdie had wanted to change the name, but Ted told her that he'd learned so much from it that he loved it as he loved her and therefore Oriana Hut it would remain. Ory was flattered but more than that, she was relieved that they had survived. 'Isn't it wonderful how they come through safely?' she wrote to Mrs Pennel. 'It makes me realise how they are as safe on the sea and in the Antarctic as at home and I feel full of hope that all will end well next year.'[20]

The crew of the *Terra Nova* had been in complete ignorance of Amundsen's success until they reached New Zealand on 2 April 1912. Now *The Colonist* reported that Captain Amundsen would be giving a lecture in New Zealand. Joseph Kinsey wanted to avoid a repeat of the 'Cook v Peary' controversy in the northern hemisphere, and enlisted Ory's help to host Amundsen at their house Warrimoo in Papanui Road, Christchurch. Determined to 'play the game', as the popular poem 'Vitai Lampada' written by Henry Newbolt in 1892, suggested. Ory braced herself to smile at the lugubrious, mustachioed Norwegian and found him 'quite pleasant but personally I am not prepossessed by him – & I don't think it is all prejudice!'[21] He read the entire lecture from a script and '… he was very handicapped by the fact that the operator at the lantern was apparently tipsy – the lantern slides were put wrong way up – back to front – sideways & every way but the right – put in the wrong order & shown when Amundsen didn't want them shown – it was appalling & everyone was very sorry – Mr Kinsey especially so on account of Christchurch being Capt Scott's stronghold so to speak …'[22] Afterwards, Ory found herself in the extraordinary position of trying to cheer Amundsen up. They all went back to Warrimoo and talked for an hour but Ory concluded that there was 'nothing much to tell but his dash to the Pole – though he says that the Meteorological observations are very interesting …'[23] For her the evening was worth it for Amundsen's reassurance that anyone who could survive a winter journey like the one her husband had been on could probably survive anything.[24]

Altogether she felt cautiously optimistic. 'I think & hope that this time I shall keep well. I know it will be a long wait when all the present excitement has gone … I know better how to take things now …' She would stay in the country rather than the towns, not go for endless exhausting short visits and if she felt low, concentrate on her needle work or practise singing – those things always cheered her.[25]

On 15 April the *Titanic* had struck an iceberg and sunk. At the time of Amundsen's visit to New Zealand they were still picking up survivors, but the total loss was thought to be over 1,500 lives. The *Titanic* was 'unsinkable'. Polar exploration was, by contrast, full of 'perilous dangers'. Ory wondered again about the reverse logic. Amundsen's lecture reviews were all but buried under the wave of mourning that broke across the English-speaking world.

Ory settled to read Ted's letters and diary and admire the sketches and watercolours. 'You can't think how the thought of you and your encouragement stirs me to get sketches done,' Ted had written, laying his art at her feet, 'it is all done with the thought of you in my heart and mind all the time, and I love it all.' He was still experimenting, using Turner for inspiration, but he was sensitive about the colour – 'in looking at them', he reminded her, 'you must remember that they were all done by artificial light, acetylene and so they look queer in daylight. The blues and yellows are apt to go wrong …' Ted didn't know what to do. He couldn't repaint them in daylight because when the sun returned he would be out and doing: 'I don't like the idea of these hundred water-colours being shown as they stand ...' He trusted her to sort it out, 'Ory ... will have the doing of anything there is to be done ...'[26] Ory, the 'U.H.' did 'the doing'. She decided not to exhibit Ted's pictures alongside Ponting's but to make a separate exhibition later on (using lawyers this time so that 'the sharper' would be properly tamed). Ory hoped by that time, Amundsen's news would be old news and, she observed: 'I trust there will be no huge strikes on.'[27]

Ory was referring to a strike at the Singer sewing machine factory on Clyde bank in Scotland in April and the threat of a transport strike in Liverpool. She decided to stay out of it in New Zealand, saving the price of a return ticket home but she did not relish the thought of being a guest. She needed that 'Oriana Hut'.

The first Ory knew of it was a visit to the dockyard in Lyttelton. A pile of planks? Kinsey told her that it was, indeed a pile of planks at the moment. A solid tongue-and-groove construction, designed by Boulton & Paul. It had been taken south by Scott as a hut for the expedition meteorologists. When it was deemed 'surplus to requirements', it was brought back to New Zealand in the *Terra Nova*. Kinsey had now pur-chased it, partly to help allay the expedition's debts and partly to provide a base for her.

Whilst Ory was trying to take in this extraordinary kindness, the Kinsey's discussed suitable names. *Uncle Tom's Cabin* by Harriet Beecher Stowe, published in 1852, was the best-selling book of the nineteenth century after the *Bible*. Ory knew all the characters. Uncle Tom was a freed slave from the American Deep South who lived in the cabin on his former owner's land. Was it Ory who named it 'Uncle Bill's Cabin' or the Kinseys?[28]

Gradually, the reality of Kinsey's offer sank in. It was perfect. Ory would have something to do and somewhere to live. Ted would love that cabin when he came back – it would appeal to his ascetic tastes. The pattern book showed a platform along the ridge line of the roof. It was like the deck of a ship, a land ship, a look out, a crow's nest you could actually live in. She knew that Ted had often found privacy in the crow's nest of the *Terra Nova*. Now they would have a nest of their own. Kinsey suggested erecting it in their garden at 'Te Hau', in Sumner. It would be basic but Ory was almost relieved to relinquish the teagown lifestyle of a decade ago and relished the opportunity.

So gradually the thing got done. The mules were engaged to drag the planks up the hill. The ground was prepared. The pattern book studied, until gradually 'Uncle Bill's Cabin' rose from the ground.[29] It was a thrilling business. But for now, Ory returned to her desk at the Kinseys' main house in Papanui Road where she could read Ted's diary in peace. It was so intimate, like a conversation, written to her as his confidant. All day when they were in the hut at Cape Evans, he had listened to grievances and confidences from the other men. 'My goodness I had hours of yesterday; as though I was a bucket it was poured into me,' and he poured it all out to Ory. 'It isn't what I should like to write to you about most of all but it is what is much in my mind last thing at night and first thing in the morning, and it is a huge comfort to me to be able to voice it to someone ...'

Soon it was May Day 1912, the middle of the New Zealand winter. 'I dreamt of you singing at the piano, impromptu, to a number of people,' Ted had written the previous May. 'You were trying to pick up a tune and every time you tried it ran into a sea-shanty that we sing down here, and that wasn't what you wanted. You looked lovely because you were sitting with your back to a large window through which was a perfect glory of buttercups in a lovely hayfield in bright sunshine. I love to think of you enjoying May sunshine ...'[30] When Ted pictured Ory, he thought of her as still in England, probably in one of the top fields at the Crippetts. It was somewhere full of summer, beauty, 'a perfect glory'.

By September 1912 she had become quite house proud, comparing her cabin to the B34 Seaside Bungalow of her nearest neighbour, out of sight at the bottom of the hill. Ory's was a real beauty, wood-lined and snug as a cigar box. The table set with imported china and the French doors opened out onto those epic ocean views. While the workmen were fixing the fireplace, Ory watched sea birds as they slid across the sky.

Harold Stemmers looked at the fence he had put up along the edge of the cliff edge, that precipice at the end of the garden. He noticed that Mrs Wilson was a slim lady and that her long dress caught the wind like a kite. It would only take one gust. After the stone 'viewing' platform was built, Ory got involved in the garden. Rockeries were all the rage. Could Stemmer use some of the volcanic rock that Kinsey had asked Pennell to bring back from Mount Erebus in the Antarctic, as ballast? They would recreate an Antarctic landscape right here in Sumner – hot-coloured flowers to represent lava and perhaps white flowers for snow. As she sat in the hut looking out at the rockery, she could imagine Ted, back from the Pole, snug in his Antarctic hut looking out at the real Mount Erebus.

In October 1912 as the balcony railing was being fixed around the flat deck on top of her cabin in the early summer sunshine, Ory turned 38. Anniversaries had never been so important. Birthdays and wedding anniversaries were days on which Ory could know, for certain, that Ted would be thinking about her.

She framed some of his penguin pictures and put them on the walls of their cabin. She thought about the lives of the Emperor Penguins, their ability to wait, to endure.

In December, the recently promoted Commander Evans returned from meeting the King, back across the globe to New Zealand with news and parcels from England. Together with Pennell, he sailed back to collect her husband from the Antarctic. Ory envied them. Pennel and Teddy would see Ted in January 1913. She would have to wait until the *Terra Nova* returned, probably sometime in March or early April 1913.

Ory often sat on the 'terrace' of Uncle Bill's looking south towards that windswept roofless 'Oriana Hut' at Cape Crozier. On 24 December 1912, as she and Constance boarded the train for Ashbuton and Christmas at Peel Forest, Ory reflected that, in the competition for creating 'a top hole living place', she probably had the edge. To Jim Wilson she confided that sometimes she felt 'I have had so much happiness crammed into my life that it can't go on.'[31]

PART 2

NEWS OF TED'S DEATH

REACHES ORY

10 February 1913

OAMARU

At 2.30 a.m., the *Terra Nova* sailed towards Oamaru Harbour in South Island under cover of darkness. Three men rowed ashore to Sumpter Wharf. One rowed back. The other two went to the Harbour Master's house and, politely refusing his wife's offer of beds, slept on the floor. The *Terra Nova* steamed back out to sea and hid over the eastern horizon.

Scott had issued specific instructions about how the expedition news should be released. A lucrative sponsorship deal depended upon absolute secrecy. A coded message would be telegrammed to the Central News Agency in London in the morning so that they had exclusive access to the news for twenty-four hours.

The two men sent a brief telegram to Kinsey in Christchurch before settling down in a field beside Oamaru station to wait for the Christchurch-bound train. When they boarded, the 'two men in seaboots' roused suspicion. Was one of them Captain Scott? The men smiled but would not divulge anything: their orders were to 'say nothing'.[1]

DUNEDIN

Seventy miles to the south in Dunedin, Ory was staying with May Moore, Kinsey's married daughter. In the early morning she woke suddenly with a strong sense of her husband's presence in her room. 'I felt Ted so near early in the morning,' she wrote, '& wondered whether he was specially thinking of me.'[2]

CHRISTCHURCH

In Christchurch, Kinsey received the brief telegram message from Oamaru and forwarded it, as per Scott's explicit instructions, to the Central News Offices in London. At some point in the day, he contacted his daughter May, giving her instructions to put Ory on the train north to Christchurch the following morning.

DUNEDIN

May Moore passed the message on to her guest. They walked down the steep hill to Dunedin train station to buy a ticket and Ory returned to pack.

CHRISTCHURCH

The New Zealand newspapers heard rumours that the *Terra Nova* was sighted off Oamaru and approached Kinsey as the expedition's agent. He told them that he only knew as much as they did.[3]

When the Christchurch train arrived from Oamaru, the 'two men in seaboots' walked straight to Warrimoo on Papanui Road. They gave Kinsey the expedition report and a note from Teddy Evans: 'I am very worried about poor Mrs Wilson,' wrote Teddy, 'I feel somehow that the blow to her will be far worse than to the others. Mrs Scott has her son, but Uncle Bill was all the world to his wife ...'[4]

11 February 1913

CHRISTCHURCH
Using the prearranged code, Kinsey telegrammed the 2,500 word expedition report to the Central News Agency in London.

DUNEDIN
Ory said goodbye to May and William Moore and boarded the train. She would arrive in Christchurch in the late afternoon.

Around lunch time, when her train drew into Ashburton, she noticed that there were crowds gathering around a notice on the station platform. Suddenly her carriage door burst open. The Dennistouns had heard rumours that a ship had been sighted and, saddling their horses, galloped from Peel Forest hoping that Ory would be on the train.[5]

CHRISTCHURCH
By late afternoon, Ory's train drew into Christchurch station. She was aware of vague rumours that a ship had been sighted but also that one of the 'two men in seaboots' who seemed to be ahead of her, was thought to be Captain Scott. Perhaps the other was Ted?

The Dennistouns knew no more than she did, but she had often told them about the wonderful reunion of April 1904. The last time Ted had returned from the Antarctic, had been one of the single best moments of their lives: 'This sort of meeting,' Ted wrote, 'beats a wedding hollow'.[6]

Over the hiss of steam brakes and the clatter of doors banging, porters wielding their trolleys and the chatter of reunions, Ory noticed that the Christchurch cathedral bell was tolling out a single note. She walked up the platform, looking for Kinsey through the crowd.

On the edges of her hearing she became aware of a newspaper hawker in a kiosk in the main station building. A loud New Zealand accent called, 'Antarctic Tragedy!'

Scott ... Bowers ... Oates ... Evans ... Wilson.

Her husband is dead.[7]

24

The Last Letters

FEBRUARY 1913

In which Ory derives some comfort from Ted's last letters and feels a strong sense of his continuing presence in her life. Ory and Kathleen are disturbed by entries in the diaries referring to shortages at the depots and begin to suspect Teddy Evans.

The two 'men in sea boots' who greeted Ory when she first walked into the Kinseys' home turned out to be Lt Pennell and Dr Atkinson (Atch). Pennell was upset. He had planned it all so carefully. He had wanted to make sure that Ory heard her news from one of them, not from a stranger, not as a gossiped rumour or a disinterested newspaper headline. Ory tried to reassure them. It was the news itself rather than the manner of hearing it that was important after all. Both men were impressed by her poise, her generous reassurance, her concern for others.

Atch handed her a worn canvas pouch. Ory recognised it as the one she had made on the SS *Corinthic* whilst discussing Tennyson with Ted. She knew that Ted admired the Navy doctor and now she asked for a detailed account. Atch told her about finding the bodies in the Antarctic. Charles Wright had been the first to see a small speck, which tuned out to be the top six inches of the tent. It had been covered with snow and looked like a cairn covered in drift. Beside it they found the skis and a buried sledge. As they began to dig it out they saw the outlines of three bodies in sleeping bags lying side by side. The tent had been pitched well and was as neat as ever, with the canvas spread 'taut and ship shape' and the inside lining free from snow.

They opened the tent flap to find Ted's eyes fixed on the entrance. He was lying in a reclined position, with his arms folded quietly across his chest. Scott was in the middle with his arm flung out across Ted. Bowers was on the opposite side. They were only 11 miles to the south of One Ton Depot. Ted had died peacefully. As a medic, Atch could assure Ory that he had passed away in his sleep.

Ory told him that she had felt her husband's presence early the previous morning. Was that normal? Atch told her that one night during the eight months they had been waiting for the polar party's return, when they heard five or six knocks on the little window above their bed. Atch had cried, 'Hullo ... Cherry they're in' and they all rushed outside. There was no one there. It was a potent mixture of hope and 'ghost work'. He thought it probably wouldn't be the last time Ory felt Ted near.[1]

Ory looked at the canvas pouch Atch had given her. The buckle was broken and along the back, where the loops threaded through his belt, it was stained with Ted's sweat. Lifting the flap she could see that inside were what looked like his diaries and sketchbooks, she knew the shape – landscape with rounded corners. She drew the diaries out. The paper was mottled, translucent. Pencilled notes.

She knew that Ted would have urged patience and scientific method, chronology and measured accumulation, but she needed to find out if he had written a note, a last note, to her. There were various letters written vertically so that the bottom of the letter was near the spine of the book. She imagined Ted sitting in his tent, reclined with his knees bent. The front cover would be on his chest, this book in the crook of his body, the page opened on his lap as he wrote.[2]

To my beloved wife ...

The writing was self-controlled, neat, the script, recognisably his. She felt the anticipation of a reunion and it was a reunion of sorts. In this book was more of Ted that she did not yet know.

... Life has been a struggle for some weeks now ...

It was a lot of new information to try to digest in a single sitting – especially as she tried to adjust to the reality that Ted, the writer, the speaker almost, was gone.

… We have been short oil and short food for so long …

Had Ted and Bowers set out for the depot and then returned, or had they never even tried? Eleven miles was not impossible. Ory remembered his attitude to his tuberculosis and acknowledged that it was more in character to be resigned to his fate than to fight it, especially where it involved the tantalising prospect of heaven.

She skimmed to the end of the letter and flicked over the page. Another diary. Another letter:

To my most beloved Wife …[3]

This letter was longer than the first, several pages. In it he referred to the first. So this had been written later. By this time he had either tried and failed to get to the food depot, or had given up the idea of even trying. Instead it seemed that he had focused entirely on comforting her, exhorting her to 'take heart and live your life out'. Their record was 'clean'. She had never doubted it.

Had Ted died hungry and cold? She couldn't bear to think about it. He seemed to answer her:

… don't imagine [me] dying in any pain or suffering or in sorrow – either bodily or mental – for I shall simply fall asleep and awake with Christ …

But he had written that before he died. Had his death been as gentle as he had anticipated? Had he just 'passed away in his sleep' as Atch described? Was it just as simple as 'passing over' as the Wilson family told? The 'not knowing' worked both ways. Ted did not know, as he lay dying in that tent in the Antarctic, whether she was alive or dead. He wrote:

> *... but God may have even now closed [your life] before mine and I may
> be coming to you by a quicker way ...*

That phrase resonated. She had first felt Ted near her the morning of the 10th. 'I may be coming to you by a quicker way ...' Was he there with her now?

She thought about his burial, about the body he no longer needed. It mattered to Ory that Ted should have had a Christian burial. Atch had assured her that he had. Eleven men had stood bareheaded around the tent as he read the Burial Service from Ted's prayer book. They removed the tent poles, collapsed the tent over the three bodies and then built a 12-foot-high cairn over the tomb. They made a cross out of skis for the top and in a metal cylinder they put a note commemorating the men: 'The Lord giveth,' the note ended, 'and the Lord taketh away.'

Ory went back over the letters, reading slowly. Unlike Ted's structured letters, they were a stream of consciousness – circular, often repeating but returning to the same themes. To read them was like watching a candle guttering. This was God's will. She must submit to it faithfully. That was his major theme. Without Ted there in body, she needed his words to become part of her – to give her the strength to carry on. There was a rhythm to them – an incantation – a creed for her to live by: 'no fear of death', 'no terrors', 'no sorrow', and then, that familiar coda, '... All is well.'

Ory focused on Ted's promise, she needed to believe in his 'absolute faith ... that if God wishes you to wait long without me it will be to some good purpose.' She knew that she could not kill herself to get there – it was against her faith and Ted's instruction to 'live your life out', but she could not bear to wait long. The only control Ory had over the length of the wait was to discover and expedite that 'purpose'. It was her ticket to Ted.

Scott's handwriting was familiar from his letters to her. Even now he remembered to write 'To Mrs Wilson (E.A.)' to distinguish her from her mother-in-law. Scott's message to her:

> *... He is not suffering, luckily, at least only minor discomforts. His eyes
> have a comfortable blue look of hope and his mind is peaceful with the*

satisfaction of his faith in regarding himself as part of the great scheme of the Almighty …[4]

Kathleen Scott was travelling to New Zealand from America. She had left on 11 February with a sixteen-day voyage ahead of her. Ory knew that they were trying to contact Kathleen, but the wireless was not strong enough to reach her until she was nearer a transmitter. As telegrams encircled the globe like an electric storm, Kathleen contemplated taking Spanish lessons to distract herself from seasickness. Scott's dying letter to Kathleen was still in his diary. It was intended for an audience of one. His 'Message to the Public', written shortly afterwards in the same notebook, had already been telegrammed to London. It was printed and reprinted around the globe. The newspapers that had covered the *Titanic* in exhaustive detail now filled their columns with this fresh disaster.

Ory was staying with the Kinseys and oblivious to this. She rose early the next morning and by 9.30 a.m. she was standing in the garden in front of Uncle Bill's Cabin at 'Te Hau' on the birding platform that had been created for her. The garden rockery, which she and Harold Stemmer had designed with Ted in mind, was at its summer best. Looking south out over it towards that too familiar horizon, she could see the *Terra Nova*, steaming in to Lyttelton Harbour with its flag at half-mast.

To start with, telegrammed condolences began trickling into Joseph Kinsey's shipping office in Christchurch. As the *Terra Nova* docked in Lyttelton, the trickle became a steady flow. Kinsey tried to keep abreast of the media demands but after Scott's 'Message to the Public' finally reached its intended audience, the flow became a torrent and they were wading through ticker tape.

'Had we lived,' Scott wrote, 'I should have had a tale to tell of the hardihood, endurance and courage of my companions which would have stirred the heart of every Englishmen. These rough notes and our dead bodies must tell the tale …'[5] Atch never told Ory that, in order to retrieve Scott's message, he had raised Scott's frozen arm to retrieve his diary from his inside pocket. The arm had snapped off with a sound which, to those standing outside the tent, sounded like the report of a gun.

The Kinseys tried to shield their bereaved guest from the full force of the public's grief, but Ory refused protection. She knew that Ted would expect cheerfulness and the consoling of others as confirmation that she was not wallowing in 'selfish grief'. Ted would never see the cosy 'shack' she had created for them but, the Kinseys assured her, it would always be there for her. For now it was too far from the centre of things. She didn't want to hide.

She posted the miniature New Zealand flag to Anne Hardy in Raikia, 'I know you will prize it <u>very</u> much – it went to the Pole with him & was found with his other flags in his tent.'[6] Anne thanked her by return. She would give the flag to the Canterbury Museum in Christchurch. Ory approved. Ted had always felt that people should 'not generally keep private collections of things but should give them to the nation'.[7]

It was the kindness of strangers, of 'anonymous friends' that touched Ory most. On 19 February she received a stuffed godwit, 'a rare migrant to this country'. The Europe-based Black-Tailed Godwit had somehow got caught up in the marathon migration of its cousins, the Bar-Tailed Godwits. The Bar Tails breed on Arctic coasts and tundra mainly in the Old World but migrate to the New World. Ory's Black Tail had hitched a ride.

She showed it to Atch. Could he see how very well it was set on its long wader's legs? A realistic stance. One could easily imagine it tipping forwards to probe the mud with that long beak. No signs of stitching, the feathers all lying flat against the body and the eyes very symmetrical. This slight, slender, elegant bird had flown halfway around the world. An everyday miracle.

On Valentine's Day, there was a memorial service for the expedition members at St Paul's Cathedral in London. Royal protocol dictated that the King should only attended royal funerals, but now he went to St Paul's. Just over 2,000 people could fit into the cathedral but three times as many came. Buses, trams and taxis had to divert as thousands stood silently in the surrounding streets. Ory's in-laws could not bear to go, holding a private service at home in Cheltenham at Westal. The world grieved, but still Kathleen Scott could not be contacted and did not know.

Emily Shackleton had read the news and now the coverage of the memorial service in the newspaper. Did she telegram her condolences to New Zealand? Sir Ernest Shackleton was in America marketing his Tabard cigarette company, but cut his visit short. He telegrammed Emily to expect his return. Emily reminded him that the *Nimrod* Expedition had not lost a man. He knew that Emily did not think him a 'Live Donkey', but it was not her opinion that mattered. Shackleton began to talk about going south, but what was left? 'Another expedition unless it crosses the continent is not much,' he told her.[8]

On Sunday 16 February, Ory went to church in Christchurch. 'I shall be at Holy Communion at 8 o'clock with him and all I love.'[9] Ory saw nothing paradoxical about attending a service in her new widow's weeds 'with' her husband. For the memorial service held there later, people came from all over New Zealand, there was standing room only. 'Mrs Wilson,' noted Lilian Burton, 'is being wonderfully brave and is full of faith and sweetness.'[10]

In New Zealand, Ory waited for Kathleen. She thought of that dreadful scene with Hilda Evans the night before their husbands left. Would Captain Kathleen remain stoically atheist? Kathleen hadn't even said goodbye to Scott lest people saw him sad.

They continued to try to contact Kathleen but the wireless signal was too weak and the Marconi grams could not get through to her ship. She was due to arrive in Wellington on 27 February but would, by then, have missed both the memorial service at London and New Zealand.

Ory was increasingly aware of newspaper reports focusing on the inaction of the relief party led by Apsley Cherry-Garrard. Cherry and the Russian dog handler had been tasked to go to One Ton Depot to restock and, if possible, meet the polar party and assist their return. Cherry had followed his orders, and done his best. Now that he knew that Scott, Bowers and 'Uncle Bill' had perished just 11 miles to the south of the depot where he had camped, the issue of what more he could have done played relentlessly on his mind.

Ory invited Cherry to visit her. She read him part of Ted's letters and assured him of Ted's high opinion of him. She allowed him to look at Ted's sketches, journals and books. She wanted to demonstrate her trust in him but Cherry could not let it rest. If he had pressed on through the blizzard, he could have left oil and food in the cairns that Scott and the others might have seen. If he had made good progress and if he had killed some dogs to feed the others, he might even have met the polar party and shepherded them home.

Ory did her best to reassure Cherry but increasingly there was talk of an enquiry. Dr Atkinson was concerned for Cherry's mental health, 'I see he is afraid that things generally are worrying me too much,' Cherry noted.[11] Ory kept Cherry close. She asked him to dine: 'Oh she is wonderful,' he said after dinner with her and May Moore at Warrimoo, Papanui Road: 'Beautiful table, good dinner, pretty girls in London frocks: what does a miserable explorer want better than that?'[12] But what he wanted was an absolution beyond that which Ory's reassurances could provide.

On 19 February the Marconi gram finally reached Kathleen's ship. But as Kathleen admitted later, it was good that she did not believe in life after death or 'surely, surely I would have gone overboard today.'[13]

On 24 February, Shackleton arrived back from America and docked in Plymouth. As he disembarked he told the waiting journalists that 'curiously he was the only survivor of the three who made the dash South on Scott's *Discovery* expedition exactly a decade earlier – Scott, Wilson and himself.'[14]

When Kathleen walked onto the Wellington quay in New Zealand three days later, Ory was there. This 'Mrs Wilson,' Kathleen noted with surprised approval, 'is behaving very well …'[15] It was the best, the only, compliment she had ever given Ory.

Kathleen wanted facts and suspected that Atch was hiding something. 'He told me the details of how he found you,' Kathleen wrote to 'you', her diary/husband, as was her habit, 'but not enough. I didn't like asking so I still ache to know more.'[16] The fact was that Scott had died with a look of agony on his face. Atch wondered if his frozen foot had begun to thaw, which would have been excruciatingly painful. Scott had thrown open his sleeping bag and undone his coat; was it hypothermia or just an effort to die faster? Was Scott the last to die? Atch allowed them to think so, but Bowers had written a final note on the back of one of Scott's letters.

Kathleen and Ory needed to assimilate information quickly and dispassionately and decide how best to present the material they had. The Antarctics waited for their verdict.

If the wives allowed each other to read their letters, they might have noticed the contrast in their messages. Scott's was all about life on earth. He told Kathleen that he had no truck with the sentimental rubbish about remarriage,[17] that when the right man came along to help her in life she should take the opportunity. Ted had never said that to Ory. Ted told her that he would be coming back to her – in body or in spirit – that they would be reunited.

Scott's letter to Kathleen left instructions for Peter's upbringing: 'make the boy interested in natural history if you can, it is better than games they encourage it at some schools.' Surely that was Ted's influence? Ted had always been relieved only to have been singed by the 1870 Education Act which began to make school games compulsory – it was the kind of instruction he would have left Ory if they had had a child. Atch gave Kathleen a note found on Scott's dead body. It was the one in which she had written encouraging him to risk his 'physical life'.[18]

Kathleen knew that the Wilsons also believed that a physical life was different to a spiritual or, in agnostic terms, an 'in spirit' inspirational one. How would Ory's faith stand this test? Kathleen wondered if Ory wished that Ted had left Scott and braved the blizzard. Was there a part of Ory that blamed Scott for her husband's death? Would she admit it to Kathleen if she did? Kathleen deliberately emphasised the nobleness of 'staying with our sick'. If Ory agreed with this principle, surely she could never now, or at some time in the future, blame Scott.

Kathleen tried to stress to Ory the reason behind her renewed determination to be cheerful. '… how dare I possibly whine. I will not. I regret nothing but his suffering.'[19]

Teddy Evans was apparently 'quite hysterical'. Perhaps he was worried about how he would come out of Scott's diary. Kathleen had never liked Teddy and now he knew she wouldn't ask for his version of events. His version would be subsumed beneath Scott's heroic truth.

Or was Teddy's hysteria just that, having been in Scott's shadow in life, he found himself eclipsed by him in death?

In their hotel, the two widows poured over their letters and diaries. They surmised that Scott regretted having made Teddy Evans his second in command and began to look at him in a different light. Cherry, who had witnessed the situation first hand, felt very strongly about it. 'I should like to see that man branded the traitor and liar he is,' he wrote in his diary, 'It would be an everlasting shame, if the story of this Expedition were told by the one big failure in it.'[20]

As Kathleen and Ory compared their husbands' diaries, they realised that the shortages at the depots seemed to result from someone taking more than their fair share. The evidence pointed to Teddy Evans' team who had returned by the same route days earlier. Was this the root cause of his hysteria?

Their husbands had been declared heroes. If this information ever saw the light of day, their deaths would be seen to be the result of unheroic selfishness or perhaps, since Teddy Evans had scurvy at the time, bad planning on Scott's behalf. What could they do? The diaries were written in pencil because ink would have frozen in the pen.

In Ted's diary he uses every line until 11 February 1912. After that date, there are gaps. On 24 February there is half a line of blank space and then three words, 'Fat pony hoosh',[21] followed by two-and-a-half lines of space. Ory wanted to leave the record 'clear' and 'clean', even if it meant a little rubbing out, even if it altered history.

In Scott's diary Kathleen knew what she wanted to be edited out, even if she did not use an eraser. On 17 January, Scott wrote, 'Now for the run home and a desperate struggle [to get the news through first]. I wonder if we can do it.'[22] But in order to emphasise that the British expedition was not just a race to the Pole, the part in square brackets was cut.

Although Kathleen and Ory had been cast as the passive 'wives-of' whilst their husbands were alive, as widows, they were active, empowered. They began writing letters and erasing letters. Ignoble phrases, critical comments and incriminating observations in their husbands' diaries were carefully edited. The diaries reached the public as 'magnificent invigorating document[s]' with which to face the world – 'wonderful record[s] of valiant clear-headed courage.'[23]

While holed up in the hotel, a telegram arrived to announce that Kathleen had been granted the rank of widow of a Knight Commander of the Order of the Bath. Soon it would be time to part, to return home. Ory tried to fend off the crowd of people, everyone she knew in New Zealand it seemed, who promised to come to Wellington to see her off. Together they composed a final message to *their* public to be published in the New Zealand newspapers:

> Before leaving this country we would like to express our very real gratitude to the Government and people of New Zealand for their sympathy and thoughtful help to us. The forethought for our welfare has touched us very deeply, and will not readily be forgotten. (Signed) Kathleen Scott. Oriana Wilson.[24]

25

Securing the Narrative

1913

In which Ory returns to Britain as a famous widow. She and Kathleen meet Lord Curzon and attempt to remove Teddy Evans from his position of power, but not to sully the expedition's heroic reputation with unheroic behaviour.

For Ory anniversaries of major events in her marriage were significant. Anniversaries had been a way of 'communicating' with Ted whilst he was away, a time when they knew they were 'particularly thinking' of each other. The fact that he not physically there was a condition she had grown used to during his long absences. On Good Friday 1903, Ory had been watching from the Harbour Master's tug as Ted waved from the deck of the *Discovery*. It had been 'the sort of meeting that beats a wedding hollow'. This Good Friday, almost a decade later, Ory and her sister Constance were on the deck of the SS *Remuera*, pulling out of Wellington Harbour. As the land receeded, Ory wondered if she would ever see New Zealand again.

In the early part of their voyage back to England, Mrs Malet, one of their fellow passengers, was suddenly taken ill on the first anniversary of her husband's death. Ory asked if she could sit with Mrs Malet. Together with the nurse, Ory stayed up all night. The ship's doctor, Dr Gibson, could not understand why the patient's heart did not respond to the injection of digitalis. Ory told him that Mrs Malet mentioned that she kept wishing to join her husband. Dr Gibson wondered if that could explain it.

Ory had not been able to be there when Ted died but she was there for Mrs Malet. She and Constance comforted Mrs Malet's daughter; 'Two finer women,' wrote Captain Greenstreet to his employer, Joseph Kinsey, 'it would be hard to find.'[1] Constance shone. She played Mendelssohn's funeral march for Mrs Malet's funeral and the coffin was let down into the sea in the path of the setting sun. The Wilson sisters were not morbid. Later, Constance was persuaded to conduct an impromptu 'glee', singing without accompaniment, using a small roll of paper as a baton. The '*Remuera* Glee Society' was in demand as entertainment for the rest of the voyage. 'Miss Souper,' continued Captain Greenstreet, '[was] really a most unselfish woman.' Constance watched solicitously over her bereaved sister, writing back to New Zealand to Joseph Kinsey:

> Oriana joins in all the board-ship life – watches and cheers on all the games – nurses the sick and comforts the sad, and laughs with the jolly ones. She is a truly wonderful woman, and you feel it more each day. <u>Everyone</u> loves her and admires her, and she is always surrounded with friends. She is looking perfectly beautiful – and now I have got used to the black, I think how lovely she looks in it, only so pathetic too, after her lovely blues.

Dr Atkinson, 'Atch', had been tasked with chaperoning Ory and her sister. Every morning at 6.30 a.m. he entertained them all by mushing the huskies he had brought around the deck 'bumping against stanchions and bolts and occasionally capsizing … It's as good,' wrote a bewildered Captain Greenstreet, 'as any Circus Play.'[2]

One day, about four days from Cape Horn, a little diving petrel was blown on board, 'such a dear, fat comfortable little thing with a blue black back and head and white breast and pale blue legs', wrote Ory in her letter to Kinsey, 'Dr Atkinson brought it to me to hold.'[3] The captain thought that they should keep it and take it home to the Natural History Museum 'but I am glad in one way that it "got away" one morning'.[4] Ory's quote marks were an economic truth. Science required specimens, but there had been enough death.

As the 'circus' ship sailed up the coast of Portugal, Ory's in-laws boarded the steam train for Southampton. Her mother-in-law, Mary Agnes, was still reeling from 'the crushing loss …'. Her father-in-law tried to distract himself with travel details. Would the *Remuera* dock? Would there be 'much waiting about of tug-work?'[5]

Kathleen's ship arrived back to London earlier and on 14 April she met Lord Curzon, President of the Royal Geographic Society (RGS). The expedition had had RGS approval – its legacy was, Curzon reasoned, their business. Whilst Kathleen talked, he took notes. They discussed a wide range of subjects, including the deaths of the men and the fact that Oates probably took opium before leaving the tent to commit suicide. Kathleen told him that she suspected Teddy Evans, and the two men with him, of having 'consumed more than their share' of food and fuel from the depots. In her husband's diary, he wrote 'generosity and thoughtfulness have not been abundant ...'[6]

Curzon, like the rest of the world, had understood the story in terms of pure heroics, something the RGS would benefit from by association. This information was a shock. Since Scott's death, Teddy Evans, as second in command, had naturally assumed leadership of the expedition. By this time, Scott's lack of confidence in Evans had become known in the exclusive polar circle. It would require some fancy footwork to demote him at this stage and Kathleen's accusations might mean a public inquest. Ory's ship was due in a couple of days. When she arrived, Curzon would seek corroboration. 'Females', in his opinion, were unreliable witnesses. Earlier that year, the RGS had finally been obliged to admit females but Curzon had been on record as saying:

We contest in toto the general capability of women to contribute to scientific geographic knowledge. Their sex and training render them equally unfitted for exploration; and the genus of professional female globe-trotters with which America has lately familiarised us is one of the horrors of the latter end of the nineteenth century.[7]

While Kathleen might have agreed with many of Curzon's views on suffrage, when she left his office, she felt uneasy. She did not want an inquest. And Curzon had mentioned presenting the widows with some sort of RGS award in the unlikely form of a casket. He would do the presenting. It would be a public endorsement, but of whom? Kathleen wondered whether Curzon was hoping to endorse his position or her husband. Whilst Kathleen was taking a cab back home through London,

Hilda Evans, sailing back to England from New Zealand, had a sudden pain in her stomach and the ship's doctor was summoned to attend her.

Teddy and Hilda Evans had left New Zealand a week after Ory on the *Otranto*. On 15 April Hilda was diagnosed with peritonitis and an operation was performed. King Edward VII's appendix had been drained in 1902 and weeks later, he had been crowned. Appendix treatment had advanced but the operation performed on Hilda was 'severe'. By the time the ship reached Naples on Thursday 16 April, Hilda was conscious and recovering. Ory's ship, the *Remuera* was just reaching Plymouth when, at half-past two on Friday morning, Hilda suffered from an embolism as a result of the operation. She became steadily worse, dying just after midnight on 18 April.

Ory had only been back for a few hours when the telegram announcing Hilda's death arrived at Westal. The widow–widower irony was awful. She could not attend Hilda's funeral, because, in the heat of the Mediterranean, Hilda had to be buried quickly in Toulon. Ory and Kathleen were informed that Teddy's return date would be 22 April and it was agreed that Kathleen would meet him at Charing Cross station, the widow greeting the widower 'with true womanly sympathy' – a 'touching scene'. The few reporters did not guess that Kathleen and Hilda had never experienced a modicum of 'womanly sympathy' for each other, or that Teddy was under suspicion.

Teddy had loved Hilda. He now added 'Russell', Hilda's maiden name, to his. Yet all the while he stayed focused on his polar reputation. He had been writing a narrative of his version of the expedition during the voyage home and went directly from his official 'touching scene' with Kathleen at the station, to continue his work at his hotel in London. The widows had anticipated this. Scott's account (after a few edits, especially of her husband's disparaging comments about Teddy Evans) was at that moment being handed over to the publishers Smith & Elder. It would fill two volumes, be priced at two guineas and appear simultaneously in English, French and German. Teddy's version would surely, be subsumed beneath the official line.

Ory went to meet Curzon fully cognisant of his view of 'females'. Like her husband and his Antarctic colleagues, she wasn't a suffragette or '-gist'. She had been nurtured to defer to men for their superior education and she had a traditional respect for the ruling classes. She had heard the rumour that when summing up after Amundsen's lecture to the RGS, Curzon had said, 'Therefore, I take the liberty to propose three cheers for the dogs,' whilst at the same time gesturing to Amundsen to keep calm.[8] Was it clumsy or brilliant? Curzon mumbled, which was irritating, but he was the keeper of the flame, the personification of the British Empire. As she entered the hallowed halls of the RGS, she reminded herself of why she was here. To remove Teddy Evans from his position of power, but not to sully the expedition's heroic reputation with unheroic (or feminist) behaviour.

The notes from Curzon's meeting with Ory are held in a box of papers in the British Library, which has only recently come to light. Ory had to corroborate Kathleen's report without giving Curzon permission to use it for the inquiry he had begun. It would require diplomacy and dexterity. By now, she was practised in both. Curzon wrote:

> Mrs Wilson told me there was a passage in her husbands [*sic*] diary which spoke of the 'inexplicable shortage of fuel & pemmican' on the return journey, relating to depots which had not been touched by Meares and which could only refer to an unauthorised subtraction by one or other of the returning parties. This passage however she proposes to show to no one and to keep secret.[9]

Teddy had no idea that his fate was being decided. Ory had given Lord Curzon the information and then told him that he could not quote it. Teddy should, in her opinion, be demoted but not publicly disgraced. Ory could be persuasive. It seems that Curzon took the hint, even from a 'globe-trotting female' and shut down the inquiry.

This uncharacteristic spirit of cooperation in Ory and Kathleen's relationship was tested over the issue of Lord Curzon and his casket. Ory had agreed to attend the RGS presentation, but she sensed that Kathleen was trying to wriggle out. Ory decided to come completely clean. 'Frankly, I could <u>not</u> have said this 18 months ago,' she wrote to Kathleen, 'but I feel it <u>very</u> truly & honestly now, – that I want to be with you at these times & I would have given <u>much</u> to have you, as it won't be at all easy to go alone. I have my people [the Wilsons] there – but that is not the same as having you.'[10] Besides, Curzon's casket was a side issue; Kathleen and Ory were off to see King George V.

Ory, attired in widow's black and a hat with a sensible brim, was characteristically perfectly turned out as she arrived at Buckingham Palace with Kathleen and Mrs Bowers for their audience. 'In his wonderfully thoughtful way, the King had arranged to see each of us entirely alone.'[11] Lady Scott went to receive the bar to the Polar Medal and then Mrs Bowers, her son's medal and then it was Ory's turn. She had already sent sketches to the Palace because, in Ted's sledging notebook, Ory had found a scribbled message:'make two sketches of the Pole for the King'. She was 'rather petrified when I found myself alone with the King – he was charming – very quiet – and thanked me for the two little polar sketches, which he had received that morning'.[12]

Prince Battenberg, at that moment standing at the opposite end of the throne room from the King and Ory, had been promoted to First Sea Lord at the end of 1912, but no one could be quite sure of his allegiance and people questioned the wisdom of trusting the secrets of National Defence to any alien-born official. Battenberg had a pronounced German accent and considerable land in Germany which he had no plans to relinquish. Regarding him sideways, Ory thought of the rumours that Kaiser Wilhelm was building up his fleet. Battenburg resisted pressure to chose a British surname, unlike the King who was changing from 'Saxe-Coburg-Gotha' to 'Windsor'. The range of Ory's iceberg stare was generally agreed, by her relatives, to be '20 paces'. Battenburg kept well out of range.

Back down to normal life at Westal, Mother and Dad had already summoned the builders to create a separate flat for Ory. On 10 May, in the midst of a slop of plaster and the sound of sawing and hammering, Ory received a letter from Kathleen offering to share the proceeds of the polar memorials she had been commissioned to sculpt. Even though it touched her, her reply to Kathleen was still formal. She addressed Kathleen as 'My dear Lady Scott' and signed herself 'Oriana F Wilson'.

The issue of money was an ever-present one. But Ory could not and would not accept Kathleen's money. Scott had expressed reservations about Kathleen getting paid for her work; to him it seemed to denigrate it as art. Ted had been loath to sell his pictures for similar reasons. Ory tried to think of an acceptable alternative, an alternative that would have been acceptable to Ted. 'What I would like you to do,' she told Kathleen, 'is to put aside what you would, in your generosity, have given me, for Peter's future.' Ory felt that Peter's future was somehow her responsibility, along with Ted's godsons. Although she had not got a son of her own, she assured Kathleen by letter that: 'I love boys & have always had so much to do with them & Peter's future will be of the greatest interest to me and his education will cost a lot of money!'[13] Ory wasn't naïve about money. She knew that, as a widow, she would need to be supported. By upper middle class standards, the Wilsons were not well off. Funds were limited and the sale of Westal was a real possibility. Scott's dying message 'for God's sake look after our people' had resulted in an outpouring from the public and the setting up of the Mansion House Fund. Accepting money from the Fund was an entirely different thing to taking money away from Peter's future. 'About the Mansion House Fund,' Ory continued to Kathleen, 'I shall be only thankful to receive anything they like to give me! Because there is so much I want to do to help with my money.' For a start she wanted to save Westal. 'I would just love to help the dear old things for Bill's sake,' she wrote, '& it will make him so happy.' She did not write, 'it would have' but, 'it will'. For Ory, Ted, though invisible, was still very much alive and watching her. Ory had taken to calling him 'Ted' at Westal but he was now famous as 'Bill' or 'Uncle Bill'.

Getting Ted's parents to accept the money was another matter and Ory was not above a little manipulation: 'I know I shall find it very difficult to make them take it from me, but I can only then say that I cannot live here! & they know how much I want to be here – & I know they want me! So I think I have a strong lever.' Kathleen became so flush that she had begun turning money away. Ory urged Kathleen not to 'refuse any money! If people are so good as to give it to us! I want only a little for myself ...' Shortly after her return, Ory received what she referred to as a 'wonderful letter from "Bill"'. Hearing news from Ted seemed natural. Mrs Oates had found the letter in her son's journal and forwarded it to Westal. For Ory it was proof that her relationship with Ted was real, it was 'just wonderful'.[14] Everything was. Then suddenly, Ory's relentless cheer was punctured by disappointment: 'What awful things newspapers are,' she wrote to Kathleen, 'I gave my little sledging flag to be hung in Gloster [*sic*] Cathedral – &

the fertile brains of the reporters of local papers made it out to be the 2 Union Jacks! One wrapped round the body in the tent. Unfortunately *The Times* copied this rubbish and I am afraid they won't probably copy the correction.' Ory began to be more circumspect. 'This is of course private & confidential' she wrote, or 'I would like all this to be kept quite private.'[15]

Ory was now a famous widow but she 'detested publicity' and avoided anything that might translate into copy in the 'awful' newspapers. Kathleen did not avoid anything. She refused to let circumstances dictate how she should live and Ory did not seem to criticise her for it. When Kathleen decided to go up in a flying machine, Ory merely added a P.S. to her letter: 'I was relieved when I saw the Monday papers to know you had not come to an end over aeroplaning [*sic*] in spite of your having made a satisfactory will!'[16]

The two were still united in battling Teddy Evans. Together they had made sure that it was Pennell rather than Teddy Evans who brought the *Terra Nova* back into Cardiff. But when Ory visited the Imperial Services Exhibition at Earl's Court, she found that Teddy had sanctioned a tasteless display of polar memorabilia. Notices claimed that the exhibition had Kathleen's consent. Ory immediately called on Kathleen, who confirmed that, 'My consent was neither asked nor given and I had no knowledge of it whatsoever.'[17] On Ory's prompting, Kathleen gave Teddy an earful down the telephone and then dictated a letter to the typist she had been obliged to employ to help her keep abreast of correspondence: 'I consider the exhibition of the Tent, wherein the Explorers died, their skis, and a novelette purporting to have been read by them, is singularly out of place and in very bad taste, exhibited as they are side by side with mannequins dressed in Wolseley underwear, advertising the firm.'[18]

Teddy's reaction was typically 'hysterical': he removed everything, 'all the articles which,' according to the exhibition manager, 'were of the greatest interest to the public.'[19] By 10 July, Teddy was persuaded to replace the exhibit without the offending novella and the advertising labels. By the end of July 1913, he found himself removed from the official leadership of the expedition.

At the RGS Memorial meeting in the Albert Hall, Emily Shackleton was humiliated and her husband 'very hurt, because by Lady Scott's request, conveyed by [Charles] Royds, he was not allowed to speak'.[20] Ory suspected that Emily, like Ernest, regarded the *Terra Nova* expedition as a failure. Amundsen did not help. He had been insulted by Curzon and his toast to the dogs. Ory had got to know Amundsen at Warrimoo on the other side of the world. She was not 'prepossessed' by him but she no longer thought him 'mean' and had tried to comfort him after his disastrous slide show. There is no record of her reaction to Amundsen's interview after the RGS Memorial where he told a newspaper journalist that in his opinion: 'Shackleton ... nearly met the same fate [as Scott] four years before on the *Nimrod* expedition. He turned back just in time.'[21]

The Beaumont Library, Bradfield College, named after Oriana's maternal ancestor, Mr Beaumont, rector of Skirbeck, Lincolnshire. (Photograph by Anthony Collieu in Blackie, J., *Bradfield 1850–1975*, 1976, p. 180)

'And yet, the wind still blows off Beachy Head, and the buildings still nestle beneath the South Downs …' A cricket match at St Andrews Prep, Eastbourne, where Oriana spent her childhood. (Spillane, P., *St Andrew's School 1877–1977*)

Oriana as a young girl in lace collar. (E. T. Wilson, *My Life* Volume 2, 1995.550.35b. Cheltenham Borough Council and the Cheltenham Trust/The Wilson Family Collection)

Edward Wilson's sketch of an iceberg in the pack ice: 'Adelie Penguins in the Pack Ice.' Undated. (Reproduced by courtesy of Abbot Hall Art Gallery, Lakeland Arts Trust)

A sketch by Edward Wilson done shortly after meeting Oriana at Caius House, Battersea in April 1897. Title: 'From Caius House. The River. June 3 1897'. (Cheltenham College Archives)

'The 19th, it was a Thursday' taken the day of their engagement. Family Album.
(Cheltenham Borough Council and the Cheltenham Trust/The Wilson Family Collection)

Edward Wilson's comic cartoon of the roof blowing off Oriana Hut at Cape Crozier, drawn for
the *South Polar Times* in 1911. (Seaver, G., *Birdie Bowers of the Antarctic*, 1938, plate pp. 216–17)

Wedding group at Hilton, Cambridge, 16 July 1901. L–R: Polly Wilson, Edward, Oriana, Constance Souper. (Private collection)

Ory. and Ted.
1901.
Westal.

At desks in the garden at Westal. (E. T. Wilson, *My Life* Volume 2, 1995.550.35b. Cheltenham Borough Council and the Cheltenham Trust/The Wilson Family Collection)

Oriana in profile in her Suffolk Hall room shortly after Ted's departure in 1901. The only picture of her late mother, Fanny Souper (née Beaumont), in a frame hanging on the wall, top left. Family album. (Cheltenham Borough Council and the Cheltenham Trust/The Wilson Family Collection)

Oriana at Middleton, Christchurch, New Zealand, 1903. L–R: Lady Georgina Bowen (Sir Clements Markham's sister) G.M. Bowen, Oriana, Commander Royds, Sir Charles Bowen. (Private collection)

Oriana (with her trusty binoculars) and Edward in Fort Augustus during the Grouse Inquiry work. 1907. (Cheltenham Borough Council and the Cheltenham Trust/The Wilson Family Collection)

Captain Scott in a boater with L-R Oriana Wilson and Kathleen Scott on the *Terra Nova*. Cardiff, 15 June 1910. (SPRI Box – 91/(08): (★7) 1910–13 BAE Various)

An Antarctic Expedition garden party given by Sir Joseph Kinsey at Uncle Bill's Cabin [Scott Hut]. 1910 (JJ Kinsey collection, Canterbury Museum, Christchurch, New Zealand)

Press photograph. L–R: Unknown, Teddy and Hilda Evans, Oriana and Edward Wilson, Sir Joseph Kinsey. Lyttelton. November 1910. (*Last Port to Antarctica* by Ian Church, Otago Heritage Books, 1997, p.27)

Oriana wrapped in a rug reading the *Morning Post* at Westal, 1911. Family Album. (Cheltenham Borough Council and the Cheltenham Trust/The Wilson Family Collection)

Edward Wilson in front of the stables, Antarctica 1911. Pose used for Kathleen Scott's bronze sculpture unveiled in 1914. (Library of Congress Archive. Herbert Ponting)

L–R: Mrs Kinsey and Oriana in Uncle Bill's Cabin in the garden of 'Te Hau', near Christchurch, New Zealand. 1912. (Canterbury Archive, Canterbury Museum, Christchurch, New Zealand)

L–R: Dr Wilson, Captain Scott, Petty Officer Evans, Captain Oates, Lieutenant Bowers, 17 January 1912, South Pole. (Library of Congress Archive)

Unveiling the bronze statue of Edward by Kathleen Scott. Cheltenham Promenade, 9 July 1914. (Cheltenham Borough Council and the Cheltenham Trust/The Wilson Family Collection)

Gathering at Westal after the statue unveiling as captioned in the family photograph album. Front row L–R: Godfrey Rendall, Bernard Wilson, A. Cherry Garrard. Second row L–R: Miss Scott, Rev A. Souper, Lady Markham, Sir Clements Markham, Mary Agnes Wilson, Mr Kinsey, Ory, Lady Scott. Back row L–R: Pollie, Skelton, Mrs Campbell, Dr E.T. Wilson, Ida, Elsie, Mrs Moore, Mrs Reginald Smith, Mr Reginald Smith. 9 July 1914. (Cheltenham Borough Council and the Cheltenham Trust/The Wilson Family Collection)

Frank Debenham, *Terra Nova* expedition, Antarctica, 1910–13. (Private collection)

Owen and Constance Bragge with baby Elizabeth, Hawkchurch, Dorset, 1916. (Private collection)

Oriana at the New Zealand War Contingent Association Office, London. Ted's watercolours on the wall behind her. *c.* 1917. (Private collection)

THE NEW ZEALAND WAR CONTINGENT ASSOCIATION.

Telephone Nos.:
Museum 3190 & 3191.

11, Southampton Row,
W.C. 1.

.... *Committee*

The French letter business is very big now & really is one person's work — but poor Audrey has to do much else —

I forget whether I told you that at last I have got a bonded store of cigarettes here — & we are saving hundreds of pounds in consequence. I went & sat at the Customs & argued all round a dry old Scotchman & then wrote a very diplomatic

Page 5 of Oriana's letter to Miss Bertha Raynham, 15 October 1917. (Private collection)

Oriana Wilson CBE. *c.* 1918. (Imperial War Museum Archive)

Oriana outside Buckingham Palace after having received her CBE, 26 March 1918. L–R: Captain Greenstreet, Oriana, Anne Harper (with whom she stayed in Wellington in 1913), Isabel Smith, Margaret Bowen, Bertha Reynham. (Private collection)

George Seaver aged 50 in 1933.
(Private collection)

Oriana in her 60s in the mid 1930s.
(George's Hospital Archive)

Oriana's sketch 'Emperor Penguins', 25 April 1912. (Private collection)
'Now and again one hears a penguin cry out in the stillness near at hand or far away and then perhaps he appears in his dress tail coat and white waistcoat suddenly upon an ice floe from the water … the whole fairy-like scene as the golden glaring sun in the south just touches the horizon and begins again to gradually rise without having really set at all.' (Edward Wilson's journal, December 1910. Seaver G., *Edward Wilson of the Antarctic*, 1933, p.211)

Edward Wilson's sketch of Emperor Penguins. (Private collection)

Still from the 1948 film *Scott of the Antarctic* directed by Charles Frend with Harold Wallendar and Anne Firth playing Edward and Oriana. Vaughan Williams composed the music for the film. The fourth movement represents the recollections of the explorers with different themes for Kathleen and Oriana, but Ory's theme was cut from the film score. (Alamy)

26

Moving On

1913

In which Ory tries to separate her 'dear old' Ted from 'Bill' or 'Uncle Bill', the public's 'saint'. Cherry delivers the Emperor Penguin eggs to a reluctant Natural History Museum and Shackleton secures the promise of the King's blessing on his Endurance *expedition.*

It was late in the summer of 1913, as Cherry walked along the cool echoing corridor of the Natural History Museum (NHM). In his hand, he held a lined basket. In each compartment, carefully wrapped, he had the three large Emperor Penguin egg shells. Each shell had a rectangular window cut into it and, separately preserved, the penguin embryos.

Apsley Cherry-Garrard was Reginald Smith's young cousin and not yet 20 years old when he first met the Wilsons at the Smiths' shooting lodge in Cortachy, back in 1907. He was still at Oxford University but had just inherited the vast Lamer Park estate near Wheathampstead in Hertfordshire. He was sporty but fresh faced and myopic when he'd volunteered himself, and substantial funding, for Scott's expedition. In the Antarctic he worked under 'Uncle Bill' as assistant zoologist, developing a strong admiration for him that was cemented in their epic expedition to the Cape Crozier Emperor Penguin colony in mid winter.

Cherry had not made an appointment with the NHM. This was Uncle Bill's world, the obvious place to analyse his eggs. Surely the museum officials would be awaiting this delivery in eager anticipation. This moment marked the end of a polar odyssey for which three men had risked their lives. Two of them, two of the men he admired most in the world, now lay dead under the Antarctic snows. He was the last of them. This donation was his sacred duty.

When Cherry reached the office to which he had been directed, he was asked to wait. He waited. Sitting on a bench in the corridor, he tried to be patient as he knew Bill would want him to be. More and more he wanted to live up to Bill's high opinion, which he could quote, verbatim, from the letter Ory had shown him. Ory's Ted had written to her in December 1911, sensing Cherry's disappointment at not being chosen to make the final journey to the South Pole. 'Please write to Mrs Cherry-Garrard,' Ted had told Ory, '… and say how splendidly her son has worked on this sledge journey. He has made himself beloved by everyone – a regular brick to work and a splendid tent mate.'[1] Ory had assured Cherry that as her husband's compliments went, a 'brick' was good but a 'regular' one was a rare bird indeed, and incidentally, she agreed. Cherry was still waiting patiently in the corridor when another visitor arrived and was shown straight into the museum official's office.

Cherry looked down at the basket where it sat on the pattern tiles and tried to control his frustration. He focused on the eggs themselves rather than what in Wilsonian was described as 'red-tapism'. Had the Magi made an appointment? Had Odysseus? In an effort to get perspective, he told himself that they were only eggs after all, pear shaped, pale greenish white and about 10 inches high with thick pitted shells. They had started with five but two had broken in the treacherous conditions of their return.

Cherry thought back to that 134-mile journey made in complete darkness, in record-breaking frost and screaming katabatic winds. In the silence of the corridor he realised that 'men do not fear death, they fear the pain of dying.'[2] Cherry's thoughts were away in the Antarctic by the time that the museum custodian finally entered *Aptenodytes fosteri* into their specimen book and took delivery of the basket and its contents – Cherry waited again. He wanted a receipt. Some time later, as he strode back down the corridor and out onto the Cromwell road, he had the distinct impression that the museum felt it was an honour conferred upon the collector that results should be accepted. As he told Scott's mother, Hannah, and anyone else who would listen – they never even said 'thanks'.[3]

As Ory waited to see whether Ted's Emporer Penguin embryos would prove Haeckel's ORP and place him in the Darwinian history books, she tackled the protocol required to present Ted's watercolours to the King. Rough sketches of the South Pole were one thing, but she felt sure Ted would want to offer some proper pictures as well. At first, the King refused: 'His Majesty feels great difficulty in depriving you of such precious possessions so near to your heart.'[4] Ory was stumped and sought out her friend, the publisher Reginald Smith: 'I wish I had you at my elbow to advise me as to what I had better do …'[5]

Between the lines of Ory's letter, Smith read her desire for masculine guidance, preferably Ted's, and humorously suggested that what Ory sought was an archangel's draft! It made her laugh. 'If you only knew how stupid my head feels nowadays,' she protested. She was so confused by the constant stream of new demands on her time that she could barely think straight. 'I knew "interpret" was spelt wrongly!' She continued, 'But for the life of me I couldn't think which letter was wrong …'[6]

Ory tried to separate her 'dear old Ted' from the public's 'Saint' and retreated to minutiae: 'Would you eliminate the dotted lines?' she asked Smith as she scanned some proofs he had sent of the expedition book, 'Doesn't it make it more obvious that they are sheets out of a note book?'[7] Ory felt that things should be done properly, though she admitted, 'I rather like them'. Informality on any level was, Ory felt, inappropriate. Ted, the man, was hers. Dr Edward Wilson, the Head of *Terra Nova* Scientific Staff, belonged to the book-buying public. To this end she vetoed a photograph of her husband smiling, in place of a serious portrait, despite the fact that it was a 'less clear negative' and he looked 'tired'.[8]

Teddy Evans was still a thorn in her side: 'Why is Teddy Evans writing to ask me to send any records of my husband's to the office as the "official records or charts are being now written" – or something', Ory wrote to Cherry, with a touch of her old froideur, '… I am taking no notice of it. I don't wish to send anything to that office.'[9] She focused on the people who mattered. The King, for example, although Ory's monarchism was challenged when King George V promised to see Sir Ernest Shackleton's *Endurance* expedition off at Cowes the following summer. Shackleton wanted to cross the Antarctic via the Pole, but his brother, Frank, had a colourful past and was being tried for fraud at the Old Bailey in October. Emily Shackleton claimed that the judge knew her husband had nothing to do with it, however for Ory, remembering Ted's view, Shackleton was a 'wrong 'un' and together with his wife, best avoided.[10]

Meanwhile, Ory began to look at on her financial position. Scott's 'Message to the Public', particularly his last diary entry, ' for God's sake look after our people', had resulted in £78,000 of donations from the public, which was organised into the Mansion House Fund. Ory was awarded £8,500 from the Fund as well as a government pension of £300 a year and a British Antarctic Expedition salary of £636. In addition, Ted had left her £626 in his will. Apart from her Suffolk Hall salary, Ory had never done 'finances' and sought advice. Her lawyer uncle, 'the Dry Old Stick' Edward Beaumont, wrote from his offices at Lincoln's Inn Fields to advise her to invest in property. Ted had chosen Ory's brother Noel Souper and his brother Bernard Wilson to be his executors. Bernard suggested shares in railways, canals and roads. Ory wasn't sure and asked Reginald Smith to translate.

Reggie's letters found Ory staying with the youngest of her two vicar brothers – Adrian 'six-foot-five inches in his socks' Souper – at The Old Rectory in Oakhampton. The legalise swam before her eyes and reading the letters made her 'quite out of breath ... because there are no stops in it! Or comparatively none.'[11] Eventually it seems that Ory went with Bernard's suggestion. Bernard was Ted's brother, the nearest thing to Ted.

When Scott's diaries were published, Kathleen sent Ory a copy with a cheque for £125 for Ted's artistic contribution. 'I don't quite know what to say to you,' wrote Ory by return, 'Always I am having fresh proofs of your wonderful thoughtfulness & generosity – but it is almost too overwhelming ...' adding that she felt, '... quite ill with nervous excitement' as the day of Scott's publication of the expedition journals drew near.[12] Scott's friend J.M. Barrie had written a biographical introduction. Kathleen hoped that her husband's reputation was now secure. On the blue cloth covers was printed *Scott's Last Expedition*. The subtitle was another study in breathlessness, but the Smiths had insisted that Ted's contribution be headlined: *Scott's Last Expedition In Two Volumes Volume I Being the Journals of Captain R.F. Scott, R.N., C.V.O. and Volume II Being the Reports of the Journeys and the Scientific Work Undertaken by Dr E.A. Wilson and the Surviving Members of the Expedition Arranged by Leonard Huxley and With a Preface by Sir Clements R. Markham.*

Ory bought all the papers and wondered particularly over the review in the *Times Literary Supplement*. 'I don't know what you can feel except a rejoicing that the world can now see a little more what a wonderful man your husband was ...'[13] The first print run sold out immediately and demand has never ceased. (Three editions were printed in 1913. In 1923 a cheaper edition was published by John Murray and sold in its thousands. The facsimile, now online, is the most visited document in the British Library.)

Cherry had been in charge of returning Ted's effects – random things, like 'a packet of silly caricatures' alongside the scientific paintings. There were a few grouse disease papers, a sketchbook (mainly empty with odd sketches of knots). He was fastidious. Ory tried to ease the burden. Ted's things were just things, though there were some that she had an affection for, the tools that they had used throughout the grouse work, for example, and some that were downright awkward – what should she do with Ted's gun?[14]

The main thing was those eggs. Ory asked Cherry what that birding trip had really been like. 'Antarctic exploration is seldom as bad as you imagine, seldom as bad as it sounds,' Cherry said, 'But this journey had beggared our language: no words could express its horror.'[15] Uncle Bill and Birdie Bowers had made it bearable.

Ted's parents were particularly impressed with Cherry's way of explaining things. Ory liked the idea of complete editorial control over Ted's legacy and suggested to Cherry that he might help her to write up Ted's Emperor Penguin work.[16] She knew Ted had wanted it to be, in his words, 'A Classic'. Cherry wanted to write something, but he had a history degree – Reginald Smith said science was for scientists. Ory was neither, but was willing to have a go for Ted's sake.

Westal, the Wilson 'stronghold', had started out as a hub for the Antarctics, but as time passed Ory watched as they moved on. The Navy men returned to the forces, the scientists to their laboratories, and it was not only in their professional lives. Griffiths Taylor and Silas Wright both took a shine to Raymond Priestley's sisters whilst writing up their expedition reports in Priestley's father's school in Tewkesbury, just north of Cheltenham. Ory's father-in-law, 'Dad', noted that 'on Nov 8 Griffiths Taylor and Wright with their fiancées came over from Tewkesbury for the afternoon'.[17]

Frank Debenham ('Deb'), along with Cherry, were the Westal favourites. Deb often stayed for the weekend. A knee injury sustained whilst playing football in the snow had put him out of the running for the South Pole, but he had worked under 'Uncle Bill' in the Antarctic and had come to admire him as much as Cherry did.

Teddy Evans had embarked on an ambitious lecture tour and Ory made herself scarce when he came to Westal on 14 November, though Dad assured her that he spoke most warmly of Ted both privately and in his lecture.

Cherry shared Ory's suspicions and while the *Terra Nova* men got on with their lives, Cherry stayed close to her. The Wilsons, Dad, Mother, Ida and Elsie, had gone for a summer holiday to Pembrokeshire. Ory demurred. Cherry invited her to Lamer – he was thirteen years her junior, but he admired Ory and the feeling was mutual. Perhaps he had even decided to study medicine knowing that it would meet with her approval. Ory was delighted and told him how happy 'Bill' would be to hear of Dr A. Cherry-Garrard.[18]

Cherry's physical similarity to Ted had been noticed by others. Kathleen Scott asked Cherry to 'be' Ted, to model for her when she was commissioned to create a full-size portrait sculpture of Dr Wilson for the Cheltenham Promenade. Ory lent Cherry Ted's corduroys for the purpose. They fitted perfectly.

Now Cherry was suddenly shy and anxious that it might not be 'proper' for Ory to come to stay with him at Lamer 'alone'. Ory was indignant, perhaps in an effort to communicate her ideas on remarriage, without either of them losing face. 'Proper to come & stay at Lamer – or not proper!' Ory wrote, freer than ever with her exclamation marks: 'I never should give it a thought – if such a harmless thing as that is not proper I am afraid Mrs Grundy's hair must be perpetually standing on end at the things I do! You must remember my great age! – & I can't be bothered to worry about what "people" say or think – I'm terribly conventional in some ways no doubt, but not in others ...'[19]

Kathleen also loved Lamer and got on well with Cherry's neighbour, George Bernard Shaw – like her late husband, Shaw was a 'lion'. Kathleen danced barefoot, Isadora Duncan-like, on the dewy grass and slept under the stars or in the rotating summer house.

Cherry wanted to write up his version of the winter journey, especially since the Antarctic Committee seemed to be sacrificing him to make Scott appear perfect. Increasingly Cherry observed that for all her barefoot dancing, 'Lady Scott's possessive instinct not only of Scott but of the whole expedition, is a very strong one.'[20]

Ory and Cherry did not get down to the monograph on Emperor Penguins, but worked together on a manifesto to save another species, the King Penguin, from extinction.[21] It would become one of the first international wildlife campaigns.

As far as they could surmise, New Zealand blubber merchant Joseph Hatch had made his fortune by boiling three million King Penguins to extract oil for lamps. Large colonies of Kings on Macquarie Island, halfway between New Zealand and Antarctica, were doomed unless they did something to stop it.

'The way they kill [King] Penguins,' wrote Cherry, 'is to club, which does not mean they are dead. They are stacked in Digesters which are large rectangular iron bodies ... and superheated steam is then introduced. Only the oil is collected and the oil from 1 penguin value on Island, less cost of freight, is about $1/2d$.'[22]

Ory was not squeamish or sentimental about birds, the Grouse Inquiry had seen to that, but abject greed and cruelty and the imminent threat of extinction meant that Ted's cause (and now Cherry's) became hers. If they did not act quickly, the King Penguins would go the way of the Moa.

Ory was not the only person championing the King Penguins' cause but she was the wife of Dr Wilson, the most famous name associated with penguins in the world at that time. She was 'useful', tenacious and eloquent and brought her now considerable influence to bear. (By 1918, when the campaign succeeded, there was just one colony of 4,000 Kings left. It was formally declared a wildlife sanctuary by the Governor of Tasmania in 1933.)

By the end of 1913, Ory was through the first stage of grief, a word always prefixed in Wilson parlance by 'selfish-',[23] but reality was beginning to bite. Christmas was at Westal and 'we were all very happy,' wrote Dad, 'but felt the empty chair'.[24] People had begun sharing their letters from Ted with her. Alfred Usher Soord, who had painted Ted's last portrait, had one that particularly resonated: 'If you are hewn down,' Ted had written to the artist, '... it will be for some better purpose than you could fulfil by standing, and I shall envy you.'[25] Ted had, as his brother Bernard referred to it, 'passed over'. Ory tried not to envy him but to identify the 'purpose' that would allow her to make sense of her life.

Ted had taken Cherry's copy of Tennyson's *In Memoriam* to the Pole. Ory promised to return it to Cherry. When they met in London, she could not. Cherry let her off. Ory was touched by his understanding and assured him that she 'had already put down that you are to have it when I die'. Ory was not planning to die, but nor was she planning, really, to live. She made sure her will was up to date, just in case. She longed for a 'peak into the future'. 'We are perhaps half-way,' Ted had written to her in 1909, '... who knows ...'[26]

Foregrounding the Science

1914

In which Ory is adopted by the Cambridge Antarctics. She is troubled by Mrs Oates' suspicions that her son's death was not just 'noble self-sacrifice', but pleased with the statue of Ted that is unveiled on Cheltenham promenade.

Weighing the small stone in her right hand, Ory examined it carefully. It didn't look much. It was a little bigger than her palm and less than an inch thick. In shape it was a sort of irregular rectangle, but she knew that when Deb, the *Terra Nova* geologist, held this stone, he was transported to the lush green forests of pre-history.

Staying with her family at Hilton, Ory commuted to Cambridge to work with Deb on an exhibition of the expedition at the University. She would walk through the dawn chorus in Christ's Pieces, take the long route via Trinity Street, passing Gonville & Caius, Ted's old college (where he had studied medicine, earned rowing colours for his Lents, was too busy to attend evening classes at the School of Art, and was sent down for fishing out of hours for trout in the Cam).[1]

Deb's company was a tonic. She tried not to have favourites among the *Terra Nova* team but she couldn't help herself. Increasingly Ory was treated with a kind of sterile reverence as if she might break. Deb, assuming she shared Ted's sense of humour, broke down the barriers, teased her relentlessly and made her laugh. But like Ted, he was serious about his science.

Ory traced the impression of tongue shaped leaves in the stone. Did Ted suspect that this rock would be the first evidence ever found of *Glossopteris* in Antarctica? It went towards proving the Austrian geologist

Eduard Suess' theory of a supercontinent (now known as Pangaea) that existed during the late Paleozoic and early Mesozoic eras. It was also vital proof of a more recent theory by German polar researcher Alfred Wegener's, known as 'Continental Drift'.

Ory wondered about Teddy Evans' attitude to 'science'. She'd heard rumours that he ridiculed the fact that Ted and his companions had refused to give up their specimens when their lives were on the line. 'It seems to me extraordinary that … they stuck to their records and specimens, we dumped ours at the first big check,' wrote Teddy to some friends. 'I must say I considered the safety of my party before the value of the records … Apparently Scott did not.'[2]

The exhibition had thrust Ory into the limelight and she wrote to Cherry to say she was looking forward to a time when she could 'retire into the background for a time, which would be a real rest'. She had been reminded of the dangers of overwork when, in February, Ted's vicar brother Jim was sent into semi-retirement for complete rest by his bishop. The news had come shortly after the discovery of Ted's death and the Wilsons viewed the situation as a tragedy, almost equal to the death of Ted.

Jim's breakdown was a kind of death, but without the leavening heroism of Ted's. His son, Michael, observed that Ory 'was the kind of lady who rather talked about nervous breakdowns with a sniff – she couldn't really encompass that kind of nonsense at all.'[3] (It may have been how she appeared to the Wilsons, but never to Cherry.)

Perhaps it was just that, increasingly, Ory's grief had begun expressing itself as exasperation. She was not a scientist and yet Ted's scientific reputation partly rested with her: 'Oh the pity of it all,' she wrote on having been asked to deliver a fair copy of Ted's notes on seals, 'if only Bill were here to do his own work.'[4] Things were getting lost, information was being scrambled. Ted had been given sub-fossil bones of a dozen or so birds from the New Zealand archipelago of the Chatham Islands by Dr Ben Moorhouse in Christchurch in 1910. Where were they now? In addition, he had been given some Moa bones, along with bones of other extinct species from New Zealand. Ted was a great supporter of his father's efforts to set up an important museum in Cheltenham and, whilst on the *Discovery* expedition, sent him things of scientific interest to bolster the growing collection. Ory was a scrupulous labeller and her labelling survives to this day, but perhaps in the excitement of unpacking, either at Westal or at the museum,[5] some bones got mixed up. This was a confusing time: the fossilised bones of the Piltdown Man had been 'discovered', fooling much of the scientific establishment into thinking it was the missing link between man and ape. On the other hand, the Natural History Museum scientists all suspected that a recent arrival, a specimen labelled 'platypus', was a clumsy hoax.

Cherry felt there were still some hoaxes left to expose. He was still sensitive about the grey area surrounding his actions at One Ton Depot and his anxiety meant he was easily irritated. It irked him that, when he handed the *South Polar Times* over to the British Museum, the label read 'Lent by Lady Scott'. The journal had been produced and printed in the Antarctic and edited by him – what had 'Lady Scott' got to do with it? But Ory was pleased that her husband's 'silly cartoons' of the Winter Journey to Cape Crozier were now on display. They showed one of the most endearing sides of Ted's character.

One set of illustrations was designed to accompany a doggerel poem entitled 'The House that Cherry Built' (composed to the metre of 'This is the House that Jack Built') where the name 'Oriana Hut' had been subsituted for the sake of humour and rhyme. For Ory, it was enough that Ted had originally named it for her and now Cherry was the only other surviving witness. Without reinforcing the name 'Oriana Hut', it was hard to justify 'Oriana Ridge' and so despite Ted's wishes, there was no feature of the Antarctic named for her.[6]

At the British Museum, the *South Polar Times* journals were a popular exhibit, particularly Ted's comic book Egyptian cartoons to illustrate a spoof 'Ancient Egyptian' text about 'Oriana Hut':

Tha–arriveh–dat th'noll and built–a–stoneut.
Thagot–fyve eggs …
The morah–lis birdsnestin–gis tu–hups inwintah'[7]
(Translated: They arrived at the knoll and built a stone hut
They got five eggs …
The moral is bird nesting is two hoops in winter)

(Anything really fantastic on the *Terra Nova* expedition was 'two hoops', though none of them afterwards could remember why.)

Ory was glad that Cherry's *South Polar Times* was drawing visitors, but she recognised a restlessness in him. When the chance came for an expedition to China, Cherry lept at it. It was Atch who put him up for it. Atch and Dr Robert Leiper were planning to investigate a parasitic flatworm which was afflicting British seamen in Chinese waters, causing Asiatic schistosomaisis. Leiper was a distinguished Scottish helminthologist, from the School of Tropical Medicine in London, who had once swallowed a fish tapeworm to monitor the effects upon his body. Ory was relieved to hear that Leiper had recruited her friends Atch and Cherry, not as living incubators for disease, but as his medical and zoological assistants, respectively.

Atch and Cherry boarded the P & O steamer SS *Malwa* on 20 February 1914, just ten months after arriving home from the Antarctic. The send off was reported in *The Times*, perhaps because Ory and Kathleen were there at the dock to wave them off. 'Among all the heroes of the [*Terra Nova*] expedition,' the *Times* declared, 'survivors state that no-one acquitted himself more usefully than Mr Cherry-Garrard.'[8] Ory hoped that the expedition to China would exorcise Cherry's lingering guilt and fire his declared enthusiasm for medicine.

Atch and Leiper discovered that the parasite entered through the feet whilst the sailors were swabbing the decks, but Cherry had already shifted his focus to a commission to write a book about the Antarctic Winter Journey to Cape Crozier. Ory continued to support him when he got home and had the dubious distinction of having the tapeworm named after her '*Tetrabothrius (Oriana) wilsoni* Leiper & Atkinson, 1914'.[9] Cherry had, perhaps, told Atch of Ory's relinquishing of 'Oriana Hut' and 'Ridge' in the Antarctic but her friends were not going to let her become invisible. Besides, like her late husband, she was becoming a serious scientist who could inspire deep affection in men – and she shared their sense of humour.

Ory was staying in her mother's family home in Highgate, London with the Dry Old Stick, her uncle, when there was a debate on the suffrage question in the House of Commons. Margaret Bowen, Ory's great friend from New Zealand, came for a visit to Westal. Margaret was the daughter of the founder of Christchurch's most successful girl's school and had ambitions to become a Headmistress herself. Dad found her charming and noted in his diary that she was 'obviously delighted' with the fact that she had the vote. Down the road from Ory on 11 June 1914, the suffragettes were spoken of in Parliament as violent anarchists who were a mortal threat to civilisation. Lord Cecil suggested deportation. Ory might have wondered whether it was worth marching for a free passage back to New Zealand.

Open-mindedness was just one of the things Ory missed about New Zealand. She did not join the Anti-Suffrage movement in Britain because she had seen suffrage succeed. Kathleen, who had also visited New Zealand, was on the Anti-Suffrage committee. Ory did not accompany Kathleen to a demonstration at the Albert Hall. If she had, she would have seen that several protesters were carried out kicking.

Around her, life carried on. In June 1914, Charles Wright got married and Ory added Edith, née Priestley, to her list of friends. Charles, known as Silas, was the Canadian glaciologist who had spotted the top of the tent in which Ted had died. Ory was always grateful for that find. Ignorance would have been a greater burden by far.[10]

Ory had a lot in common with the headmaster's daughter. Edith, like Ory, was a worker: 'the Mrs kicks if I waste time,' wrote Wright proudly. Wright had last seen Ory's husband on 21 December 1911 at 85 degrees South, now he intended to keep Ory close as the link to a man he viewed as one of the finest characters he had ever met.[11] Ory felt the pressure of substitution; it was as if Silas assumed Ted's wisdom and saintliness had somehow percolated into her. When Silas and Edith's second child, a daughter Patricia, was born, Ory was asked to be godmother.[12]

Most of the time, Ory heard nothing but praise for her husband, but occasionally she had to deal with, albeit passive, criticism. On 4 June 1914, Mrs Caroline Oates called at Westal. Ory was guarded. Mrs Oates had been interviewing *Terra Nova* survivors to establish the exact nature of her son's suicide or, as Ory would have put it, 'noble self-sacrifice'. Ted had been there, one of the three men in the tent who had let him 'walk out to his death'. Herbert Ponting told Ory that he recalled a memorable talk with Oates in his darkroom at the back of the hut in the Antarctic in 1911.[13] The point was raised as to what a man should do if he were to break down on the Polar Journey, thereby becoming a burden to others. Oates thought that a pistol should be carried, and that 'if anyone breaks down he should have the privilege of using it.'[14] But Caroline Oates would not be persuaded.

For Ory, the most important point was the drastic implications for Ted's reputation. 'I have never seen or heard of such courage as your son has shown,' Ted had written to Mrs Oates, 'He died like a man and a soldier, without a word of regret or complaint.'[15] Did Mrs Oates believe that Ted was Scott's accomplice or even that he had displayed partiality in his job as the expedition doctor?

It was not the first time the expedition had been challenged. Ory had helped to defend Cherry against accusations that he should have stayed at One Ton for longer. She had helped to erase diary entries that implied that Teddy Evans had eaten more than his fair share on the return sledge journey, leaving the Polar party itself short, with possibly fatal consequences. Mrs Oates' position was more insidious and more public.

Ory would not see Teddy Evans or send any records to his 'official office'. Kathleen would not see the Shackletons. Mrs Oates could not believe her son's suicide. For the moment, the sense of a widening split in the polar community was still only discernible to those directly involved.

It was 8 July and a cloudy summer's day. On the Cheltenham Promenade, there was standing room only. For Ory the sharp pain of bereavement had evolved into a dull ache. Around her there were people whose lives would go on – people who would marry, have adventures, have children, have grandchildren. Amongst the crowd standing on the Promenade were Antarctic explorers and visitors from New Zealand. A hush fell and Sir Clements Markham began to speak. Ory and Kathleen sat either side of Ory's mother-in-law, Mary Agnes. A Union Jack flapped lazily from the canopy of a plane tree over their heads. In front of them was a column made out of a white sheet suspended from a wooden frame.

Ory knew what lay behind the sheet, she had visited the bronze statue many times in Kathleen's art studio. The pose was taken from one of Ponting's portrait photographs. It was typical of Ted, hands on hips, weight on his back leg. The only question was what Ted would have thought of a statue at all. When the statue was finally unveiled, some of the crowd gasped, others reached for their handkerchiefs. Kathleen Scott was indeed a talented sculptress, the bronze statue glowed.

The party retired to Westal for the wake, where Dad recorded wearily that 'there was a good deal of entertaining and standing about'.[16] A group photograph taken under the mulberry tree shows that only Ory was dressed entirely in black. All the other services had been for the group, not specifically for this man as a husband, brother, son. Rather than being buried in the ground, Ory's husband was now raised on a plinth, the newly burnished bronze, shining for all to see.

'The Infection of Good Courage'

1914–15

In which Ory hears that war has been declared. Constance gets married and Ory discovers new purpose working with the New Zealand wounded. Her faith is shaken when her brother is killed on the first day of the Somme.

On 28 June 1914, just three weeks after the unveiling of Ted's statue, in Cheltenham, Archduke Ferdinand and his wife Sophie were assassinated in the Bosnian city of Sarajevo. They had died quickly and together. Ferdinand's last word was 'Sophie'. The threat of war that had been hanging heavy in the air suddenly condensed and the country waited while the government tried to hold off the inevitable.

Ory remembered that Ted would rather kill himself than another man. Kathleen recalled that Scott thought a war in 1914 would have suited him, allowing him to put his Royal Naval torpedo training to good use. At Westal, Ory's father-in-law ranted about 'the invertebrate government'. On 4 August, his wish was granted, Britain declared war on Germany. Ory's brothers and brothers-in-law were clergy and teachers, but Bernard Wilson was gazetted Captain in the 6th King's Own Yorkshire Light Infantry; 'a true patriot,' noted Dad approvingly, 'if ever there was one.'[1]

Ted's Antarctic colleagues signed up. The military amongst them were already in place. Cherry had donated Lamer as a fifty-bed Red Cross hospital for wounded officers. Ory's very good friend, Deb, heard that the war had started as he arrived home to Australia by ship. Reboarding the same ship, he returned immediately to England to offer his services. Deb's was the kind of patriotism Ory admired, typical of the Antipodeans who had fought alongside the mother country in the Boer War and would fight alongside again.

Shackleton, on the other hand, had left for his next polar adventure on the *Endurance* within sound of the Flanders guns. He had offered his ship to the Admiralty for the war effort but been telegrammed to 'Proceed' south. Ory kept a weather eye on Shackleton's 'White Warfare'.

For Ory, this was the perfect opportunity to become 'useful' but her usefulness had Antarctic momentum and the change to war 'usefulness' dawned on her slowly. Ory was not a qualified nurse. Through her New Zealand contacts she heard that a New Zealand War Contingent Association (NZWCA) was being set up in August 1914 to provide comforts for the troops. Ory immediately recognised a need and sent a donation to the Officer's Family Fund in New Zealand. It was the money she had made from selling Ted's prints – Ted would surely have approved.[2]

From April 1915, the hospitals began filling up. Gallipoli was carnage on an unprecedented scale. Atch was appalled at what was going on and told Cherry that 'the public have not the smallest inkling of what happened'.[3] Ory was drawn to the injured New Zealanders but distracted by events nearer home.

Constance had fallen in love with a soldier, 38-year-old Captain Owen Charles Bragge, and had married him in St George's Church, Hanover Square, London. By the time Owen boarded his boat back to Egypt, Constance was pregnant. Ory had no time to be wistful, or concerned, about the happy fecundity of her nervous sibling, or her choice of husband; in September she began her second stab at independence, her second proper job.

Ory had enrolled for training at The College, Tadworth. The course was designed to prepare her for work at the NZWCA Headquarters. From their offices at 11 Southampton Row, London, Ory would be responsible for the comfort of injured New Zealanders in hospital in the UK. This involved visiting them in hospital, finding accommodation for convalescents and also keeping soldiers in touch with their relatives. It would be an enormous logistical challenge.

By November 1915, the New Zealand wounded being nursed in hospitals near Cairo were moved to a large Italianate villa near

Walton-on-Thames. It was the first of four NZ hospitals in England. Ory began moving her things from Westal to a pokey flat in an eight-storey red-brick apartment block in Hammersmith with an inappropriately Germanic sounding address: 33 Fitzjames Avenue.

'It's a drawback to have such a very hideous address,' she told Cherry. 'It's rather deadly work arranging a home for oneself.' Ory was surrounded by 'stacks of [Ted's] pictures everywhere and no carpets [except for] the wardroom – & it's certainly not going to be called the drawing room as its my only sitting room – for writing, reading, smoking and general work.' Cigarettes were being issued free – 'Smokes for Soldiers'. For Ory smoking was more about respite than Ted's delighted 'Oh, the joy of tobacco.' There was no doubt that the flat was 'supremely uncomfortable' but Ory spotted a couple of Coal Tits and hung up coconut shells to 'see if I can get them to take a fancy to my window ledges.'[4]

Ory was practical. She cut her hair short: it made her look even more beautiful, framing her face with curls. That hadn't been the aim. It was just quicker to wash. She had a uniform, a fitted two-tone jacket with brass on the shoulders and a badge saying 'Assistant Hon Secretary' and a tie. Her skirt was mid-calf and her handmade leather shoes were in mint condition. She kept a clothes brush on her desk and made sure that there was never a hair out of place. She had a telephone, a travel frame with a picture of Ted and two of his water-coloured seascapes framed on the wall behind her.

All day New Zealanders trooped in and out of her office 'with thrilling & awful stories of the Dardanelles business'.[5] Ory played down the 'awful' in her letter to Cherry. To start with, Cherry had joined up hoping that barrack life might match Antarctic camaraderie. He wrote to Farrer: 'It's just Kipling in real life!'[6] He soon became disillusioned. After joining an armoured car division in France, he collapsed and was diagnosed with ulcerative colitis. The condition was linked to anxiety and he was invalided home.

The British government had authorised an evacuation from Suvla Bay, on the Aegean coast of Gallipoli, on 7 December. The last troops left Helles on 9 January 1916. The Anzacs had been there less than a year but, all told, 46,000 people had died. On 29 January, Sir Clements Markham died when a candle set fire to his bed clothes. Ory put the debilitating numbers to the back of her mind and went to Markham's funeral.

Quite unexpectedly, three of her four 'parents' became suddenly ill. Her loyalties were divided, but she went to Hilton and looked after her father. It was difficult. For all her new career woman skills, she was still expected to drop everything and be a dutiful daughter and daughter-in-law. How could women balance work with home duties? But when she returned to the office she was delighted to find a new colleague, a lawyer from Wanganui.

The lawyer knew 'ladies of Wanganui who wished to do something'; Ory knew that feeling. As 'Assistant Hon Secretary', she had to define and manage that 'something'. Soon her in tray, already piled high with carbon paper copies of letters to the New Zealand Government, was piled even higher with '33 pairs of socks, 21 shirts, 30 undershirts, 4 scarves and 3 pairs of mittens and 22 pants'.[7] She was particularly pleased with the pants, 'it is getting increasingly difficult to buy these. We have to pay a great deal more now than we did originally, and the quality is not nearly so good, so that it is a great help to have these parcels coming from time to time.' Really 'pants' were not her department. She was on the 'Visiting Committee' but if the ladies of Wanganui were kind enough to send pants, she felt she could hardly expect 'the lawyer' to reply!

In February 1916, Ory was given leave to go home to Westal. 'The great Teddy [Evans] "honoured" my father and mother-in-law by calling on them with his bride the other day …' Ory wrote to Cherry with endearing honesty, 'I was in the house and badly wanted to see her, but I did not go into the drawing room & he did not know I was in Cheltenham – I think the in-laws thought it was horrid of me!'[8] Ory already knew who 'she' was: the Norwegian, Elsa Andvord, whom Teddy had met and instantly proposed to, as was the way in those uncertain times. It was two and a half years since Hilda's death and Teddy had found love. It was four since Ted's and Ory hadn't. Kathleen Scott was still single – 'she seems to be very hard at work at munitions making,' Ory offered when Cherry enquired, 'not at all bad work I should think.'[9]

Back in London, it turned out that office work was not for Ory. 'My temper [is] being sorely tried,' she confessed to Cherry, 'With people coming in and out constantly & I couldn't get any satisfactory work done ...' Partly it was the 'bevy of girls'. Women, girls, were bevying in the 'City businessman' territory, and it did not suit Ory, it did not suit her at all. She was a man's woman, always had been. The men were either dead or wounded. 'I now make everyone do the hard work, [everyone being the girls] & I interview & organise & trot about the country to inspect the NZ Hospitals & see how the workers are getting on ...'[10]

Whilst 'trot[ting] about the country', Oriana Fanny Wilson met Fanny Wilson. Fanny was the woman Ory might have been. She was the same age but shorter, more substantial and with a pronounced New Zealand accent. Her father had fought in the Crimean War and owed his life to Florence Nightingale. She became a theatre sister at the New Zealand Stationary Hospital near Cairo and was mentioned in dispatches. Fanny moved with the hospital to Brockenhurst, the No. 1 New Zealand General Hospital in England. In June 1916, by the time Ory visited, Fanny had been appointed as sub-matron in charge of the 1,500 wounded housed in the converted Balmer Lawn Hotel.

The summer of 1916 was the start of the Somme offensive and many of Fanny's patients suffered from gas poisoning. Despite all Fanny and Ory could do for their health and comfort, many of the patients remained in a critical condition.

Ory could not help comparing those hot, violent, degraded deaths with the familiar cold Antarctic death in her imagination. She had not been there to witness Ted's last moments. These New Zealanders were far from home. Perhaps, on some celestial scale, being there for these men was being there for him. But throughout, Ory tried to remain business like. Medical care was Fanny's department, hers was 'comfort'.[11]

'The killing part about it,' Ted had observed in his Davos diary whilst undergoing TB treatment, 'is the lack of occupation, nothing but idle loafing, terribly depressing and demoralising.'[12] Ory could do nothing for the worst gas victims, but depression and demoralisation were within her remit. She wrote to relatives, she listened at bedsides, she provided 'occupation' and, purely by being the wife of Dr Edward Wilson, the 'infection of good courage'.[13] There were many satisfied customers. One Brockenhurst invalid who had lost his left leg below the knee and had his right leg mangled, wrote home: 'I do hope you won't worry over me because we are treated like lords here ... you would be astounded at the fun that goes on. No one is allowed to be gloomy in this place.'[14]

Ory witnessed the horrors, but knew that to stay a 'Useful Help' she had to keep her head. She paced early each morning from her flat to the office in Southampton Row – wholesome exercise and it took in all the birds in Hyde Park from Queen's Gate to Speaker's Corner. Ory was, by this time, an active member of The Royal Society for the Protection of Birds, started by the indomitable Emily Williamson in her front room. In its early days the RSPB was dominated by women; its first major campaign had been to ban the import of exotic plumes for women's hats. Women could be effective, there was no doubt. Having deferred to men all her life, Ory found herself managing them. She could be frosty and her staff quickly learned not to take advantage: 'The great Classey has been sent away,' she told one of her secretaries, 'I felt a brute – but he was too lazy and naughty to keep.'[15]

After a short time back in London, Ory's niece, Elizabeth Bragge, was born and it was time to exchange her office uniform for an apron. Ory realised that she needed a second in command and was given Bertha Raynham as a secretary in charge. Bertha had worked as a secretary to the London editor of *Vogue* and for *Vanity Fair* in New York before applying to become Ory's assistant secretary. She was glamorous, her shorthand and typing were excellent and she was versatile. As a 'Useful Help' she was difficult to beat. Ory quickly grew to rely on her warmth and efficiency.

The Bragges lived at The Glebe, a cottage in Hawkchurch, Axminster, which was, as relations remember it, very basic. Ory was more of a homemaker than her sister, but she had no experience of babies and felt out of place. She also increasingly recoiled at the way her brother-in-law treated Constance, whose low self-esteem was getting noticeably worse. 'I do wish I could come back to work,' she wrote to Bertha. Her small niece was a 'young minx – but rather a delightful one'. Constance was shattered in spite of the wasp-waisted maternity nurse. The baby refused to sleep 'like a Christian' at nights and she and Constance took turns as Owen snored through.[16]

Soon, she was back in the office. This time it wasn't pants, but legs. Wooden ones. A great friend of hers had come into the office to show her his new leg, a 'very special one,' Ory wrote to Cherry, '& I'm not sure if the NZ government will pay for it as they only sanction one kind apparently – but I told him I should much enjoy presenting him with one – such a nice & useful present to give!'[17]

Ory continued, becoming more jocular: 'I take special interest in this "Horatio" which seems to be the name for new legs.' The new one was such an improvement on the Long John Silver version that, 'I would defy anyone to say which was the artificial leg … it is all the more wonderful because he only has a short bit of stump to fit it on to …' Horatio's owner was the kind of plucky character to whom Ory warmed. 'He wants to go into the flying corps,' she went on, becoming slightly garrulous, 'apparently they do take one legged men sometimes as Pilots – though it seems impossible.'[18]

For the moment, Cherry was conducting a private war, languishing at home. Ory had not meant to rub salt in Cherry's wound by her mention of the one-legged pilot, but weeks later Cherry would receive a white feather in the post. Ory was 'disgusted'. She tried distraction, asking Cherry to send her a box of some of the bulbs he'd ordered when they'd last met. She asked outright. She recognised the change in herself. Was it the war?

Cherry and Ory both followed the war through the newspapers. As the surviving Antarctic names flickered through 'presumed missing' to 'dead', their spirits sank. On 31 May 1916, Harry Pennell had gone down in the *Queen Mary* at the Battle of Jutland. On 1 July 1916, a month later, Ory's 39-year-old brother, Noel Souper, waited in the newly dug trenches in northern France with his troop from the Royal Berkshire. He and his wife Rosalie had left their farm on Vancouver Island to join up. Together with his twenty fellow officers, his orders were to take 656 men over the top at Casino Point to capture the German trenches. His brother-in-law, Ted, had never baulked at what he believed was his 'duty' except where he was required to kill another man. Noel had a rifle. Shooting Fritz from a distance was one thing, but when he reached the German trenches, hand-to-hand combat would be quite another.

Noel was part of a massive offensive plan that had been masterminded from London. Ted had been one of five, Noel was one of thousands. At the end of the day, the survivors of the Royal Berkshire assessed the damage: 350 wounded, 89 dead – a small proportion of the 19,000 who had lost their lives that day.

The following day Ory and her sister-in-law Rosalie learned that Noel, that 'gay, adventurous plunger' was one of the seven officers who had died.[19] He was one of seven, he was one of 19,000, but to them he was one of one. Inconvenient truths shimmered. How could a loving God allow this to happen? If there was no God, Ory's sense of judging everyday actions against Ted's approval would disappear. Was her belief that Ted and Noel's deaths had meaning, a self-sustaining illusion? Ory's Christian faith collapsed – a silent implosion, a tragedy quite as profound as any bereavement she had yet sustained.

At the end of the summer in 1916, two years and twenty-two days since leaving Plymouth in the *Endurance*, Shackleton was finally heading home to Emily. His ship had been crushed by pack ice and in an almost super-human effort he had achieved the rescue of his men stranded on Elephant Island. Kathleen Scott sat down at a dinner party, where the man next to her opened by asking if she was pleased that her husband had been found? Kathleen immediately realised that he had mistaken her for Emily Shackleton. She was not impressed. Kathleen, Oriana and Emily were interchangeable at a time when the country was filling up with widows. Women looked to them as models of stoicism in the face of the mass bereavement of the war – 'missing presumed dead' or just plain 'dead'. How long could Ory keep it up?

Then on 26 December 1916, Reginald Smith jumped to his death. He had been seriously depressed for some time, the loss of his closest friends had not helped, and he was known to be suicidal. Nurses had been placed on round-the-clock duty but, in an unguarded moment, he got out of bed and jumped out of the fourth-floor window of their home at Green Street in his pyjamas and crumpled onto the street below. Later Isabel told her that his feelings of worthlessness had manifested into a conviction that he polluted water when he washed in it.

For Ory it was a grotesque end to the year. When Ory met Kathleen at Reginald's funeral, she was suffering a crisis of faith as well as intense grief. It was a frigid mask of self protection, the same expression Kathleen had first identified on board the tug, the *Plucky*, six years before. It was the expression Ory adopted at times of extreme mental distress. But, on that bitterly cold December day in 1916, in a church surrounded by the rubble of London, Kathleen, equally shattered, had no more time for the sphinx – Ory had reverted, in her mind, to being 'not much use' and was now just 'an absurd prig'.[20]

21

The Search for Purpose

1917–20

In which Ory tries to adjust to a post-Christian mindset. She frets about whether she could be doing more for the men in France. Ted flickers in kinematograph in the trenches. The war finally comes to an end and Ory is awarded a CBE.

It was midwinter in London, a cold dark night and Ory woke suddenly from a deep sleep. What had woken her? The previous year, Ory might have thought it was Ted. It was difficult to adjust to this post-Christian reality. It was like leaning against a familiar tree to find that it had been cut down. She found herself continually tripping over the stump. The worst of it was that there was no one to comfort her. Her father and surviving brothers were all priests, as was her politically radical brother-in-law Jim, who had recently experienced a vision of Christ dressed in working clothes. Ory's new bereavement was as private as losing Ted had been public – where that was heroic, this was taboo. Her grief was necessarily disguised in an increasing brusqueness, lest her relations suspect the truth.[1]

Since she had first met Ted, every action had been judged against his approval. Now she realised that Ted was not watching her, never had been. He was not waiting for her. They would never work together again. The heaven that had been her life's goal still shimmered on the horizon, only now she saw it for the mirage it was. Living without the promise of ultimate reunion with Ted was living hell. The pain of loss was a blow that could never heal. Physical wounds, such as those Ory had witnessed amongst 'her' New Zealand soldiers, either healed or killed. Spiritual wounds were invisible. Hers could never heal.

Yet there, strangely, was Ted in the trenches. Not photograph-Ted of the bedside table, but living-breathing-moving Ted. Perhaps this was the afterlife. It was incredible that Ted, who could never have killed another human being, still had an impact on the war effort. Soldiers everywhere were watching Ory's husband flickering in a kinematograph of Ponting's film. It was doing the regimental rounds. Their enemy was not the Antarctic but the Germans. 'We all feel,' wrote a grateful army chaplain, 'we have inherited from Oates and his comrades a legacy and heritage of inestimable value.'[2]

As the clock beside her bed showed midnight, she tried to go back to sleep. There were rumours of Gotha bombing raids crossing the Channel. Wrapping her woollen shawl around her, she peered through the curtains into the blacked out street below. What did she really want? Along with many other women who had worked during the war, she realised that 'I should never be content to do only home work ...' It wasn't just about empowerment and a reluctance to return to her pre-war domestic status – she just couldn't face home work '... unless I had someone to do it for ...'[3] But the more she saw of relationships, particularly that of Constance and the increasingly brutal Owen, it made her wonder whether she could ever contemplate another one.

She had been fretting about being a more 'Useful Help' to the New Zealand soldiers. Was there a better *modus operandi* than the current NZWCA set up? Suddenly she realised what had woken her. A dream. In her previous belief system she might have called it a revelation.

In the morning she tackled a Mr Elgar at the office, who was delighted and suggested that she should go over to France immediately to act upon it. It would be dangerous, but hands-on, and she could carry on her work with the New Zealanders more effectively. Why had none of them thought of linking up with the Red Cross before? Ory prepared to go over to Boulogne in early June 1917, then on to Étaples, Rouen, Saint-Omer, etc. 'They are making us out passports to last for ten days so we shall have an interesting little trip.'[4]

But it was not to be. None of Ory's relatives were keen for 'Abroad' to become a reality. The Home Front was the proper place for a woman. Ory was all the Wilsons had left of Ted. She had an obligation to stay 'safe'.

Ory's mother-in-law, Mary Agnes, an enthusiastic and entertaining correspondent, was on doom watch: 'What dire times we live in DIRE TIMES. The combing out of every man under 57 is perfectly dreadful – we shall have to be a nation of women left behind.' The 'Rules of Raal' as Ory's mother-in-law called the old social order, are 'very queer nowadays!' She looked up from her writing desk and through the sash windows of Westal. 'What is the point of a lot of lawn?' But her daughter, Elsie, would not be prevailed upon to plant potatoes in it, saying 'it's not a lady's job!'[5] Thankfully, her son Bernard Wilson had contacted his farm agent from his regimental headquarters in Étaples to send a bag of potatoes. Mary Agnes was grateful. There were rumours that ration cards would be introduced for sugar, meat, flour, butter and milk.

'The great Teddy [Evans]'[6] as Ory now called him, was, of course, at the forefront, commanding a new destroyer. HMS *Broke* had survived the Battle of Jutland in which Pennell had died, limping into the Tyne with a broken bow. In the subsequent Battle of Dover Strait on 20 April 1917, Teddy ordered the *Broke* to ram one of six German destroyers, *G-42*, almost breaking it in two. The two ships became locked together and for a while there was close-quarter fighting on the *Broke's* deck until it managed to break free. The German destroyer sank while the remaining German warships escaped.

The action made Evans a popular hero, feted in the British press as 'Evans of the Broke'. Now that Teddy had now reinvented himself as 'of the Broke', perhaps he would leave Scott to be '... of the Antarctic'. But to Ory's intense irritation, Teddy continued to let people believe that he had led the party who had discovered her husband with the bodies in the tent. It made her 'fairly boil inside'.[7]

The Wilson women were not literally or figuratively ramming ships; they were working quietly and steadily on the home front (all except Ory, who was 'boiling' at the New Zealand War Office). Lily and Polly were 'raising 140 chicks and 20 rabbits'; Lily particularly had 'lost 1.5 stone and was going grey ... What that Kaiser has to answer for,' wrote her mother. Mary Agnes was determined to put her pre-war farming skills to good use, but the gardener was going off to the war. 'When he does we shall be up a tree for we can't manage the vines and crop of grapes … valuable for they say this year's apple and pear crop will be very poor.'

Apples and pears were the least of it: 'Do you see those horrid vile Huns are now contemplating Polygamy as the right way of life for their nation,' Mary Agnes continued unevenly, '… and every man to have as many wives as he chooses after the war! It's too terrible oh how one does hope and pray they are to be beaten.'[8] Outside her window, the Whishaw–Wilson family mulberry tree quivered.

Polygamy and pears? Sometimes Ory felt more understood at the office than she did with her own family. It was as if she lived in another country – 'Zeadequate', a little satellite of New Zealand.[9] In 'ugly street', Ory acquired New Zealand flatmates when Margaret and Laura Bowen came over from South Island to help with the war effort. It was lovely to have company and to 'talk' about things rather than 'talk around' them, as Ory was beginning to realise was the English way.

In the office and in the flat, the main news concerned New Zealander Ettie Rout, serving as a nurse in Egypt. Rout maintained that venereal disease should be treated as a medical issue, not a moral one. She had designed prophylactic kits and sold them to the troops on her own initiative. A letter to the *New Zealand Times* advocating condoms and clean brothels caused such outrage that for the rest of the war her name was forbidden to appear in print on pain of a £100 fine. But her letter persuaded the New Zealand authorities to sanction the free issue of her kits to the troops abroad.

'The French letter business,' Ory confided wryly to Bertha Rayham, 'is very big now & really is one person's work.'[10] She had been dealing with clothing and cleanliness, but this? Although trench foot was a problem, a man was more than five times likely to be what Ory would still call 'invalided out' suffering from syphilis or gonorrhoea. Ory organised for French letters to be posted to the troops. It could not be beneath anyone's dignity – these 'kits' might contribute to winning the war. But was this her 'purpose'? Ory was tired of it all.

It was midway through 1918 when Ory learned from Cherry that Atch had received horrific injuries from an explosion aboard HMS *Glatton* in Dover Harbour. Although burned and blinded, he was able to rescue several men before escaping. Atch, who had walked from

Oamaru in person to tell her about Ted, lay in the naval hospital where he had worked as a doctor, his head swathed in bandages, and wondered that he had ever tried to persuade burns victims that life would be worth living. He did not want visitors.

Finally, on the eleventh hour of the eleventh day of the eleventh month of 1918, the war was over. Whilst the Allied Countries negotiated The Treaty of Versaille, Ory gathered statistics for the New Zealand War Office. The total population of New Zealand was only 1.1 million. Just under 10 per cent served overseas. Over 18,000 New Zealanders had died and nearly 50,000 more were wounded. They had paid the highest price of any allied nation. Ory felt keenly that her country would be forever in their debt.

Ory didn't stop work – the New Zealanders were still in hospital, they didn't just 'pick up their bed and walk'. Repatriation was the biggest logistical task she had tackled so far. How did one ensure that a recently discharged man survived a six-week voyage? By March 1919 Margaret Bowen described Ory to Bertha as 'washed out and tired with perpetual headaches ... She is not allowed to come back to the office yet, which is a good thing.'[11]

She was standing still as a stump in her 'wardroom', the now congenial 'not-drawing room' of 'ugly street', trying not to think of the war. A pair of Coal Tits were pecking at the precious rationed food she had strung out on her window ledge. Below her, she saw the postman picking his way over the stumps of iron railings that had been requisitioned for guns. Would there be a letter for her?

A Whitehall postmark? A Mrs E. Wilson?

Ory had, by now, become an expert at extracting the essence of such a letter, however deeply embedded in official jargon. She was amazed, in fact, never more amazed. Oriana was now a Commander of the British Empire. From the day she opened the letter, she reverted to her own initials. Mrs O.F. Wilson CBE.

'A CBE ... I think how amused and pleased Bill would have been.' (Still, after five years and a world war, her first reaction to anything of consequence was to imagine what her late husband would have thought.) 'I am very pleased,' Ory wrote to Cherry with studied under-statement, lest he thought it had already gone to her head, 'I am very pleased to be identified with NZ in this way ... When the Order of the Empire was first instituted,' Ory wrote, still trying to keep the smile off her face, 'I thought it would be a very nice thing to have – but never dreamt it would come to me & certainly not the Commandership!'[12]

Ory would have to go to the Palace for her own sake rather than for Ted's. She dressed up for the occasion. She bought a new hat and polished her already shining shoes. Ory had met King George V when she had studiously avoided Battenburg (anglicised to Mountbatten in 1917). She was so proud to be in the first batch of people to receive the new order in the war and was 'absolutely electrified over it all'.[13] She was ushered into the throne room, went up with a line of people. Suddenly the King looked at her again as if he had seen her before – 'and he had of course – but I moved on and it was over'. She was sorry that the King had not been told who she was, for 'I knew he would have been interested because of my husband.'[14]

Outside the Palace, Ory had a crowd of well-wishers; amongst them the incomparable assistant Bertha Raynham; her flatmate Margaret Bowen; the man who had brought her back from New Zealand in 1913, Captain Greenstreet; her dearest friend, Isabel Smith; and her youngest brother, the Reverend Adrian Souper.

She was photographed for the *Daily Sketch* wearing a glamorous feather boa, which, according to the rules of the RSPB, was 'allowed'.[15] 'Mrs E. Wilson, widow of Dr Wilson of Polar expedition fame, a CBE'. Ory's identity was still 'wife of' – as friends observed, 'the loss of him still clung to her'[16] – but now she was officially more than a widow.

Ory could be proud of the turquoise enamel medal given her by the King, but outranking servicemen was more awkward: 'One girl I know whose husband is a D.S.O. is most annoyed to think that I would take precedence of [sic] him on any public occasion!!' Ory had not put her life in danger, but 'her great organising capacity [was],' according to the appointers of her CBE, 'of inestimable value'. Some of her New Zealand friends wondered if it made her a Dame, 'No my dear,' she replied to Anne Hardy in Rakaia, 'I am not Dame Oriana, though I would rather like to be!'[17] Ory's CBE made her more passionate about New Zealand than ever.

'I am truly disgusted,' she opened her letter to Dr Bennett, 'by your account of the lack of medical comforts on the *Paparoa* – and have at once given orders that the things you were wanting should be put on future transports, whatever class of men are taken …' The British Navy's ranking system was iniquitous, and what was worse, she had been told that her Red Cross supplies were languishing uselessly in the discharge depot! 'I feel very mad about the whole thing.'[18]

'Dear Mrs Bill,' wrote Deb on 26 October 1919. It had been a year since the war ended and gradually the New Zealand hospitals in England were closing. He wasn't sure where to send the letter. To 'ugly street' or to Binfield on the outskirts of London where he'd heard she was buying 'The Little House'. Deb had been severely wounded in August 1916 and was invalided home with shell shock. All through his recovery he wondered whether there would be enough survivors of the expedition left alive to write up the *Terra Nova*'s science when it finished.

The Scott Memorial Fund, raised through public contribution in 1913, had reached £78,000. Even after the widows and children had been provided for, there was money over. Deb had just found a tidy sum of £10,000 set aside for a Polar Research Fund. He dreamt of building some kind of polar institute, a dream he had first discussed with Ory when they were working together on Ted's Glossopteris rock, in Cambridge, before the war.

Ory had asked him when the idea had first come to him.[19] Like Ted, Deb was meticulously truthful: 'in a blizzard, spent in Shackleton's hut early in December 1912.' Originally he'd suggested 'A Polar Centre', but now he thought 'A Polar Institute' sounded more scientific. Besides, he needed a job. If this scheme worked, he planned to 'wangle himself' onto the staff.[20] He had married Dorothy Lempriere in 1917, and now there were more mouths to feed.

As far as memorials went, the statuary, he knew, was Lady Scott's particular niche (but in Deb's opinion, 'statues got scrawled all over'[21]). This, Deb told Ory, would be a really 'useful' memorial.

In soliciting Ory's support, Deb used words like 'practicable', 'useful' – a 'practical museum of Polar equipment (not the things one sees as relics in the R.G.S. but the things explorers want to see and handle and know the use and cost of such as camp gear, instruments, clothing etc.)'.[22] Deb understood Ory well and liked her. That list was to her what sweet nothings would have been to your average girl. How could the 'Useful Help' resist a litany like that?

Ory liked the idea of an institute and her support encouraged Deb. What would he call it? Deb told her that the name was a tricky business. He supposed it should be named after Scott, although Ory knew of his disappointment in Scott. While in Antarctica he had written to his mother, 'There's no doubt he can be very nice and the interest he takes in our scientific work is immense, he is also a fine sledger and as organiser is splendid … But there I am afraid one must stop. His temper is very uncertain and leads him to absurd lengths even in simple arguments …'[23] Ory knew that Scott could be salty. Ted had witnessed him cursing subordinates who, according to the rules of naval discipline, could not retaliate. But he had always been charming to her.

Deb confessed that, 'If I were asked to pick out the best all round men, I should place Wilson easily first,' and that was why he wanted to call the institute after Dr Wilson. 'Though I called the work I did over the PRI "in memory of the Pole Party" it was really in memory of Bill.'[24] 'The Wilson Polar Research Institute' – Ory tried it for size, it had a kind of ring. Deb reminded her unnecessarily that her husband had been Chief of the Scientific Staff after all and the institute had started life as part of the Cambridge University Geography Department. What could be more appropriate – a scientific institute named for one of the University's most famous scientific alumni? What would Ted have thought? They both knew. It would have been inconceivable for it not to have been named after Scott.[25]

Deb had to satisfy himself with the Wilsonian dictum that it was all about the intention, not necessarily the final result. In order to achieve the institute, whatever it would be called, they needed funds. Should they ask Cherry for cash? Cherry saw it coming. The Labour government, 'the yelling pack',[26] was bleeding landowners like him dry – he had no money to spare – and the institute should have been a government-funded initiative – at least that is where they should go for the shortfall. Deb agreed: 'I fear the people who would like to help have been robbed like you and those who have helped in the robbing do not recognise the need ...'[27]

The main thing that Ory could do for Deb was to give Ted's watercolours. But she held back from giving. Perhaps a loan? At least until she knew who would be involved. As a 'polar' institute, she supposed it would have to include Shackleton and Evans – legitimising their actions. Ted had broken with the first and been betrayed, as she increasingly saw it, by the second.

She promised to loan Ted's pictures – if the plans included a suitable gallery so that they could be on display rather than gathering dust in the vaults of the RGS, as Ted himself had suspected they might. Deb agreed. They could do better than the RGS. They would have a gallery. The Wilson Gallery.[28]

The plan for the Scott Polar Research Institute was forwarded to the trustees in November 1919 but they did not meet until the following March. On 20 December 1920 Deb read out a description of the aims of the institute at the RGS, which was printed in the *Journal* in 1921. By now it had members including Teddy Evans, Atch and Cherry, Victor Campbell and the brothers-in-law Charles Wright and Raymond Priestley. Deb did not want to give up on the idea of a memorial to Bill. One idea he wanted to discuss with Cherry and Ory was that special parts of the building should be endowed, such as:

the Wilson Library of Geography ... Another idea and I think a better one as far as Bill's name is concerned is to have a Readership endowed in his name. That is all the more proper from his close connection with this University. Perhaps a Readership in Vertebrate Zoology would be the most apt under ordinary circumstances, but if our idea goes through it should certainly be the readership in Geography, so as to keep the connection between the R.F. Scott building and the E.A. Wilson Readership.[29]

Ory found her 'Wilson' name was sandwiched between those of Teddy Evans and Shackleton. It was iniquitous but inevitable. She decided to 'fairly well abstract myself', as she had in the office during the war.[30] She was living with a deaf cousin, Geraldine de Courcy, at 'The Little House' in Binfield. But with polar politics threatening to demand her attention again she became restless and, besides, she wanted to thank New Zealand for her CBE. She bought a ticket via Australia. It was winter in the Northern Hemisphere. Deb gave her contacts – part of him wanted to come too.

PART 3

DARWIN, NORTHERN AUSTRALIA, 1921

'So far,' wrote Ory from Darwin, Northern Australia, in 1921, 'I have not been successful in catching small mammals. There seem to be none here.' Her letter was addressed to Michael Oldfield Thomas, a zoologist working at the Natural History Museum in London. His mentor, Major Gerald Barrett-Hamilton, was the co author of *The History of British Mammals*, an important book illustrated by Ory's husband. In the fifteenth edition of *British Mammals*, published in March 1914, Barrett Hamilton included a eulogy to Dr Edward Wilson. In it he described Ted as 'a dreamer of great dreams ... it was sometimes necessary to call him to earth.' Both Oldfield Thomas and Barrett-Hamilton could see that Ory was no 'dreamer' and that, where Ted 'revolted against the minute detail inseparable from mammalogy', his wife would embrace it. Oldfield Thomas was devoted to his own wife, the heiress Mary Clark, and they often went on collecting trips together. He knew from experience that women could be excellent field scientists.

Ory was fanning herself in the shade on the verandah of the Lloyd Apjohn's clapperboard house in Darwin, Northern Australia. It was hot and humid up here in the Top End and, best of all, there was absolutely nothing 'post-war' about it. She had decided to come to thank New Zealand for her CBE, taking in a little light adventure en route. And so here she was, writing to Ted's friend, Oldfield Thomas. She wanted her letters to be upbeat and chatty and perhaps a bit witty, like Ted's, which is why she teasingly told him that there seemed to be 'no mammals in Australia'.

Ory was enjoying herself. She was off up the East Alligator River, and hoped to have better luck collecting there, 'unless I am collected by a Crocodile or a Cannibal! Both of which live near the part of the country I shall be in.' Ory was venturing to a place 150 miles from the nearest white man and out of communication altogether with the outside world, a place to which no white woman had ever been. Oldham Thomas recognised in Ory a woman with nothing to lose, a woman cheerfully inviting danger. On one hand it made for a valuable collector, on the other he advised her to make haste to link up with a Mr Sherrin.

Ory listened to the rhythmic slap of the canoe paddles on the river, resisting the temptation to trail her hand in the water, as she might have done from a punt in the Cambridge Backs. The saltwater crocodiles, rather than alligators, that slipped off the river banks into the murky waters had developed a nasty tendency to treat humans in their territory as prey.

Ory fanned herself with one hand and held her binoculars with the other as the canoe glided through deep cliff-sided canyons. The rustling eucalyptus fluttered with splashes of bright turquoise – the Hooded Parrot. And later when they began trekking inland through the pine creeks, the White-Throated Grasswren, White-Lined Honeyeater, and Chestnut-Quilled Rock Pigeon.

'I have got a good few ants,' she told Oldham Thomas, 'and I am sending home any butterflies and moths I can get direct to Dr Graham.' She did not want to take on airs, as she was an uneducated enthusiast, but had worked alongside Ted as he illustrated Barrett-Hamilton's *British Mammals* and remembered their discussions on different species. Ted's pictures of bats had prompted Barrett-Hamilton to speculate that every species 'has its own modes of evolution and development, which are peculiar to it and to it alone'.[28]

Paddling past the white sandy beaches of the gorges, marvelling at the rock formations, Ory wondered if Oldham Thomas was a 'splitter' or a 'lumper'. Barrett-Hamilton, who had died suddenly of a heart attack on a collecting trip on South Georgia Island in 1914, was an enthusiastic splitter. He delighted in describing structural variations among a group of animals, which could then be used to separate them into a new species or, more commonly, subspecies. When challenged by the 'lumpers'

he explained that his aim was to 'throw light, however dimly' on varia-
tion and that, in his experience, the animals themselves flatly 'refuse to
accommodate themselves to any scheme which man can invent'.[29]

Finally Ory and her guides trekked from the river to their destination,
the Kintore Caves, a complex karst limestone cave system that included
caverns 100 yards long and 6 yards high. The guides showed her flaked
tools. These caves had been used as an Aboriginal tool-working area for
thousands of years. They entered the underground cave. It was a darkness, blacker and more complete than any wartime blackout she had
experienced. They relit the lanterns, 'throwing light however dimly' on a
stone forest of stalactites and stalagmites.

After hundreds of yards of powdery pathways she saw ancient paintings high up on the walls. The light flickered so that each picture seemed
to come alive, like the frames in Ponting's Antarctic kinematograph. They
reminded her of the Japanese artists and that extraordinary economy of
line that Ted had admired so much. But Ted was not with her. Which is
not to say that she was alone. In the darkness she could hear the chirrup-
ing of thousands of little animals. Bats.

Ory remembered all the bats Ted had painted for Barrett-Hamilton,
the Long-Eared, the Pipistrelle, the Noctule. In one of the more remote
and inaccessible caves, Ory found bats that might belong to the genus
Miniopterus, but amongst these was one much paler in colour than any
she had seen before. On her instructions, her guides 'collected' some
specimens for her and, taking them out into the light, Ory began to
examine them scientifically.

The dead bat was still warm in her hand as she turned it over and
spread its skinny wings to examine it more closely. It was nearly uniform
pale brown but she knew that would not be specific enough. She noted:
'undersurface cinnamon, the inguinal region a little paler. Head faintly
greyer than black.' On her makeshift table, she took careful measure-
ments: she measured the forearm, the head and body 57mm, the tail
47mm, the third finger, metacarpus 40mm, first phalanx 10mm and
second phalanx 34mm.[30] She unpacked the dissection kit she had used
for the grouse work with Ted and began.

Wilson Takeover of the Natural History Museum

1922

In which Ory hears that Kathleen Scott has remarried. Ted becomes the hero of the moment again courtesy of Cherry's best-selling memoir The Worst Journey in the World *and Ory becomes a recognised collector in her own right.*

At the end of March 1922, Ory climbed the stairs to the platform on the top of Uncle Bill's Cabin in Sumner, Christchurch. 'I am so happy to be back in N.Z. again,' she told Anne Hardy in a letter sent on her arrival, 'but find it very difficult in Ch. owing to all the many associations with the expedition – I wish I could stay in any other place.'[1]

Ory resolved that she would use the Cabin as an office. She knew that Dmitrii Gerov, the expedition's Russian dog handler, had used it after she left. It was good that it had been used. The door opened easily with the key Kinsey had given her. She opened the diamond-paned French windows facing east. The familiar briny air and the smell of the newly mown grass on Kinsey's lawn. Waves breaking on the cliff beneath, the light breeze rustling the leaves of the bush in front of her rockery, the cry of gulls.

On the table, she had a new light-blue canvas book. Beside it, an envelope stuffed full of newspaper clippings. She had read some of them with Mr Nolan in Auckland. Mr Nolan, one of her good friends from the war, had been given a CBE for his work at the New Zealand Officer's Club in London. His home was just the place to read out a gathering storm in the newspaper letters' page. She had a trunk of books that Isabel Smith gave her for the voyage out, most of them philosophy. She had visits to arrange. She had purpose, and yet the Cabin was such an eloquent reminder of the past.

Kathleen did not live literally or metaphorically 'in' the past. On 22 March 1922, Kathleen married the politician Hilton Young in ten minutes flat. Austen Chamberlain and the 11-year-old Peter were the only witnesses. Ory had not been invited. No one was. Kathleen had perfected outwitting those 'gentlemen of the Press'.

The idea that Kathleen 'South Pole' Scott could marry again reopened the possibility that Ory might. No one said it outright, which made it worse. For Ory: 'The marriage of older people always seems to me to be full of a real romance & a lasting friendship.'[2] She discussed it with her friend, the New Zealand poet Ursula Bethell. 'Perhaps [she] does not like living alone & therefore imagines others don't like it? It's bad for a woman no doubt. She is apt to acquire peculiar quirks & cranks! But unless you can find just the right person to live with – why worry?'[3]

But Michael Wilson remembers that the Wilsons were not keen to lose Ory, and thereby connection with Ted, through remarriage. Bernard and Geoffrey both wanted to write Ted's biography. Ory wrote to Isabel Smith: 'but could you imagine my going through or reading to them extracts from my private letters?'

Increasingly, Ory fled from, albeit well-intentioned, interference by the Wilsons in her version of Ted. She is rumoured to have inspired one of Ursula's poems and a line from 'Time' (From *A Garden in the Antipodes*) expresses her attitude well: 'for I am fugitive, I am very fugitive ...'

Would Emily Shackleton consider remarriage? At the beginning of the year, her husband had died suddenly of a heart attack on 5 January 1922. He'd reached South Georgia on the *Quest* and the ship's doctor, Alexander Macklin, was on his way home with the body when a message came from Emily that she'd rather he was buried where he died. On 5 March Shackleton was buried in the South Georgian whaling station, Grytviken.

The blue canvas book on the desk in Uncle Bill's Cabin was not Ted's biography – though he was the hero of the story. *The Worst Journey in The World* (or the weirdest birding trip in history) was Cherry's account of the Cape Crozier trip to collect the Emperor Penguin eggs. The book was very good, but where was the embryo research? Both Ory and Cherry had chivvied any number of 'minor custodians' at the NHM. So far they were told that there had been a war on (they had noticed). Richard Ashton, the specialist embryologist tasked with analysing them, had died (and they were still looking for a replacement a decade on). What was next? A dawn raid?

Back in 1904, Ory remembered Ted's stated ambition to make his monograph on the Emperor Penguin 'a classic'. Later, in 1911 he had collected the eggs with one aim, to prove Haeckel's theory. Now it turned out that the German biologist had been fudging the data – inaccurate illustrations – that ugly word, 'fraud'. Ted's classic was now on its way, but under Cherry's authorship. Kathleen Scott might have wished Ted had written it. In Cherry's version, Scott was described as 'weak' and 'peevish', which she regarded as 'very offensive'.[4]

Beside the blue canvas book on her desk was her envelope of press clippings. Ory read that Cherry's handing over of the eggs to the museum was represented as a comedy of manners. ('This ain't an egg shop ... Do you want me to put the police onto you?'[5]) George Bernard Shaw weighed in on Cherry's side – the newspaper letters' page was, after all, his spiritual home. Although no one else cared, for Ory it was bad timing. Ory worried lest her friend Oldham Thomas got caught in the crossfire. Besides, Ory's wooden specimen boxes from Darwin, marked 'Mrs Wilson', were due to arrive on the NHM doorstep any day now. Would they think that it was a sophisticated Shavian joke?

Ory decided to say 'nuthin'. For Christmas she stayed with Sir Joseph and Lady Kinsey – knighted for services to Antarctic expeditions in 1917. Anne Hardy's father had just died: 'I know what a chum your father was to you,' Ory wrote, and 'how terribly lonely you must feel.'[6] She urged Anne to join them. Loneliness avoidance required imagination. Birds of a feather and all that. Ory had experience. At the Kinseys' she would be in good, predominantly female, company – the norm after the devastating loss of men through the war. Joseph Kinsey and his wife were the only couple, and they decided to see the New Year at 'Te Hau' in Uncle Bill's Cabin at Clifton. It was a lovely idea but Ory needed Anne's support. She suggested that Anne might come back to the UK with her: 'many of the things I work for come off – so I am going to wish and scheme for this plan – and if you add your wishes – it will help.'[7] Ory was fascinated by willing or wishing things to happen, having just finished a book on 'Autosuggestion' by psychologist Charles Baudouin.[8] His theory held that if a patient/client could impregnate their subconscious mind with a goal, say 'becoming free of rheumatic pain' or 'getting a million dollars', it could materialise. Bernard Shaw talked of the Antarctic's 'triumph of human will over adversity'. The 'triumph of will' interested the newly agnostic Ory; she clung to it as a kind of religion for a brain programmed to think along spiritual lines.

It was here, in Christchurch with the Kinseys, that Ory learned that late in 1922, Oldfield Thomas had published her bat. He registered it as a new animal in the NHM's official list and named it after her. 'I am much complimented by your calling a bat after me! ... I long to go back to Darwin again ... I believe I could do a good deal there if I could 'enthuse' helpers ...'[9] Or perhaps she could go to Sudan (although she'd heard rumours of a terrible sleeping sickness epidemic there) or what about Dutch New Guinea: 'is that a useful place to collect in ... I fancy bats more than anything.'[10]

It seemed extraordinary that whilst her bats, shipped weeks before, had already been analysed and registered – Ted's eggs, received almost a decade earlier, had not. And perhaps even more extraordinary that a new species had been named after her, not him. As she was fond of saying when she was in New Zealand, the world was indeed upside down.

But even ten years on, and many Australian trips and specimen packing cases later, she still didn't feel she had enough clout. Ted's penguin eggs were briefly on display at the NHM in early 1934, alongside a loan of maps and pictures from the newly established Scott Polar Research Institute, to be known as SPRI. The exhibit was very popular, many people came, but Ory was abroad at the time and when she returned it had been taken down. 'I am rather tired of being told by people that the [Emperor Penguins'] eggs are not on view!' wrote Ory to Mr Kinnear at the NHM. 'When such ordinary birds and eggs are shown it would seem a bit peculiar ...'[11]

And today, Ted's penguin eggs are still one of the most talked-about exhibits at the NHM. Ory's bats are only a few metres away. Two of the three examples of *Miniopterus orianae* that Oriana prepared in the heat of Katherine, Australia, in 1922, can still be seen, perfectly preserved and minutely labelled. Ted is centre stage. Ory is tucked in a drawer.[12]

Wartime Friendships Renewed

1926–28

*In which Ory organises a NZWCA reunion of friends made during the war,
women with whom she had 'laughed and joked … when most they wanted
to cry'. She continues her migratory lifestyle, avoiding pressure to authorise
Ted's biography.*

It was 25 April 1926 and Ory was now 51. She remembered the first
Anzac day a decade ago in London. She had just started work at the
office in Southampton Street when the New Zealand soldiers, the
'Knights of Gallipoli', had marched through the grey streets of London,
carrying their colours high. It would always be a special day whichever
side of the world she was on.

Now, as she walked up Clifton Hill, the air smelt of tarmac rather
than brine and there were houses being built all along Kinsey Terrace.
There was scaffolding between Uncle Bill's Cabin and the view south.
But most people were only building to one storey – only British
people seemed to disdain the word 'bungalow': they perhaps suffered
from 'vernacular disease'.

Ory was pleased to be over this side whilst unrest boiled on the
other. Negotiations were under way to avert a general strike, osten-
sibly in defence of miners' wages and hours. She was torn between
the traditional patriarchs such as Cherry and Deb, and the more lit-
eral Wilsons such as her brother-in-law, Jim. The patriarchs thought
the workers, the 'yelling pack', should know their place. Jim was at
the sharp end in his parish of Sneyd in Burslem, one of the Pottery
Five Towns. He rang the Lord Mayor to tell him about a family who

had been evicted from their house and were sitting outside in the rain on their meagre stack of possessions. 'You can't do this to a dog you know' he told the Mayor.[1]

In New Zealand things seemed more peaceful. The pavlova, a meringue-based pudding had just been created by a Wellington chef in honour of the visit of the Russian prima ballerina, Anna Pavlova. She had recently appeared in the newspapers posing in front of a flock of sheep. Pavlova, her fifty-strong dance troupe and twenty-two member orchestra, had delighted audiences with a sell-out tour of thirty-eight shows in thirty-nine days. Ory witnessed this demand for culture. Ballet, opera and the theatre generally was what Ory would have described as 'a hyacinth to soothe the soul'. Culture was a 'hyacinth to soothe the soul'. She determined to contribute somehow to New Zealand's desire for high culture, for objects of aesthetic and literary value. She had thought of gifting Ted's paintings to a new gallery that was being built in Wellington, but where would that leave Deb's SPRI?

Coming up here to Uncle Bill's Cabin every time she was in New Zealand had become a ritual now. She had to see it, to climb those stairs, to lean on the rail, to look south over the horizon. Just to look. An albatross? She couldn't be sure. It was too far off. Just a tiny fingernail moon shape hovering in the far distance. She put her faithful Zeiss binoculars back in their patched leather case. They were still good but were they getting heavier? Maybe she should leave them here. They were Bill's after all and this was his cabin. Her eyes weren't quite as keen – sometimes she wondered whether she had the equivalent of snow blindness – all that sea travel and refraction.

Ory left Uncle Bill's Cabin and headed north to Wellington. It was windy but she loved it and it wasn't Christchurch. Through the NZWCA, she had met the 'eminently practical' Burnetts, who absorbed Ory into their extended family with all its highs and lows. When she expressed a wish to put down roots in New Zealand, they offered Ory a plot on which to build the 'shack' she had dreamed of. 'Aunt Bill's Cabin' perhaps: 'High up looking across the Bay to Wellington and out to the sea and a lovely range of snow mountains in the South Island.'[2] She would stay with the Burnetts and then go on to a reunion she had helped organise in Wanganui up on the west coast of North Island in two days' time.

Wanganui had been the source of all those pants in her in tray. These were the New Zealand friends she had made as they worked alongside during the war, the people with whom she had 'laughed and joked … when most they wanted to cry'.[3] Ladies like these had shown the world just what women were capable of. 'I cannot see that it helps anyone to be cynical about the Modern Girl,' observed Ory. They did not, as the traditionalists maintained, play 'fast and loose' with life.[4] They had been 'Useful Help[s]' during the war and were, in her opinion, the 'persona grata' of the future – the cynics had jolly well better catch up.[5]

As the dining room of the Chequers Hotel filled, Ory saw the Wellington-based *Evening Post* correspondent carefully noting her turquoise medal 'CBE', together with the other medals in the room: 'MBE, Royal Red Cross, Florence Nightingale Medal, Oak Leaf (mention in dispatches); Serbian Order of St Sava, the Serbian Red Cross, the A.R.R.C, the médaille de reconnaissance (Belgian Order), the V.A.D Medallion, the N.Z. War Contingent Association Medal, and the Russell Square N.Z.S.C. Medal.'[6] It was like those legal documents she had waded through after Ted's death – hardly any punctuation. It made one breathless, like trying to classify an aviary packed with exotic birds.

These women gave her faith in her new religion: 'an immanent spirit of goodness, a divine principle making for righteousness, alive in the world'.[7] The sense of community she experienced when she was with them helped replace the Christian community in which she had grown up. She felt secure amongst them, loved. Around her were frequent cries of: 'Why, I saw you last in London,' or 'France', or 'Egypt' or 'Serbia'.[8] And Ory realised that she was not the only one. The bonds had grown stronger over the years. Together they had found solace and perhaps even Ory's elusive sense of purpose.

A hush fell as the 77-year-old Hester MacLean RRC, the grande dame of women war workers, rose to speak. Hester was the only woman in New Zealand to have been awarded the Florence Nightingale medal. It was the equivalent, in Ory's previous belief system, of an outright sainthood. The six medals covering her chest glinted in the electric lamp light like Boudicca's breastplate. Ory smiled, remembering that Hester was not without detractors; Jessie Bicknell had trained under Hester and found her quite impossible.

Hester MacLean fought against the introduction of the eight-hour day, believing that nursing was essentially a 'charitable occupation', which required eleven-hour shifts. Jessie Bicknell had been one of the eleven-hourers. Eleven hours, seven days a week until the government had prevailed upon Hester to give the Jessies of the hospital a day off!

Ory had given up regretting that she had never become a nurse. She hadn't saved lives as had many of those taking their seats around her now, but Hester was keen to acknowledge Mrs Wilson's 'great organising capacity' in realising the gathering of women here tonight.[9] Mabel Thurston, another friend of Ory's and nearer her in age, replied, formally, to Hester's welcome.

Mabel was English but had worked full time from NZWCA headquarters in London alongside Ory and had also been appointed a CBE. As Mabel finished her speech, Ory looked about her. Unlike the majority of those present, she had been married. These women had, of necessity, reinvented spinsterhood, opting for all-consuming work as a substitute for marriage. There was a profound shortage of marriageable men following the war. They were pretty, Vida McLean was prettier than Ory; they were practical, Jessie could graft even better than Ory; they were funny, Fanny Wilson was far funnier than Ory – well known for being a brilliant and witty conversationalist.

Ory loved these women. Loved them perhaps as Ted, Bowers and Cherry had loved each other on that birding trip in the polar winter – adversity did that. It was love that had pulled them through. But straight after dinner, Ory tore herself away. She boarded her ship to England and sailed relentlessly north on the migratory forces of familial duty to which she could not help but respond. Ory's sister, Constance, was ill with depression and Ory had been summoned. Ory arrived back to an England reeling from the effects of the General Strike. Jim Wilson hoped the ruling classes would see sense. He told Ory that the strike had cleared the black smoke from the Potteries' air and that even now, Norah, his wife, was able to grow flowers in the vicarage garden, which had hardly thrived before.

By January 1927, Constance seemed to have rallied and Deb was waving Ory off to New Zealand again. Ory hated rushed visits, and now she argued that she must return to finish where she left off. She was off again to the country where she now had 'as many friends ... as in Britain'.[10]

This time she had a letter to deliver. It was from Deb to Joseph Kinsey. A begging letter. Deb still did not have sufficient funds to realise his dream of a dedicated Scott Polar Research Institute. It was currently in one room in the Sedgwick Museum of Geology in Cambridge, where he was lecturing. Deb was at pains to point out that though it was a 'begging letter', Mrs Bill was 'innocent of complicity in the matter'. To Kinsey he confided that he regretted that she was leaving England again: 'but that's because New Zealand is such a nice place. I was bold enough to urge her to cease her wandering and settle down one side of the world or other, but since I'd like her this side, and she prefers the other the argument didn't get very far ...'[11]

The truth was that as soon as Ory set foot back on English soil, Ted's siblings had renewed their efforts to write their brother's biography. Ory's reluctance was thrown into contrast by Emily Shackleton, who had authorised Dr Hugh Robert Mill to write her husband's within a year of his death in 1923. But Ory's family did not realise that this had been motivated by necessity, namely to clear £40,000 of debt that Shackleton had left.

Ida, Ted's mystically religious spinster sister, claimed she had found 'just the man' to write her brother's biography. If he was Ida's friend, he was probably a priest. While Ory was away, Herbert Ponting wrote to the *Morning Post*, 'The really Great Man of the Expedition was Dr Wilson, and it seems a pity that more should not be written about his life.' Ida's 'just the man' had 'had a long talk with him (Ponting) on Saturday and he told me much of interest about life at the hut'.[12] Much of it was off the record.

Even from New Zealand, Ory was aware that the net was closing. Ted would be biographised. The only variable was her endorsement. Isabel Smith, her wise and sympathetic friend, had, she assured Ory, also found, 'just the man'. Isabel's publishing pedigree was more reassuring that Ida's spinster crushes.

By mid 1928 Ory was back in England, not because of the biography but because Constance, worryingly, was ill again. '... I can't get away to NZ where I want to build a shack,' she lamented, '... until my sister is much better she has been so ill.'[13] She had come back 'hurriedly' for Constance but now that she was here, she could no longer avoid meeting 'the man'.

In the years that came afterwards, Ory was always fond of telling the story: 'I will tell you how the book came to be written for it is an interesting history.'[14] It was interesting, mystical almost, because by some extraordinary coincidence, Ida's man and Isabel's were the same.

Romance with a Small 'r'

1927–29

In which Ory falls in trust with George Seaver and whilst picking at the scab of memories of her life with Ted, engages in romance with a small 'r'. But when things get too intense, she escapes back to New Zealand.

It was trust at first sight. George Seaver was sixteen years younger than Ory but physically very like Ted when she had last seen him in sixteen years before. He was tall and lanky with 'well appointed' features and a robust approach to physical exercise. He had been a soldier during the war, worked in Africa as a Native Commissioner and recently returned home to become ordained. When George first met Ory in the autumn of 1927, it was as a windswept motorcyclist. He'd motored for several hours over the North Wessex Downs from Melksham and was hot and dirty. Ory stood in the door way of The Little House and watched him clatter towards her in a noisy cloud of exhaust fumes, peeling off his leathers to reveal a dog collar and clerical frock coat. For his part, George immediately noticed her eyes, which were, as Ida and Isabel had warned him, still that piercing ice-berg blue. George was not frozen by them, quite the opposite. His name had been put forward for his subtle writing skills, but now they deserted him and he could only think in superlatives: 'glorious', 'won-derful' and 'perfection'. He had always been fascinated by the epic of Scott's Antarctic expeditions, and by the part played by Dr Edward Wilson in particular.

'Mrs Wilson kindly put me up for the night – in the Garden!' George wrote to Ted's sister Ida, 'At my own request!'[1] Before the war when

Cherry worried about whether it was 'proper or improper' for Ory to stay with him at Lamer, she had told the Mrs Grundys to go and jump. This was entirely different and Ory made up a single bed for George in her summer house.

George was completely bowled over. Ory was just simply 'wonderful, wonderful'. This was the woman his hero had chosen 'till death do us part', except it obviously hadn't. It was as if Ted was there with them at every meeting, conjured by their conversation. Once George had recovered control of his lower jaw, he realised that, in addition to her Ted-like attitude, she was graceful. Grace was a quality George had always found most attractive, particularly when the purveyor of it was blissfully unconscious of this herself. The atmosphere that pervaded their every meeting was a tonic to Ory, who had not felt so understood since she was married over sixteen years before. George was 'a Padre', Ory confessed to Cherry, 'but not of the usual type or else he would not be my friend.'[3] George was the most un-clerical clergyman Ory had ever had the pleasure of meeting. And it was a pleasure, they even had the same sense of humour. 'George', she told him, mischievously, was not a name she loved. She preferred 'Derek'. Derek! Why Derek of all names? Ory was not used to being asked to explain herself and so (only to her) 'Derek', George became.[4] Similarly, Ory began respectfully as 'Mrs Ted' (as the family referred to her) or 'Mrs Bill' (as she was known to all the surviving members of Scott's team). Within days, all the 'Mrs-ing' went out of the summer house window, and she became Oriana and then Ory.

Ory had shown George the precious chest of Ted's letters she had been guarding for so long. She also 'offered to make me a present of a complete set of the reproductions ... Well,' said George, 'I didn't know whether to sink into the earth or to soar into the sky.'[5]

By October Ory and George found it necessary, for biographical reasons, to spend the weekend together at Wolf's Craig, Melksham, where George lived with his father. On 17 October, straight after Ory had left for the London train, George wrote to Ida, 'It has been a wonderful time for me,' he told her, 'We also spent much time in discussing matters of faith and exchanging ideas as well as "yarns" about our travels etc. I appreciate very much her point of view and can sympathise with it – we found so much in common ...'[6]

They had only known each other a month and yet Ory, still head-turningly beautiful in her early 50s, had found a soulmate, and a handsome one at that.

George, at his writing desk, was bringing another gushing letter to Ida to a close, 'I admire her wonderful character more and more and I can see what a source of inspiration she must have been to your Brother.' He confessed that he had 'expressed some confidences about myself [to] Mrs Ted,' he was careful to use the name by which Ida referred to her. He wasn't generally incontinent with secrets but there was something about Oriana. If he felt naked as a result, he comforted himself that, whatever she had thought of his deepest secrets, 'it was a help to me. She is very strong with the strength that comes from sorrow.'[7]

Melksham was beautiful, all honey coloured stone and, in the centre, St Michael and All Angels, George's exquisite church. Ory stayed there with George throughout the hard winter of 1928–29 and brought the Antarctic of his schoolboy dreams with her. She introduced him to Cherry. She introduced him to Deb. It was exceedingly cold. 'Debenham said that, for the first time since Antarctic days, he had felt a touch of frost-bite and Cherry's racing Vauxhall was frozen solid in its shed,'[8] but there was warmth, cheer and excitement on offer for visitors to Wolf's Craig.

George helped Ory to gain some perspective on Teddy Evans' 'lack of generosity' at the food and fuel depots on his return journey from the last camp before the Pole in 1912. Atch visited and revealed that, from the research he had conducted on the nutritional value of Scott's rations, the polar team's food allowance was generating less than 50 per cent of the calories they required. These figures seemed to explain the starvation of the polar party. Regarding the shortage of cooking fuel, the chief reason for the shortage was leakage. Thinking back to the threat of an inquiry by Lord Curzon in 1913, Ory must have been grateful that she had followed Ted's advice to say 'nuthin' at least in public, and that she had secured Curzon's promise to keep their interview confidential.

When the Antarctics had departed, and a cosy silence settled on Wolf's Craig, Ory made a significant decision. 'There was an evening when she brought into the room where we were sitting some pages of thin paper written over in pencil, scarcely traceable. They were her husband's last letters, filmed with his frozen breath, from the tent in which he died.' Ory said: 'I have shown these to no one else, except the Reginald Smiths. I think I will go out while you read them.'[9]

It was the most profound act of trust she had made since she gave herself to her husband in marriage back on that scorching summer day in 1901. These letters were 'sacredly intimate', her most precious possession, her private self, and yet now she revealed them to him.

It seemed odd, impossible almost, that George had never even met Ted. Would Ted have approved of him? George needed to know. 'Only once … did I venture a question, diffidently enough, as to the possibility of personal friendship with [Ted] had I known him …' To Ory, the situation seemed self-evident. 'But of course you would have got on together famously. Besides you have so many of his ideas.'[10] George's birthday was on the same day as Ted's. George had many of Ted's ideas. If Ory hadn't lost her faith in God, she would have believed that George Seaver was God-sent.

Ory's wifely home-making skills had been gathering dust. Now she lavished them on a man who had never been married. Ory cooked for him as she had for Ted. George found her dishes 'as delicious as they were wholesome: if bread-making be the test of culinary skill, her home-made wholemeal loaves were the perfection of bakery!'[11] In George's company, she recovered her generosity of spirit and her appetite for food; eating in good company relaxed her. Once he chided her for 'what seemed excessive generosity'. But Ory was ready for him: 'it is only what you told me … you said we ought to circulate the gifts of God!'[12] On New Year's Day 1929 she gave him the two-volume copy of Cherry's book, *The Worst Journey in the World*, inscribed 'G. Seaver from ORW in Mem. EAW. And underneath 'To Derek from Ory' and under that 'Our Heart's Brother'. She had, she told him using Rudyard Kipling's phrase, found 'The Thousandth Man'.[13]

With 'our heart's brother' agnosticism was not taboo but it was difficult for George because Ory could be convincing. He often found that 'one's own faith burns down, as mine does so often' and appreciated a letter from the devout Ida which detailed the miracle of a friend's healing.[14] It was not just God that they discussed, the philosophical debates that Ory had longed to have with Ted had been queuing for too long. She could not remain dispassionate. George was on the receiving end of not just 'a strong intellect', but 'an unexpected zest for philosophical debate'.[15] There was so much that Ory wanted to talk about. Ted had died in a 'prehistoric time'. So much had changed. Ory challenged George upon the new range of issues that had emerged since female suffrage. By this time Ory (over the age of 30 and with the minimum property requirements) was one of 8.4 million women in the UK eligible to vote, following the Representation of the People Act in 1918. In George's presence she did not feel inhibited, she felt alive. Their discussions were passionate: 'often vigorous and sometimes tempestuous', especially when the subject was one on which 'men and women have always mostly agreed to differ'.[16] George had been put forward by Ida and Isabel for his way with words and yet he was now tongue-tied with contradiction. Perhaps his grammar was suffering because 'always, mostly' they differed about love.

For Ory, going through Ted's letters again felt like picking at a scab. Ida asked George how the book was getting on and he replied frankly that, 'Mrs Ted began the task but found it difficult to continue on account of the pain that old memories brought & so this is in abeyance at present.'[17] Ory's father-in-law, Dad, died in 1918, leaving a handwritten memoir of Ted. Ory asked Ida if she could get it typed and bound. Perhaps that would satisfy the family's desire for a biography, and she and George could just be friends.

George did not want to rush her. Ory had, after much mental struggle, become successful at living in the present rather than the past, and dragging her back there seemed almost cruel. He hated to see her upset and felt protective. He assured Ted's family that 'your brother's life will be forthcoming in due course, but the time may still be distant. In the meantime,' he continued, 'I don't advise hastening Mrs Ted in the matter in any way or indeed mentioning it to her.'[18]

Increasingly, George was becoming so familiar with Ted's ideas that he could quote them verbatim. Conversations became three-way affairs. George had never known Ted but now he felt that he 'knew him in spirit'. In some strange way, 'I came increasingly to recognise in him a kindred soul who has thought my own thoughts before me and carried them further ... I am sometimes positively frightened to find such an extraordinary coincidence of outlook with my own.'[19]

Things were getting fearfully intense. In an effort to ward off the fear that they both felt for different reasons, they took breaks from their right and dutiful work on Ted's biography, and set off into the countryside. George soon learned that walking was Ory's favourite recreation, especially if there was wildlife to observe. George was no naturalist, but Ory was a willing teacher. George had a motorbike. After a time, Ory agreed to rides in the wicker sidecar. She didn't care that it was a 'precarious contraption'– it was exciting, it was adventure and it was with George. The best excursions were spontaneous 'for a "treat" was all the better when it came as a "surprise"'.[20]

Some 'treats' had to be planned in advance. Treats were not trysts but shared moments – there were some that were so romantic, so perfect, that neither of them would ever forget. One evening they sat in deckchairs under a full moon in Regent's Park watching the Old Vic's performance of Shakespeare's *Tempest*. Had Ory ever done anything so perfectly, frivolously romantic with Ted? There never seemed to have been the time.

In George's company she remembered how much she had enjoyed sport. Ted hated compulsory school games but her father was a games enthusiast. In 1933 George took her to Wimbledon to see John Crawford of Australia against Henry Vines of America. Before a crowd 15,000 strong (no standing room and the gates had been closed for hours) the match began. Crawford took shots of whiskey between matches when things got tense and went on to win – it was exhilarating, a truly 'unforgettable match'.[21]

With George, Ory had ceased to be lonely and remembered how to 'frivol',[22] but perhaps she was becoming too dependent on him and George had other single female friends. George began to realise that Ory was 'frankly jealous of her friendships and somewhat exacting in them too'.[23] Eventually it seemed that she declared herself to him. George tried to decline tactfully: 'she offered me more than I desired or deserved and beyond my power to reciprocate,' he wrote afterwards with studied ambiguity.[24] Ory began to retreat; she had to remember how to live as she had before meeting George. She had been completely open. She had given him her 'chest full of letters'. She had put herself and her past, not to mention her house, entirely at his disposal. Now she felt vulnerable. Migration was her instinctive response. This time, for good. Ory was aching to get back to the other side of the world! She was 'dreadfully homesick for [New Zealand] for the mountains and bush and my friends there …'[25]

On 22 February 1929, Ory heard that Atch had died. He had recovered from his war injuries – terrible burns so that only one side of his face was recognisable – to become surgeon-captain, but when his wife died in 1928 he had suffered a nervous breakdown. Recently he had recovered and remarried and Ory had gone to his wedding, but now he had gone and most suspected that he had jumped overboard. Ory was beside herself. She did not pick up the telephone but, as was her custom, instructed Cherry to write to *The Times* putting the search party record straight. Atch may have received the Albert Medal for bravery, but still she couldn't bear his Antarctic contribution to die without the fullest recognition she could arrange.

A few days later Ory's beloved father, the Reverend Francis Souper, died in Cambridge. Ory's relationship with some of the Wilsons had become somewhat strained. Ida heard about Ory's father's death from George, not from her. Ory then heard that her mammologist friend, Oldfield Thomas, had committed suicide aged 71. It was a year after his wife had died, a blow from which he had never recovered. Ory knew how close they had been. Working side by side as field scientists, as Ory knew from her experience with the Grouse Inquiry, could do that. But Ted had told her expressly in his dying note that she did not have that option. She must live her life out. 'Slog on, slog on.'[26]

Money was short following the failure of many of the investments made by her brother-in-law, Bernard Wilson, on her behalf. It was on the cusp of the Great Depression when Ory wrote frostily, 'Of course I have often wondered, why you invested it in the Indian and NZ stock at only 3.5%! When I could get 5% to 5.5% quite safely. But I am afraid it could cost more to sell out now.'[27] She sold 'The Little House' to Lily and Bernard Rendall and arranged for Ted's paintings to go on loan to the SPRI in Cambridge, where Deb had offered to sort out the storage and insurance.[28]

Ory was about to set sail for New Zealand once more when Kathleen Scott contacted her out of the blue. Would she sign a joint letter to the press? Last time they had done this was when Ory had been leaving

New Zealand to return home in 1913. Now she was leaving England to return home to New Zealand. Ted's biography was unfinished.

> Sir,
>
> With the passage of time letters and other relics of the Scott Antarctic Expeditions and other Polar Expeditions will increasingly pass from the hands of their original holders, who treasured them.
>
> May we through you, and before it is too late, call to the attention of such holders the Scott Polar Institute at Cambridge which has been founded for the express purpose among others, of providing a safe keeping for documents and other relics of Polar travel.
>
> We have ourselves given, or shall give, what we can of this sort to this institution, to the British Museum, or to some other public institution. We may perhaps, be allowed to express a hope that others will do the same, and so both make them available for study, and save them from commercial traffic.
>
> Yours truly,
>
> K. Kennet (Scott)
>
> Oriana Wilson
>
> Leinster Corner, Lancaster Gate W2.[29]

Earthquakes

1931

*In which Ory arrives in New Zealand just as the Napier earthquake strikes.
She returns to her default war work helping to organise the relief effort, but
serious concerns about Constance cut short her visit.*

The day had dawned warm and still. It was early on Tuesday, 3 February
1931, and she had escaped Christchurch and its memories for Wellington.
Ory was staying in the Burnetts' cabin, trying it out for size and position.
She had visited Uncle Bill's Cabin in Sumner and gained some perspective on George. He was, after all, a confirmed bachelor and a vicar and
she wrote to ask him whether he could write a less intimate history
of her husband. The biography should be about Dr Edward Wilson the
artist and scientist, not about Ted or 'Uncle Bill'.

Just along from the house was the site that the Burnetts had so generously given to her '… for building my longed for shack!'[1] It was south
facing, high up on the hill with a view over the channel to South Island
and the Malborough Sounds. Reflections in the Cook Strait were so
perfect they made it seem as if there were two worlds, the real world
and its equivalent upside down. It was on mornings like this that she
felt anything could happen. Suddenly the ground gave a gentle bump.
It was as if someone from the upside-down world was knocking on the
door. Several seconds later there was stronger rolling and shaking, with
sharper interludes.

The epicentre, she later found out, was Napier to the north but
for two-and-a-half minutes the 7.5 magnitude tremor could be felt
throughout the southern half of the island. Ory and the Burnetts rushed

north to help but the main roads were blocked by mountains of rubble and the train tracks had buckled. By the time they reached Napier that evening, the town was unrecognisable, the ruins still smouldering, the smell of building dust and charcoal choking the air. Some of the buildings had withstood the earthquake only to be gutted by fire. Many of those who were trapped were burnt because, since the water mains had broken, the fire brigade was unable to operate. The Auckland-based *New Zealand Herald*'s headline said it all: 'Napier Like Ypres'.[2]

It was thirteen years since Ory had worked with the wounded New Zealanders and been awarded her CBE. Now she threw herself into helping her fellow countrymen, British sailors whose ship, HMS *Veronica*, had been in port at the time. Together they joined survivors to fight the fires, rescue trapped people and give them medical treatment. Efficient systems were quickly put into place using the *Veronica*'s radio to request assistance. Soon cruisers were dispatched from Auckland with food, tents, medicine and blankets, as well as a team of doctors and nurses.

During the war, Ory had worked in an office or 'trotted about'[3] visiting hospitals. Now she was at the epicentre, it was like a Gotha bombing zone, 525 aftershocks for a fortnight after the first quake. Ory worked through the tremors never knowing whether the next would be fatal. She visited the 400 patients in hospital, navigating newly opened 'crevasses' all the way. The death toll included 161 people in Napier, 93 in Hastings and 2 in Wairoa. Strong aftershocks meant even more admissions to the already crowded hospitals.

When the shocks subsided, Ory was left with mixed emotions. Having pulled through the disaster, she felt even more solidarity with her adopted countrymen – half New Zealander and half British. Neither fish nor fowl. But then, as Ted said, she had always been different: 'You from the first have always been different, yes, from the very first ... and I am the man you have blessed above all.'[4] It was all very well being different, and the Napier wounded felt cherished, but sometimes Ory felt so torn. She had been planning to emigrate, but was it sensible to put down roots in a country where the ground shook? And what about those she loved in England?

Shortly after her work in Napier came to a close, her brother-in-law, Owen, telegrammed to tell her that Constance had taken a turn for the worse. As Ory boarded the SS *Port Huon* in Auckland and took her familiar route north, she was haunted by the memory of that 1913 journey home. Constance was the most popular person on board the Remeura. She had won Captain Greenstreet's prize for singing. He described her as selfless, supportive and courageous. What had happened in the intervening years?

On paper, Constance had everything Ory wanted, a husband, children, a home, but she had not found love with Owen and she had not really made a home. Owen was a 'frightful skinflint' and Constance, neither 'strong willed or strong physically',[5] could not stand up to him. Family life could, as Ory was increasingly coming to realise, 'be a terrible thing'.[6] Constance had suffered her first bad nervous breakdown from overwork thirty years before, at the mission school whilst Ory had been awaiting the *Discovery* in 1904. Ory had continued to describe Constance as 'ill' to her Antarctics, but without defining the illness. Despite brief moments of respite, Constance had never really recovered. By this stage Ory had been a widow for nineteen years, Constance had been married for most of them. Ory's organisational capacities threw her sister's inability to cope into sharp contrast. Sadly, as Constance's daughter remembered it, Ory's visits and confrontations with Owen increasingly threw Constance into a state of panic.

Two days before reaching England Ory saw a beautiful rainbow and her heart sank. 'For in my life whenever I have specially noticed a rainbow … it has brought tragedy in its wake.'[7] Ory requested to be disembarked first. To Isabel Smith, waiting for her 'dear friend' on the London dockside with a telegram in her hand, Ory seemed well and happy as she looked over the side of the ship. It was awful to see. It was the end of a journey, like the train journey up from Dunedin to Christchurch in 1913. There was no way to soften the blow. Isabel held the fatal telegram out to Ory in her hand.

As Ory had been on the final leg of her journey home, Constance, now so ill that she was entirely unbalanced, had left her children at home in Glebe Cottage and walked out of the garden into a nearby field with mower fuel and a box of matches. Ory was too late. Constance died the day her sister arrived back from New Zealand to be with her.

The Coroner recorded: Thirty First August 1931. Constance Mary Bragge. 52-year-old female. Cause of death: 'Shock due to self inflicted burns. Suicide whilst of unsound mind.'[8] There was no post mortem. Constance had left no message.

Her death was desperate, tragic and complicated. It was a death that would haunt her relations forever, at least those who were allowed to know.[9]

Birth of the Book

1931–34

*In which Ory rents a house as a home briefly for her nieces and then resumes
work on Ted's biography. After being chipped away at and hauled over, the book
is born, the reviews are written and the reprints begin.*

Bereavement from suicide was a pain Isabel and Ory now shared. Ory
stayed with Isabel at Green Street in London, as she needed a refuge.
Betty and Eleanor, Constance's daughters, were 15 and 10 years old.
They were only a couple of years older than Ory and Constance had
been when they lost their mother. Constance knew what it was like.
How bad had life been to inflict that pain on her children too? Ory
recalled an incident when Constance's flimsy evening dress caught
light as she was holding a candle whilst stoking a fire before going to
bed. Constance screamed for Owen who had put the fire out, but her
neck and arms were burned. Afterwards, she wrote to Ory hoping she
wouldn't be badly scarred. It seemed so chilling that Constance turned
to this as a way out.

Ory blamed her brother-in-law, Owen – he was cruelly selfish, and
she did not think he would feel any remorse. Ory had been with the
Bragges through some of the worst times '& could have gladly shot him
& now here I am doing all I can to help him in every way …'[2] She
had no choice. She was joint-guardian of the girls and she didn't want
to be cut off from them even if it meant 'the purgatory of being with
their father'.[3]

A short time after Constance's death, Ory rented a cottage, No. 78
Bushey Heath in Hertfordshire, opposite her sister-in law, Polly, and

her husband, Godfrey Rendall. Her two nieces, Eleanor and Betty, often stayed. Within a couple of months, Eleanor, the youngest, was introduced to Rous, a smiley lady with a cloud of hair. Rous, Eleanor understood, was the woman her father had always wanted to be with. Shortly after Constance's funeral, Rous became Eleanor and Betty's stepmother.[4] Ory adopted the role of generous aunt and, as her niece Eleanor later remembered, 'One Christmas we stayed with her and she came in with an old fashioned wheelbarrow with wattle sides and it was full of presents.'[5]

As 1931, the *annus horribilus*, closed, Ory tried to collect herself but her mind felt rather blank. There was no extrinsically beneficent ordering of the world; how could the Reverend George Seaver argue otherwise?[6] To the Wilsons, particularly Ida and Jim who would 'quote God at her', Ory replied vaguely '"life", "God" call it what you will ...'[7]

Ory tried to clear her mind. Isabel Smith gave her philosophy books: Epictetus suggested that it is not death or pain that is to be dreaded, but the fear of pain or death. It was Lao Tzu who gave her courage. The Chinese philosopher maintained that being deeply loved by someone gives you strength, while loving someone deeply gives you courage. She still had a chest full of love letters. Even though that was now in what she now always referred to as 'prehistory', it was the only source of strength and courage she could rely on.

For Ory, it was back to birding, as she tried to find the energy to 'slog on'. She knew she should stay in England for her nieces' sake, but she could not settle. She tried to put her house in order and wrote to Dr Lowe at the NHM, where he and Dr Kinnear were trying to push through Ted's storm petrel as a 'Wilsoni'.[8] Ory wanted Ted's *Terra Nova* diaries and zoological drawings back but had forgotten that she had left instructions for them to be sent straight from the Museum to the Scott Polar Research Institute. Her blank-minded inefficiency embarrassed her: 'I am so very sorry to have worried you ... I had completely forgotten ...'[9]

Ory needed a friend. Once Owen and Rous had married and her nieces seemed to be finding a routine, George was once again a constant visitor at No. 78. He did not push Ory, sensitive to the impact of her sister's terrible death, but took things gently. Instead of working, they would take the train into town and go to an exhibition. They admired Chinese art at Burlington House, where inky birds darted like figures of calligraphy over a silk screen of blossomed branches.

Sometimes they discussed adventure, George described Africa – the 'dark heart', a place full of exotic wildlife. She should go there. He could give her contacts. Despite the noise of everyday life – the loathsome telephone, the wireless, the increased volume of motor cars through Bushey, the talkies – George and Ory chose to live in a bygone era, to read to one another out loud of an evening by an open fire.

George worked in a study upstairs so that he wasn't disturbed by any friends who came around and had a lovely large bedroom next door to Ory's. Meanwhile, working like an 'iconoclast' in the garden, Ory gouged out ancient rose hedges and moved azalea bushes at the wrong time of year – pleased to see that her green fingers meant they didn't turn a hair or a leaf. In his breaks, she and George indulged in fiction (though never 'novellas'), although Ory tried not to forget the science. Those blessed Emperor Penguin embryos for a start. Where was the NHM report, for goodness sake? She asked George to write to Mr Kinnear, Head of the Bird Department – being a man perhaps he would get a straight answer. However, it appeared that nothing had been published, the material had been passed from pillar to post and now some of the specimens were missing.[10]

Perhaps they should publish Ted's excellent satirical pairs of cartoons parodying the contrast between the cosy museum scientist and the collector risking life and limb. But would the NHM have a sense of humour?

What was the net result of their achievement? As George put it in the biography, 'Three Penguin's eggs. Worth the cost of them? A thousand times yes …' The page was entitled 'The Worth of it All'. George's skill as a writer made Ted come alive. Ory realised that Ted had been slipping away. The world had moved on and Ted seemed to be an anachronism. Yet George made Ted walk across the page, out into the blizzard to return safely with his penguin eggs. And the more they worked together, the more Ted lived, until it began to seem as if he really might be there with them.

Since Reginald Smith's death, John Murray's had taken over Smith & Elder. Their principal 'reader', Leonard Huxley, had edited *Scott's Last Expedition*. Huxley was the son of the famous T.H. Huxley and father of two famous sons, Julian and Aldous. Unlike his sons, he was not a scientist but a classical scholar, and unlike them he was not an agnostic but a Unitarian. Huxley's reception of the manuscript was severe and George felt 'like a schoolboy reproved for a bad essay'. He and Ory were told that 'the public won't be interested in all this natural history ... And all this religious material too. If you jettison a good deal of this ...' Ory was shocked by this rough handling, but she magnanimously conformed to professional advice. When Ory asked Cherry to write the preface, she told him what Huxley had said. 'Oh, that old pedant', he remarked wearily. Cherry's manuscript had had worse journeys through publishing houses and he was now immune.

Ory sent it to Isabel Smith, who had generously offered to subsidise the illustrations. Ory was adamant that Ted's artistic skill should be properly displayed without pricing the book beyond the 'everyman', their intended readership. But Isabel felt George had made Ted too sentimental. 'I was interested by your objection to the phrase "they loved each other" at the end of the Winter Journey,' wrote George to Isabel, 'because I have myself wondered if it would be construed as sentiment. No one else had drawn my attention to it. My point was that some other factor than physique or morale pulled them through; for example, Wilson could never have got Scott and Shackleton through that journey.'[11]

The Wilson family felt it made their Ted 'too smooth'. Bernard knew his brother as a man with much rougher edges, his temper for a start. Deb felt it made his boss 'out to be too saintly.' 'Uncle Bill' was far wittier than any saint Deb knew. But Ory would deliver her husband to posterity, it had become her 'purpose'.

Ory and George felt 'chipped away at' and 'hauled over' by editors, readers and friends but by 20 September 1933 the first copy was due to arrive at No. 78. It was George and Ory's baby. George arrived in time to be there for the delivery and together, he and Ory sent out announcements.

For Ory, 'the relief was great when the book was really printed for all this time it has been a scrape – scrape of the "wound" so to speak going over old times ...'[13] Mary Agnes had died three years before, but the remaining Wilson's expressed their reservations. In a letter to Isabel, Ory revealed her exasperation:

Lily has written – a perfunctory letter of thanks for my present of the book – nothing more. Godfrey's only remark was 'why was the tern picture done in such an odd floppy way? I nearly broke out – but held myself in! – (he only showed his crass ignorance of birds by this remark). Ida was glad I had 'roused' myself at last to have the book written! (I wasn't aware that lethargy was one of my faults!) So perhaps you can imagine a few of my feelings in this time of stress ...[14]

Sales of *Dr Edward Wilson of the Antarctic* exceeded all expectations: five reprints were made in the first year and sales increased steadily thereafter. *The Observer* asked 'Who are a nation's great men? If you read this book you may have to revise your estimate entirely.' *The Times* noted that 'its subject stands out from its pages as large, as steady and dependable as a rock.'[15]

Ted was not the only Wilson in the newspapers. Just as the biography was sent in to be reviewed, one of the national newspapers published photographs of the Red flag in Jim Wilson's church in Sneyd, Burslem. Alongside the flag, they printed a picture of Lenin that Jim had hung on the vestry wall and a photograph of Jim 'suitably touched up', according to his son Michael, 'to give him a villainous look'.[16]

Since his vision of Christ as a man in working clothes, Jim had been working to support the poverty-stricken workers he saw in his parish in the Potteries. Influenced by Conrad Noel, the left-wing vicar of Thaxted and founder of the Catholic Crusade, he had become a member of the Labour Party and addressed his fellow clerics as 'comrade'.

The final straw was what the Bishop believed was Jim's attempt to align the words of communism and Holy Communion, the sharing of bread. During the General Strike in 1926, Jim had marched with the unemployed, but now in 1933 just as Ted was lionised, his younger

brother was demonised. The very newspapers that now published glow-
ing reviews of Ted's biography were denouncing Jim.

Jim left Burslem, dangerously depressed. For Ory the territory
was fresh and horribly familiar – she did not hesitate. Recent tensions with in-laws became irrelevant. In a manner brusque and
businesslike, she offered herself as a 'Useful Help'. Reading reviews
in *The Daily Express* and the *Daily Mail* on the train, Ory descend
upon Burslem, plucked her niece, Joan, from the factory smog (she
had Wilson lungs, what were her parents thinking!) and whisked her
back to fresh-air Bushey. Propping open *The Gloucestershire Echo* on
the hall table (some of the 'glaring headlines ... made George Seaver
wince'), Ory forced herself to use the hateful telephone to enrol Joan
into the local school. Ory took care that Joan only saw the good
'glaring' headlines about her uncle, rather than the bad press about
her father, and distracted her with a surprise present – a bicycle. She
made sure that Joan had a good breakfast before sending her off every
morning. While Joan's parents slid into despair, their daughter sat at
the breakfast table in No. 78 drinking 'a second large cup of tea ("she
has never taken more than one")'. Ory was proud of the fact she had
a child in a familiar routine under her roof but she did not want to 'be
mother' indefinitely.

Ory was off to Africa soon. George had prescribed it after the strain
of the biography and had given her contacts from Northern Rhodesia.
She would probably go on to New Zealand and, while she was away, Jim
and Norah could live in her house. She shared her plan with Joan, who
was so delighted that she told Aunt Ory 'that she would be "pulled up
for dreaming in class today"... and there,' wrote Ory to Joan's parents,
'I left it.'[17]

By March 1934 Jim and Norah were installed at No. 78 and Ory
was in East Africa, but book reviews, personal and impersonal, were
following her. A Mrs Benton thanked her, as many had, for sharing
such private letters with the reader. In an illuminating reply, Ory
explained that:

George Seaver wrote to me saying that the picture of my husband
would be so incomplete and one sided without them and that

although when he was on this earth his life was his own ... now he 'belongs to the ages' and that somehow he felt he would no longer mind these bits being published. I am so very glad I let him include them.[18]

She visited Kenya and rode 50 miles on a cassava lorry to visit the missionaries, or as she called them 'Mishies', in the interior. She couldn't understand Swahili, but felt so removed from this superstitious version of her former faith it amazed her that grown people could believe in it. Churches, once her spiritual home, were now architectural curiosities and church services a kind of serious entertainment. She could still be impressed with the patience of the Mishies and the resilience of the locals but it was an objective appreciation.

Crossing spate rivers in a bullock cart, she had time to wonder what would have happened to her marriage if Ted had survived. Would their relationship have stood her loss of faith? What would she have done if he had chosen to pursue his Caius Mission dream of teaching the catechism in 'Africa probably', a dream sustained through his last meetings with the Bishop before the *Terra Nova* sailed?

Looking back, Ory realised that they had changed places. At that first meeting, she was defined by her Christianity with science and travel as side issues. Ted was focused on the science of medicine and the idea of travel, albeit in the context of his Christianity. Now it was science and travel that defined her.

Or would Ted's faith have sustained hers? What would a post-war Ted have been like? Was it even possible that their ideas and beliefs, if put through the mill of the horrors of the world at war, would have evolved along the same lines?

Ory travelled in order to keep such thoughts in abeyance. She visited Beira in Mozambique and moved between George's contacts in Rhodesia, before returning to South Africa with its comforting memories of blubber and Bower Birds.

35

Farewell to New Zealand

1934–35

In which Ory becomes involved in the theatre, nurturing actresses and artists that she admires using funds from the royalties from Ted's book. In New Zealand, the Kinseys have grown old, but the influence of the Wilson name endures.

Ory held onto the rail as she climbed the external stairs to the roof platform of Uncle Bill's Cabin in Christchurch.[1] She would be 60 next birthday. After twenty years exposed to the elements, both the stairs and the climber were a little less robust. Removing her spectacles, Ory took up her faithful Zeiss binoculars and looked towards the familiar southern horizon. It was just as it had always been. Ted was still there in the frozen South, still the same age. His widow was grey and her tiny teagown-waist just a shade more matronly.[2]

The fashion was so much more practical than it was back then. Ory had the black and white Brownie photograph of her and Mrs Kinsey standing on the same platform back in 1912. They both wore floor length skirts, whale bone corsets, starched high collars and hats. Now dresses were shorter and looser and collars lower and softer. The sweet-tempered Lady K stuck to her Victorian fashion, and Sir Joseph still wore his boater on a jaunty angle but he had become impossible: 'How Lady K has stood it I can't think. I feel furious inwardly … but I think the poor man hates getting old … people seeing that he is not able to do what he used to do.'[3]

Ory was writing to Isabel Smith who, realising that Ory needed an outlet for her fury, had invited her to air all grievances to her. She and Isabel agreed that it was one of the worst pitfalls of being single. One had no one to 'grouse' to. Even Ted had admitted that, when the *Terra Nova* men had used him as a bucket for their grievances, he was grateful to be able to pour it all into Ory's bucket in his letters.

George Seaver insisted on Ory sharing in his author royalties. While she had been in New Zealand, she wondered if they should be used for the sponsorship and support of deserving talent, actors and artists. Increasingly, Ory found culture essential. She went often to the theatre, to galleries, to recitals. Ted had loved nature but also its sublime translation through art. In the post-war depressed New Zealand, selling art was a forlorn hope: 'in these bad times people can't or don't afford much in picture buying … Any artistic people are so starved in NZ for lack of pictures and music.'[4]

Ory did not want to make a public splash but began putting plans in place to create an unofficial 'Wilson Art Fund'. The fund would combine the royalties from Ted's biography, with the money from selling his prints, to 'do good' without identifying Ory as the 'do-gooder'. Part of her was confident that Ted would approve, and perhaps another part wanted autonomy. If she had gone public, or become 'official', the Wilson family might have become involved.[5]

Ory was a popular guest when she was in New Zealand. One afternoon when she was in Wellington, she was attending a quintessential English afternoon, all tinkling china tea cups and piano keys. Suddenly, in the midst of this gentility, there was a terrible cry and the sound of smashing china as a young man sitting beside Ory, began fitting and fell to the floor. It was Ethel Burnett's son-in-law, the painter Esmond Atkinson: 'it was so pathetic to see his expression as it was coming on,' wrote Ory, 'and so terrible to hear his cries.'[6] Afterwards Ory described Esmond's fit as war epilepsy. He had served in the Royal Navy Volunteer Reserve patrolling the English Channel and North Sea. Later it would be known as 'shell shock'.

Ory immediately determined upon 'drastic action'.[7] She decided 'there and then' to use her new educational scheme to ease Esmond's suffering.[8] Her decision was a gut instinct. Should she have taken more immediate and 'drastic action' for Constance? Perhaps helping Esmond was a way of trying to redress the balance.

When it was time to leave, Ory booked her passage. The Wilson name still opened doors in New Zealand and when it didn't, Ory was not above a dusting of frost when the situation required: 'The Young man behind the counter asked me if I minded a top berth. I said I wished for a cabin to myself, he then asked my name and changed his manner!'[9]

She wasn't really leaving, or at least she was but she was taking sponsored artists with her, a little bit of New Zealand to keep her company in Bushey. It was all secret but Esmond would follow her and go to a London art school. Ory found her new role as an undercover patron thrilling. Esmond was just the beginning. There was his sister, Rosalind, such a talented actress. And so on …

Ory had become so accustomed to this migratory way of life: transition meant stability, familiarity. It was the way of living that most suited her. She would be, as usual, in the company of strangers, a hermit in society: 'for I am fugitive …' Before she left, Ory spent her sixtieth New Year's Eve with the Kinseys in Christchurch but it was not easy.

Ory's letters to Isabel were her private face. They were an internal commentary – the kind of honest unedited observations that she would have made to Ted: 'I have to face a visit from May Moore [née Kinsey] … I think I had better freshen up by going away from a not too congenial atmosphere! She upheaves the whole house when she comes and poor little Lady K had a very bad heart attack on her last visit – she gets so bewildered and fussed and May tries to make her feel she is very old and ill and can do nothing – it's a pitiful state of affairs.'[10]

For the public face, Ory knew that Kinsey was planning to send all the letters he received to the Turnbull Library in Wellington. Alexander Turnbull, a pupil of Kinsey's at Dulwich College, had requested a set of Ted's prints; it would be a worthy archive to feature in.[11] As Ory eased herself into her 'lovely chair' on board the SS *Port Hobart* in March 1935, and took out her writing things, she composed herself. She owed it to New Zealand, the country to which she had lost her heart. She owed it to the Kinseys, who had, despite recent decrepitude, always been there for her. This letter would be, in some ways, an 'after life'. As she had done with Ted, she had softened her rougher edges for posterity, this letter would be her New Zealand swansong.

My two very Dear friends at Warrimoo,

As I think I must have often said – I cannot thank you enough for all you have done for me – in giving me a home whenever I come to N. Z. and I was thinking only yesterday, that it gave me a feeling of security, to have Warrimoo at my back so to speak – and when one has lost a good deal in life, it is a very great thing to have that feeling – it is what home gives to children – and it is a very great help when that feeling is given to elderly people like myself.

I think you couldn't have given me a more beautiful ending to this visit than you did this afternoon in taking me for that lovely drive – my mind was full of the old 'Discovery' days and of Constance's and my breathless rush over the Port Hills from Sumner to Lyttelton on the morning of the arrival of the 'Discovery' and I was living a great deal in the happy past ...'[12]

36

'The Lame Ducks?'

1937

In which Ory gives her blessing to a second book on Ted. The results of the Terra Nova *are summarised and Ted's legacy is secured. Ory becomes increasingly keen on helping the younger generation to realise their dreams.*

'It was my husband's great wish to produce a book on Natural History and to illustrate it with his own drawings. He had planned to do this on his return from the Antarctic.'[1] It was April 1937 and out of the window she could see the sky beginning to brighten over the red tiled roofs on the opposite side of Bushey High Street. Ory was writing the introduction to a second book on Ted's work. The first had been such an extraordinary success that she and George were now working on *Edward Wilson: Nature Lover*. It was quiet at this time of the morning and Ory could hear the nib of her fountain pen scratching on the paper. There was always so much office work and more now that George – who had kept all the natural history Huxley had jettisoned – was using it to create a second book. It was one in the eye for 'the old pedant' – it turned out that the public, far from being bored by 'all this natural history', wanted more. Ted was a pin-up, the Gilbert White of his day. If Ted loved natural history, so now did his fans. George and Ory were delighted to oblige them.

Ory wrote by hand but she would get her New Zealand 'lodgers' to type it up – the 'Modern Girl' could be an efficient secretary. George, rather unfairly, referred to them as 'lame ducks', but it was Ory that was lame now, as she had broken her ankle and would have to rest.[2] Anyway, they weren't lame ducks. They were just 'Bright Young Things', as Evelyn Waugh called those types in his influential novel *Vile Bodies*, published in 1930. Ory's 'BYTs' were starting out on their artistic adventures. Ory either loaned or paid their fare to England out of her still unofficial Wilson Art Fund and they found their feet at No. 78. 'My Husband was content to work behind the scenes so to speak – his one great object in life was to be of use to people but to keep in the background himself.'[3] It was a noble 'purpose' – one she hoped this secret fund would allow her to live out.

It was also a way of Ory living in New Zealand without actually emigrating. Two of Ory's favourite New Zealand BYTs were Averil Lysaght and Rosalind Atkinson, who both made No. 78 their base at this time. Averil was a biologist and artist, later well known for her work on the eighteenth-century naturalist and botanist, Sir Joseph Banks. Rosalind, who later added Wilson as her middle name, was an actress, whose career was launched by the Wilson Arts Fund. She became famous on stage and screen playing alongside, amongst others, Sir John Geilgud and Peggy Ashcroft. Ory had always loved the theatre. Following Rosalind's career and going backstage to meet these stars was 'electrifying'.

Ory took a Wilson niece to the pictures at Golders Green to see Alfred Hitchcock's *Juno and the Paycock*, set in a Dublin tenement during the Irish Civil War. She took Evelyn Ferrar, daughter of *Discovery* geologist Hartley Ferrar, to *Peer Gynt* at the Old Vic.[4] Evelyn, later Evelyn Forbes, came to live with, and later to look after, Ory. She confirmed Ory's delight in helping younger people, noting, 'She reminded me of an eagle and she reminded me of an iceberg which sounds cold and horrible but she had this tremendous interest in people and heart for helping especially young ones.'[5]

It was nearly eight o'clock in the morning as Ory, sitting at her desk in No. 78, finished her introduction to *Nature Lover*, and reached for her crutches. It was so irritating to be lame in the spring, with all those birds arriving on Stanmore Common. She would hitch a lift up to the Common with her in-laws, the Rendalls, who still lived across the main road in Bushey. By now Ory was reconciled with her Wilson relatives, after all, their disparaging comments about Ted's first biography had been proved irrelevant by its sales figures. She could still sit on the bench with her binoculars and enjoy the spring sunshine.

She heard movement. Her lodgers knew not to set foot abroad until the carriage clock chimed eight o'clock. It must be her teenage nephew, Michael, Jim's son. She would send him birding before breakfast.

'What does a Willow Warbler look like, Aunt Ory?'

'Greenish brown above and off-white to yellowish below – the wings are plain greenish-brown with no wingbars. (Juveniles are yellower below than adults.) And importantly pale pinkish-yellow legs and a long pale bill.'

'And where will I see him?'

'With the other males, Michael, singing his heart out at the top of a tree.'

'Is the song a bit like a robin?'

'A robin?' said Ory. 'Nothing like it at all.'[6]

It was insufferable. How could this boy call himself a Wilson and not be able to tell a Willow Warbler from a Robin, let alone a Chiffchaff? Broken ankle or no, it must be corrected at once!

'Listen,' she said leaning on her crutches, having got a lift up to Stanmore Common. 'Listen, there is the call, and it falls away like a waterfall.'

It was imagery, poetry, ornithology all in one nature package. Michael had heard his elders and betters referring to Aunt Ory's iceberg stare but, far from being put off by her brusqueness, he was hooked from that moment. It was something about being with Ory. There was an atmosphere of excitement, of possibility. 'It was said in the family,' said Michael, 'that in the field she was as good as Uncle Ted on her birds.' High praise. Ted was the family paragon – he was 'the' Wilson but he had died before Michael had been born. Ory was the nearest he would ever get to the 'superhero' that was his uncle. 'I loved Aunt Ory. She was, she was super.'

Once Ory had regained her desk, she put her ankle up on a footstool and filled her pen. Michael could not defy his genetic inheritance and now she had set him on the right track, the birds could do the rest. 'That done', she tried to get back to the introduction. She cited letters and requests from all parts of the world, from correspondents known and unknown asking for more words and more of Ted's illustrations. But somehow, Michael was still bothering her.

She started a fresh letter to Sir John Murray. The Oxford Press had approached George Seaver to write a *Boy's Own* Life of Edward Wilson. Both Ory and George, who did not have children, agreed that 'it is a great mistake to write "down" to boys'.[7] They'd heard that *The Boy's Life of Colonel Lawrence* (of Arabia) was 'poor'. She licked the envelope and placed the letter on her desk. Michael could take it to the postbox when he came back from the Common – pleasing symmetry.

Ory returned to her introduction. Now that it had been established that the expedition was more than the sum of its parts (the immeasurable part, 'inspiration', having been dealt with in narrative form in the first book), Ory was content for the 'parts' to be summarised under the heading: 'Estimate of the Experts'. Together, George and Ory concluded that, 'Wilson had three notable contributions to make the scientific discovery: in the departments of ornithology, physiography and geology.'[8]

The first concerned the penguins' eggs, where 'the results were 'disappointing'. Twenty-three years after they had been collected, the eggs had finally been added to the collection at the NHM in London. Zoologist C.W. Parsons, who was eventually assigned to study the eggs, concluded in 1934 that these three Emperor Penguin embryos were too close in age for them to make a decisive impact on the knowledge of penguin embryology.

Regarding the second. Ted's old comrade Charles Wright concluded that his own report on the *Physiography of the Beardmore Glacier Region* owed much of its value to Dr Wilson's accurate sketches. Finally, Deb's department, geology. The fossil samples Ted collected on his return from the South Pole, 'settled a long-standing controversy between geologists as to the nature of the former union between Antarctic and Australasia.' As usual, George dedicated the resulting book, *Edward Wilson: Nature Lover*, 'To O.F.W.' Almost immediately it sold out and was reprinted.

Ory hoped that this scientific book would bring the focus on Ted's science rather than his religion. By the time of the second reprint in 1938, George had published his second polar biography on Birdie Bowers, Ted's tent mate. The next one would be on Captain Scott.

George approached Kathleen Hilton Young (Scott), now Lady Kennet, about the Scott biography early in the hot summer of 1939. Whatever George chose to write about her first husband, Kathleen told him that she would 'rather be left out of it altogether. The life I lead now – doing everything I like – is very different from the kind of thing you are writing about. It belongs to the past for me. Another world. And I am a different person.'

Ory was part of the past. Their last recorded meeting had been at Reginald Smith's funeral, and neither had sought the other's company since. The general view amongst the Antarctics was that they were 'poles apart', or at the very least, not 'focsle friends'. But they would always have that intense time in 1913–14 in common. When Kathleen's niece married, she took the trouble to seek out a copy of *Edward Wilson: Nature Lover* and sent it as a gift with good luck for the future from Aunty Scott.[9]

At the start of the Second World War, Evelyn Ferrar remembered Kathleen's son Peter Scott, turning up at No. 78 in his Royal Navy Reserve uniform, all navy blue serge, brass buttons and shoe polish. Peter looked just like his father, square set and strong, although Deb described him as 'unfortunately undersized'. His personality and ambitions were not undersized, he was ebullient, artistic and ambitious like his mother but also military and tough like his father.

In 1933 Peter had his first solo exhibition of bird paintings in London. His birds were not painted from stuffed museum specimens but from birds that he had observed in flight. They were realistic, they were sensitive, they were alive. In some ways it demonstrated Kathleen's success in following her husband's dying instruction to 'make the boy interested in natural history, they teach it in some schools.' But Peter's passion for bird painting was more specific than that. It was not only Ory's Antarctics who observed that one of the most powerful influence on Peter's life had been his father's best friend, Dr Edward Wilson. For the moment, as Ory welcomed Sub-Lieutenant Peter Scott RNR into No. 78, she would have acknowledged that his genetic father's influence was, for the moment, in the ascendant.

Only this visit of Peter's is recorded, but he and Ory seem to have had a good relationship. Peter Scott kept a piece of his parents' wedding cake in an old pink jewellery box with a note from Oriana. The cake is wrapped in a doily, presumably from the wedding reception: 'I am so sorry,' Ory wrote, 'that this has got so squashed – it was in my husband's tailcoat pocket after the reception & I am afraid he sat on the pocket!

... So many thanks for letter OFW.'[10] Ory felt a special connection with Peter, he was a fellow birder, and Ory loved to talk birds. During that particular visit, Evelyn records, Peter told Ory he had just been lecturing on Pink-Footed Geese. In fact, he had just bagged eighty-eight of them.[11] Ted's interest in birds had started with sport and evolved through art to conservation. Ted hesitated to shoot any animal unless it was for science or food. Ory told Peter that, thirty-five years earlier, Ted had written about the desperate need for conservation in New Zealand, his desire to halt the march of extinction, of species 'dying out before one's eyes'.

Perhaps these conversations inspired Peter with his passion for conservation. As Evelyn later said, young people were drawn to her because 'life was always exciting with Oriana'.[12] The year after Ory died Peter settled in the nearest wetland to Cheltenham and made his headquarters at Slimbridge on the River Severn. From there, in 1961, he founded the most important conservation organisation in the world, the World Wildlife Fund (now the World Wide Fund for Nature) and the less well-known Society of Wildlife Artists in 1964.

The Disappearing Point

1938−45

In which Ory has a breakdown and then a stroke. She burns all Ted's letters to her and hers to him in a bonfire at the bottom of the garden. Seven years later she dies in a nursing home in London at the end of the Second World War.

Ory was depressed over a rheumatic pain in her back that, despite 'auto-suggestion', just wouldn't go. Perhaps it was the heavy cans of water she had been lifting in the garden. Ever since the creation of the volcanic rockery at Uncle Bill's Cabin in Sumner, she'd loved pottering about in the garden, particularly in the very early morning dew when her guests, following her explicit instructions, were still abed – but now, time seemed to drag: 'Why is 3 o'clock & before & after in the afternoons a difficult time?' she asked her Ursula in a letter. 'Of course I know that highly strung people feel always better at about 6 p.m. onwards – 'nerves' are not jangly then & life seems better & more hopeful. Why?'[1]

It was a bitterly cold day in January 1938 and 63-year-old Ory was returning from a funeral service in Bushey Heath. When she turned the last corner of the road, she found it difficult to lift her feet or to walk straight.

Her 'daily factotum' found her collapsed downstairs at No. 78 and, together with a neighbour, got her comfortable and summoned the doctor. While she recovered from what was diagnosed as a stroke, her friends rallied round. Margaret Bowen, now headmistress of a girls school in Yorkshire, came to live with her over the school holidays. Isabel Smith took her out in the country, with Ory wielding her trusty Zeiss binoculars to spot birds from the passenger seat of Isabel's capacious motorcar.

Evelyn Ferrar did all the cooking and correspondence ('no light job'). She was 'a perfect jewel' but eventually Ory had to have the St George's nurses from Ted's old hospital and finally, the freelance 'Nursey'.

'So often I seemed to nearly "go out" & felt very comfortable over it generally & then I would hear the Nurse say to the other one – give her a (such & such) injection – & then I was floated back into living uncomfortably!'[2] Even after a year she was not herself. Her raison d'être was to be the 'Useful Help', but here she was, 'quite useless'. What was the point?

Her friends tried to help. Ursula tried to reignite Ory's interest in the (still unofficial) Wilson Arts Fund, and suggested some members of Ursula's (also unofficial) Salon who might benefit.[3] Ory had always trusted Ursula. She embraced artistic secrecy and published her own poetry either anonymously or under a pseudonym Evelyn Hayes. Ursula became Ory's New Zealand agent, using the funds to help those in her unofficial salon. It was purposeful to feel that Ory could support Bright Young New Zealand Things from her bed half a world away.

Ory tried to travel to New Zealand in her letters and to Anne Hardy she confessed that 'as a result of my illness and a nervous breakdown – my nerves feel as if they are being stretched out always – what a pain this is.'[4] She was horribly familiar with nervous breakdowns. Had she been sympathetic enough to Constance? She was still haunted by her death. Or the three Antarctics – her long-term friends Cherry and Atch, and also Dennis Lillie – for whom the expedition seemed to have precipitated mental health issues?

Whatever Ory might have thought about it, three of Scott's, and at least three of Shackleton's crew, had developed mental health issues in later life. Were they deranged by their near-death experiences or did the Antarctic attract people with extreme personalities who were not just looking for the edge but already near to it?[5] For both the main protagonists and their families, it seemed that whatever one's state of mind, polar exploration could be destabilising, life changing.

Ory decided the time had come. She put 'the perfect jewel' in charge, she trusted Evelyn with her most precious possession, her chest of letters. She wanted her to 'see that every scrap of it burned'.[6] She wanted nothing left.

'She gave a lot to me to burn, when she was in bed with the stroke,' remembers Evelyn, 'and I remember taking them down and Oriana said make a bonfire in the garden ... which I did ... and I think they were mostly Ted's letters ... done up in little packets ...'[7]

Evelyn held the little packets into the embers with the garden fork, burning Ted's sketches of Ory, his love letters, his early, immature ruminations on the nature of God, his critical comments and all the 'rougher' edges of the man. Ted's siblings remembered he had a temper, Deb remembered his irreverent sense of humour but Ory and George Seaver had made sure that he was remembered as a saint. Every man has a 'shadow side' but the Ted that Ory intentionally left for posterity was a man who, as Cherry had so succinctly put it in his preface: 'will give you courage; and this is what the world has wanted since he died and never so much as now'.[8]

Soon Ory's chest of letters, the source of courage to live her 'life out', was empty but Ted's legacy was secure. Ted's words would not 'go father-less', as Socrates put it. Michael, her nephew, understood.

By the time war was declared in 1939, she regained some strength staying with her relations, her stepmother 'old Mrs Souper in Battersea', and also with her niece, Elizabeth Bantoft (née Bragge), in Henley-on-Thames. Sometimes she was too ill and had to be in a nursing home in Frogmore House in Windsor. Her writing had not been affected by her stroke, nor her sense of humour: 'I have a lovely outlook from my window – bombs are dropping very near – and also incendiary ones – why the Germans come here each night I can't imagine!'[9]

On 29 November 1941, she wrote to a stranger, a Miss Oriana Anne Walker, having scanned the marriage announcements in *The Times* the day before. 'I was so interested to see,' she wrote, 'your first name Oriana – for except in the case of my own family and in the title the "Oriana Madrigals", I have never come across anyone with this name.' At the end of her letter to the stranger, Ory wrote the P.S. 'I must tell you that my husband Edward Wilson ...'[10] It was four months after what would have been their fortieth wedding anniversary. Ory realised that, though she had been married for ten years, Ted had been away for half that time. Now she was in her seventh decade, only a small fraction of it had been spent with him and yet he was still the defining feature of her life.

Ory gradually succumbed to, as George put it, 'an illness which a sound physique and a natural vitality served only to prolong'.[11] As the Second World War gathered momentum outside, she lay in bed in a nursing home in 3 Broadhurst Gardens, Finchley, London. She lay quite still and she thought of the shack she had built in her mind. It was something like 'Uncle Bill's Cabin' at Sumner, but it was bigger, big enough in fact for her and Ted to live in forever and it looked over the sea to the snow-capped mountains of the South Island, New Zealand, and on to the far South where Ted also lay 'quite still' wrapped in his white blanket of snow.

Ory's bed was needed for wounded soldiers but Isabel Smith, Rosalind Atkinson and George Seaver were at pains to remind the nursing staff that she was no ordinary old lady, she was the 'Widow of Edward Wilson'. George sat beside her bed for hours working on his biography of Scott. He was working with Mrs Ted again, but only in so far as he was working in her presence. The room was quiet, her steady breathing and the scratching nib of George's pen the only sound.

Ory died on Anzac day, 25 April 1945. Two weeks later, peace was declared.

On 25 April 1912, thirty-three years earlier, Ory was just making her farewells on the Canterbury Plains in South Island. The Studholmes had been warm and generous hosts, helping her to get over the disappointment of Ted's decision to stay in the Antarctic for an extra year. To thank them for their hospitality, Ory wanted to leave the Wilson signature, a penguin sketch, in their visitors' book.

Leaning forwards slightly in her chair in her writing position, Ory's soft lead pencil moved carefully across the surface. She was not an artist, as Ted was, but the Studholmes had been generous and kind and she wanted to leave them something. Slowly, the two Emperor Penguins emerged from the page – the only one of Ory's drawings to survive. In Ted's signature sketch, a large Emperor Penguin is placed in the foreground on the left, with a recently hatched chick balanced on his feet, while on the right a crowd of penguins stand at the foot of a cliff. But in this sketch made, although she didn't know it, a month after Ted had died, Ory drew just two penguins – a larger penguin in the foreground on the left, while in the background to the right, a smaller solitary penguin, its black back turned with flipper wings extended like arms, walking away.

In Ted's sketches, the penguins were always set in a recognisable Antarctic landscape – under a cliff with a clearly drawn distance, a disappearing point. Ory's landscape was just a couple of roughly drawn horizontal lines. She wasn't confident about what that distant shore actually looked like.[12]

The Reverend George Seaver stood strangely out of place in Ory's secular church, the recently built Golders Green Crematorium. He had not reversed her agnosticism but had helped her to a faith in 'an imminent spirit of goodness, a divine principle making for righteousness, alive in the world'.[13]

Fifty million people had died in what was now becoming known as the Second World War, but to the small group who gathered on that April morning, and to Ted, the lady in the coffin before them had always been unique. George quoted Ted's tribute to her: 'You from the first have always been different; yes from the very first … and I am the man you have blessed above all.'[14]

As the May blossom came out on the trees in the grounds of Lamer, Cherry received a package in the post. It was the copy of Tennyson's *In Memoriam* that he had lent Ted. Cherry was touched. It was not only the Antarctics who had been brave. That small leather-bound book of poetry had helped Ory to 'live her life out' – she had demonstrated a rare species of grace under pressure and he would miss her. He sent a letter to *The Times*, reporting the book's significance and its return.

Shortly after Ory's death, George moved back to the Seaver's ancestral family home, in Kilkenny, Ireland. There was nothing to keep him in London now. He trawled back through the parts of Ted's letters that he had noted and never used. He was astonished that, months later, letters of condolence kept coming in from all over the world – from Africa, Australia, New Zealand and many 'unexpected persons' young and old, men and women, all expressing 'the debt that they owed [Ory]'.[15] George was familiar with getting letters from people inspired by Ted, but these were not about him. What had Ory meant to these people? Who, in fact was she? When George thought about it and tried to distil it into words, it seemed to him that her chief legacy was courage, 'The infection of good courage' at a time when people had never needed it more.[16] She was also without self-pity, as he knew she would want him to be now.

In 1946 George published a slim volume, *The Faith of Dr Edward Wilson* – an elegant book with the rejected 'all this religious material' held between sky blue covers, sprinkled with stars. If Ory was right and there was no heaven, it could not hurt. Ted had believed in Heaven and now, with his 'faith burning low', George needed to as well.

Some of the letters George had received he wished he could have shared with Ory. One that Ted had written to his sister, Polly, was forty-four years old. It had been folded and unfolded many times and yet it was fresh and keen and somehow alive with hope as if it had been written yesterday:

My very dear old Poll,

I feel I must trust to you all to forgive me for spending all my available time and energy in doing my very best to make things more bearable for Ory. She is wonderful Poll, and I want to help her to keep so. You can have some idea, because you know her, but not as much as I do, how splendid a thing her love must be to keep her going as she has since I left. However much I trusted her, I never quite expected that her love <u>could</u> overcome her self in this way, and how I admire her for it you can guess. I miss her badly sometimes of course and there's a chronic undercurrent of a bad want, but its place will gradually be taken, as this time goes on by a chronic undercurrent of 'le bon temps viendra'.[17]

Postscript

On an icy windblown ridge on the edge of Cape Crozier there is a ring of volcanic rocks with a gap that might have been an entrance, long ago. After more than a century of screaming katabatic winds, it still echoes with the memory of the first ever journey to be made in the polar winter. Inside the ruined walls there are penguin parts, shreds of canvas, wind-worn wool clothing, a test tube, rope, and some unlabelled tin cans, all preserved in the Antarctic deep freeze. The hut is classified as a Category 1 Heritage Site (Historic Monument No. 21) by the Antarctic Heritage Trust.

Beside the ruin there is an angled rust-red frame at about knee height, with four metal plaques bolted on. In four languages, the raised capital letters read:

> Wilson's Igloo, Cape Crozier. This site is an historic monument and preserved in accordance with the provisions of the Antarctic Treaty. It commemorates the Winter Journey of Scott's party to Cape Crozier, who built this igloo in June 1911.

The New Zealand Geological Survey Antarctic Expedition 1958–59 named the hut 'Wilson's Igloo' and the ridge 'Igloo Spur', so these are now the names that appear on the map of the bottom of the world.

However, should anyone find themselves on that ridge in the near future, on the next page is a list of what else to look for. It is the kind of inventory that appealed to Ory – things that Ted left in the hope that they would be a 'Useful Help' to anyone who came after him:

1. Box of pickling solutions and all the apparatus.
2. A sledge.
3. A pick.
4. Some bamboo.
5. A variety of odd clothes.
6. A down sleeping bag which was so solid with ice that nothing could be done with it.
7. A note [tied] to the handle of the pick where it couldn't be missed in a match box.

We will probably never know what is inside that unmissable match box, but perhaps it reads something like the note Ted wrote to Ory in his journal on Sunday, 16 July 1911, their tenth wedding anniversary:

> *... and I called it Oriana Hut, and the ridge on which it is built Oriana Ridge.*[1]

Notes

Chapter 1

1   Ted to his mother, see George Seaver, *Edward Wilson of the Antarctic: Naturalist and Friend*. London: John Murray, 1933, p.35.
2   Ory to Isabel Smith, 21 February 1935, MS559/145/3 SPRI. Letter talks of Aunt Emmie Hopkins, her stepmother Henrietta Escreet's sister. Aunt Emmie was always a particular friend to Ory. She died in 1935 in Sherbourne.
3   'One little brat came with a bandage over his eyes.' Seaver, *Wilson of the Antarctic*, p.34.
4   David M. Wilson et al., *Edward Wilson's Nature Notebooks*. Cheltenham: Reardon, 2004, p.47.
5   Seaver, *Wilson of the Antarctic*, p.61.
6   Ted to John Fraser, 25 January 1909, MS1577/6/14;D SPRI.
7   Barrett Hamilton quoted in Seaver. *Wilson of the Antarctic*, p.167.
8   Ory to John Fraser from NZ, 3 October 1903, MS1577/8/1;D SPRI.
9   This is how David Wilson's father Michael later described Aunt Ory's eyes in their recorded interview held at Cheltenham Borough Council and the Cheltenham Trust/The Wilson Family Collection, 2004.
10 For Ted's thoughts on mission work in Africa see Seaver, *Wilson of the Antarctic*, p.37.

11 Ory to Jim, 20 December 1912, from Christchurch, New Zealand, 1995.550.106 (v), Cheltenham Borough Council and the Cheltenham Trust/The Wilson Family Collection.

12 See Wilson et al., *Edward Wilson's Nature Notebooks*, p.51.

13 Seaver, *Wilson of the Antarctic*, p.57.

14 Seaver, *Edward Wilson of the Antarctic*, p.45.

15 Ted to his mother, quoted in Seaver, *Wilson of the Antarctic*, pp.35–36.

16 Seaver, *Wilson of the Antarctic*, p.36.

17 Oriana to Kathleen Scott, 10 May 1913, MS 195 1453/190/1.

18 James and Eliza Beaumont lived in Highgate, London, and had ten children of which Ory's mother was the fourth. There is a library at Bradfield College called 'The Beaumont Library', which was partly funded by a Beaumont relation.

19 Paul Spillane, *St Andrew's School Meads: A Centenary History 1877–1977*, 1977, p.9.

20 Spillane, *St Andrew's School. A Centenary History 1877–1977*, 1977, pp.9–10.

21 Leach is quoted in John Blackie, *Bradfield 1850–1975*, p.60. Privately published by Warden of St Andrew's College Bradfield, 1976.

22 For Rev. Souper's views on diet, education and report-writing see Spillane, *St Andrew's School*, pp.8, 11.

23 Spillane, *St Andrew's School*, p.8.

24 Philip Dottin Souper (1801–61) was an English Colonial Administrator and Railway Company Secretary. A controversial character, he sided with the planters during the 1833 Slavery Abolition Act. He married his first cousin Oriana Jane Reinagle (1804–90) in Trinidad in 1827. Her father, Philip's uncle, was the well respected Royal Academy portrait and animal artist, Ramsay Richard Reinagle who painted their engagement portraits. (Her mother was called 'Oriana Bullfinch'.) Philip Souper's first job was as Colonial Secretary of Trinidad and last Register of the Supreme court of Mauritus. According to the Cambridge University Alumnus information, he also worked as a surgeon. Francis Abraham Souper (1849–1929), Ory's father, was the third of eight surviving children. The seventh, Jessie Georgina, married Gerald d'Courcy O'Grady, whose deaf daughter, Ory's cousin, lived with her in The Little House in Binfield after the war.

25 Dr E.T. Wilson, *Notes for a Life of Ted Wilson*, handwritten illustrated version of memoir, p.74, MS750:BJ SPRI.

26 Seaver, *Wilson of the Antarctic*, p.45.

27 Ibid., p.45.
28 Cheltenham College has a memorial window to Ted in the chapel, a plaque (a copy of one commissioned from Kathleen Scott) and an impressive Wilson archive.
29 Spillane, *St Andrew's School*, pp.7–8.
30 Ibid., p.302.
31 When Ory was 6, Francis Souper's 52-year-old cousin Josephine arrived from Singapore and was registered as 'Matron (Dom Serv)' at St Andrews, Eastbourne, in the 1881 census. At a time of rigid class separation, this was controversial. Perhaps it was Ory herself who asked for her Suffolk Hall job description to be adjusted?
32 Public Record office reference RG 13/2465, Cheltenham 1901 England Census, column 13, third line up from the bottom.
33 Dr E.T. Wilson, *Notes for a Life of Ted*.
34 Ory to Jim, 20 December 1912.

Chapter 2

1 Eleanor Forbes to David Wilson, interview at 10 Summerfield Cambridge, 11 August 1995.
2 There was a battle with the windows at Westal. Ted always wanted them open. The cure for TB was inactivity and fresh air, but Ory talked of his mother's general dislike of open windows at Westal to Jim in her letter of 24 April 1903, 1995.550.106, The Wilson Collection Cheltenham. I have assumed for this chapter that Ted and his father overruled his mother when Ted became ill.
3 'I have got me a bit soot-sodden', Seaver, *Wilson of the Antarctic*, p.45.
4 There is no conclusive evidence on whether Ted actually had TB or another serious respiratory disease. Isabel Williams suggests an alternative diagnosis of chronic pneumonia, with the mycobacteria seen under the microscope being non-pathogenic (rather than TB's pathogenic) contaminants. Isobel E. Williams, *With Scott in the Antarctic: Edward Wilson: Explorer, Naturalist, Artist* (The History Press, 2008), p.51.
5 Wilson et al., *Edward Wilson's Nature Notebooks*, p.54.
6 'Biography of Oriana', included in twenty-sixth impression (1959) of Seaver, *Wilson of the Antarctic*, p.304.
7 Seaver, *Wilson of the Antarctic*, p.46.
8 *Nature Notebooks*, p.38.

9   *Family Faculties Book.* A record of family members and characteristics drafted by Dr E.T. Wilson as part of early research into genetic inheritance, for which he won a prize. 1995.550.61 The Wilson Collection, Cheltenham.
10 Ory to Cherry, 3 May 1918, MS559/143/1-25;D SPRI.
11 *Family Faculties Book.*
12 Seaver, *Wilson of the Antarctic*, p.51.
13 Evelyn Forbes, interview with Dr David Wilson, 11 August 1995, Cambridge. Evelyn, the daughter of Hartley Ferrar, the *Terra Nova* geologist, came to look after Ory during her last years in Bushey Heath.
14 Seaver, *Wilson of the Antarctic*, p.61.
15 Mary Agnes Wilson, *The ABC Poultry Book*. London: Cassell, Petter, Galpin & Co, 1880 [Held by the Wellcome Trust Library, London].
16 Ibid., p.47.

Chapter 3

1 Seaver, *Wilson of the Antarctic*, p.56.
2 Ibid., p.51.
3 *Edward Wilson: Diary of the 'Discovery' Expedition to the Antarctic Regions 1901–1904,* Ann Savours (ed.), from the original manuscript in the SPRI, London: Blandford Press, 1966, p.30.
4 Ory to Apsley Cherry-Garrard, 22 February 1929 (collection of twenty-five letters). M559/143/1-25 SPRI.
5 Seaver, *Wilson of the Antarctic*, p.56.
6 'Biography of Oriana', p.303.
7 Seaver, *Wilson of the Antarctic*, pp.55–56.
8 Ibid., p.57.
9 Dr E.T. Wilson, *Notes for a Life of Ted Wilson*, p.86.
10 Ibid.
11 Seaver, *Wilson of the Antarctic*, p.61.
12 'Biography of Oriana', p.304.
13 Dr E.T. Wilson, *Notes for a Life of Ted*, p.86.
14 Ibid., p.87.
15 Seaver, *Wilson of the Antarctic*, p.61.

Chapter 4

1 Seaver, *Wilson of the Antarctic*, p.63.
2 Ibid., p.62.
3 Ibid., p.63.
4 Ibid., p.103.
5 'Biography of Oriana', p.303.
6 Seaver, *Wilson of the Antarctic*, p.64.

Chapter 5

1 Dr E.T. Wilson, *Notes for a Life of Ted Wilson*, p.91.
2 Seaver, *Wilson of the Antarctic*, p.72.
3 Seaver, *Wilson of the Antarctic*, p.68.
4 Ibid., p.61.
5 *Edward Wilson: Diary of the 'Discovery'*, p.26.
6 'Everything seemed against him but he had obtained the written consent of his future wife …', E.T. Wilson, *Notes for a life of Ted Wilson*, p.92.
7 At the end of her life Ory, suffering from a nervous breakdown, instructed her friend Evelyn Forbes to burn all the personal letters between herself and Ted.
8 Seaver, *Wilson of the Antarctic*, p.195.
9 Ibid., p.185.
10 Seaver, *Wilson of the Antarctic*, p.102.
11 Seaver, *Wilson of the Antarctic*, p.102.
12 Ted to John Fraser, 27 February 1901, MS157/6/2 SPRI.
13 Ted to his mother, 29 November 1901, Dr E.T. Wilson, *My Life (1832–1918)*, Vol. 2, p.101. 1995.550.35B Cheltenham Borough Council and the Cheltenham Trust/The Wilson Family Collection.
14 *Edward Wilson: Diary of the 'Discovery'*, p.25.
15 5 January 1901, Wilson, *My Life*, p.280.
16 *Family Faculties Book*.
17 Dr E.T. Wilson, *Notes for a Life of Ted*. It is understandable that Mary Agnes was worried; their daughter Lily had just had a stillborn son, but at least she had survived the birth.
18 See Lieutenant-General William Bellairs' pronouncements on officers' marriages in 1889. Myna Trustram *Women of the Regiment: Marriage and the Victorian Army*, Cambridge: CUP, 1984, pp.233–35.
19 Seaver, *Wilson of the Antarctic*, p.75.

Chapter 6

1 Ory to John Fraser, 8 March 1904, MS1577/8/1 SPRI.
2 Dr E.T. Wilson, *My Life*.
3 For details of Ted and Ory's wedding and first two weeks of married life as described by Ted see Savours Prologue, *Edward Wilson: Diary of the 'Discovery'*.
4 Information in St Mary Magdalene Church, Hilton, Cambridgeshire.
5 Ted to John Fraser describing wedding, quoted in Dr E.T. Wilson, *Notes for a Life of Ted Wilson*, p.96.
6 Ted to John Fraser, 25 January 1909, MS 1577/6/13 SPRI.

Chapter 7

1 Ted to John Fraser, 30 July 1901, MS1577/6/4;D SPRI.
2 Ted to John Fraser, 25 January 1909, MS1577/6/13;D SPRI.
3 Savours, *Edward Wilson – Diary of the 'Discovery'*, p.30.
4 Ibid.
5 Ted to Polly, 29 November 1901, 2015.29.6, The Wilson Collection, Cheltenham.
6 Ted to his mother, 17 December 1901, Wilson, *Notes for a Life of Ted Wilson*. p.101.
7 Seaver, *Wilson of the Antarctic*, p.79.
8 Ibid., p.80.
9 This bird was different to numerous other petrels in South Trinidad because it was brown and nested earlier and higher on the cliffs than the pale-bellied petrels. It was named *Aestralata wilsoni* but years later it was reclassified as a subspecies of the Trinidad or Herald Petrel. Recent scientific debate has reopened other possibilities, however, and the issue is still not resolved. Everyone who knew Ted then or who knows him now through books wants that petrel to be named after him. I hereby add my vote and Ory's *in absentia*.
10 Seaver, *Wilson of the Antarctic*, p.81.
11 Ibid., p.103.

Chapter 8

1 The experience of daily life during the voyage and the spotting of albatrosses from the deck were gleaned from George Bulleid of

Oamaru, New Zealand, and Kensington, London, who sailed this route aged 6 in 1922. Email to the author 31 December 2012.

2   Believed to be the first play performed in Antarctica, *The Ticket of Leave* script was found in rubbish around Discovery Hut during its restoration in 1963–64. The programme for the evening is held in the archives of Canterbury Museum, Christchurch, NZ.

Chapter 9

1   Scott's original letter to Ory, written in 1911, is held in Cheltenham College Archive. Quoted in Seaver, *Wilson of the Antarctic*, p.116.

2   Ibid.

3   Seaver, *Wilson of the Antarctic*, p.106.

4   David Crane, *Scott of the Antartic: A Life of Courage and Tragedy in the Extreme South*, London: Harper Perennial, 2006, p.227.

5   What exactly were those 'hard words'? Ted may have been more explicit. The letters no longer exist. In 1922 Albert Armitage published the account related to him by Shackleton: One morning Ted and Shackleton were packing their sledges after breakfast, they heard Scott shout, 'Come here you BFs.' They went to him and Wilson quietly said: 'Were you speaking to me?' 'No Bill,' said Scott. 'Then it must have been me,' said Shackleton. He received no answer. He then said: 'Right, you are the worst BF of the lot, and every time you dare to speak to me like that you will get it back.' Albert Armitage quoted in Crane, *Scott of the Antarctic*, p.240.

6   Ory to Jim Wilson, 24 April 1903, 1995.550.106 Cheltenham Borough Council and the Cheltenham Trust/The Wilson Family Collection.

7   Wilson et al, *Edward Wilson's Antarctic Notebooks*, p.115

8   Ibid.

Chapter 10

1   Seaver, *Wilson of the Antarctic*, p.116.

2   Mrs Armitage was, as Skelton put it, 'a hell of a woman'. Scott's mother had warned him of the scandal in a letter delivered to the Antarctic in the *Morning*'s mail bag. The affair is mentioned in David Crane, *Scott of the Antarctic*, p.238.

3   Ory's state of mind at this time, what she chose to do about it and her favourable impressions of New Zealanders is detailed in a letter to John Fraser, 8 March 1904, MS1577/8/2;D SPRI.

4   Ory just missed meeting the much-loved school's founder Basil Holt Wilson 1872–1902. Though I have not been able to find a family link (Wilson being the seventh most common surname at the time) the school's motto and Woodford Souper's employment suggest some connection.

5   Ory to Jim Wilson, 19 December 1904, 1995.550.106 (v) Cheltenham Borough Council and the Cheltenham Trust/The Wilson Family Collection. It was easy to send letters home, as the New Zealanders had been typically practical. One penny universal postage from New Zealand to anywhere in the world had been introduced in 1901. Many had predicted that Post Office revenues would fall, but mail volumes increased sharply and by the time Ory wrote to Jim Wilson and John Fraser in 1904, all losses had been recovered.

6   Curragh Cottage, Ferrymead Heritage Park, Christchurch, NZ. Leaflet produced by Friends of Ferrymead 2006, text by Deborah Westlake.

7   In the same letter to John Fraser, Ory describes her concerns about Constance's condition as well as her own health and their stay in Sumner with Aunt Connie. Ory to John Fraser 8 March 1904.

8   Seaver, *Wilson of the Antarctic*, p.141.

9   Ibid.

Chapter 11

1   Ted to Joseph Kinsey, 25 June 1904, posted from Falklands, Kinsey Collection, Alexander Turnbull Archive, National Museum, Wellington, NZ.

2   All Ted's quotes on New Zealand wildlife are from *Historical Review* Vol. XVII No. 1 typescript at the SPRI. Also in Ann Savours (ed.), *Edward Wilson: Diary of the 'Discovery'*, Chapter 22.

3   Ibid.

4   Ory's letter to Ethel Wilson giving a full description of the *Discovery* Ball is on Coker headed paper. Private collection.

5   Seaver, *Wilson of the Antarctic*, p.143.

6   'Biography of Oriana', p.302.

7   Ory to Ethel Wilson.
8   Ted to John Fraser, 15 July 1904, posted from Falkland Islands 25 June 1904, MS1577/6/8;D SPRI.

Chapter 12

1   Seaver, *Wilson of the Antarctic*, p.146.
2   George Seaver, *Of the Making of Books*, Chapter XIII from his unpublished autobiography, courtesy of the Seaver family.
3   Seaver, *Wilson of the Antarctic*, p.152.
4   Ibid., pp.169–70.
5   Ibid., pp.70–71.
6   Ibid.
7   Coventry Patmore, 'The Angel in the House'. This poem published in 1854 exemplifies the Victorian theory of separate spheres.
8   Seaver, *Wilson of the Antarctic*, p.154.
9   Ibid, p.161.
10 Dr E.T. Wilson, *Notes for a Life of Ted Wilson*, pp.124–25.
11 Ibid., p.123.
12 Letter from Emily Shackleton to Hugh Robert Mill, 27 May 1922. H.R. Mill et al., Rejoice my Heart: the Making of H.R. Mill's 'The Life of Sir Ernest Shackleton': The Private Correspondence of Dr. Hugh Robert Mill and Lady Shackleton, 1922–33. Santa Monica: Adelie Books, 2007, p.21.
13 Robert Scott, *The Voyage of the Discovery*. London: Smith Elder & Co., 1905.
14 Seaver, *Wilson of the Antarctic*, p.156.
15 Ibid.

Chapter 13

1   Ted to John Fraser, 31 December 1905, MS1577/6/12;D SPRI.
2   To give a more detailed idea of what Ory was required to do, Ted's father describes the work: 'From the first it was decided to make a skin as far as possible of every bird and some 2,000 skins were prepared during the inquiry. Besides this the crop contents had to be weighed and the most accurate notes taken as to the sex, plumage, weight, damage from accident or disease of external or internal organs which was found to exist. It was eventually found to be a

minute threadworm.' Dr E.T. Wilson, *Notes for a Life of Ted Wilson*, p.130.

3   Ory to Kathleen, 1913, discussing where Mansion House Fund money should go. MS1453/190/1-5;D SPRI.

4   Letter from Shackleton to Lady Invernairn (Elspeth) 1906, dated 'Monday', as seen in the National Maritime Museum in Greenwich.

5   Ted to John Fraser, 25 January 1909, MS1577/6/14;D SPRI.

6   Seaver, *Wilson of the Antarctic*, p.160.

7   Ibid., p.161.

8   Ted to John Fraser, 25 January 1909.

Chapter 14

1   Shackleton to Ted, 12 February 1907, included in Regina W. Daly (ed.), *The Shackleton Letters: Behind the Scenes of the Nimrod Expedition*. Norwich: Erskine Press 2009, p.22.

2   Ted to Shackleton, 14 February 1907, Ibid., p.23.

3   Shackleton to England, 18 January 1908, Ibid., p.127.

4   Ted to Shackleton, 15 February 1907, Ibid., p.27.

5   Ted to Shackleton, 28 February 1907, Ibid., p.51.

6   Michael Wilson talking to Dr David Wilson, recording at Cheltenham Borough Council and the Cheltenham Trust/The Wilson Family Collection, 2004.

7   Shackleton to Ted, 15 February 1907, Daly, *The Shackleton Letters*, p.29.

8   Fredrick Cook, *Brooklyn Daily Eagle*, 8 October, 1893, cited in Robert M. Bryce, *Cook and Peary: The Polar Controversy, Resolved*. Mechanicsburg: Stackpole Books, 1997, p.50.

9   Seaver, *Wilson of the Antarctic*, p.169.

10 Ibid., p.178.

11 Ted to Shackleton, 28 February 1907, Daly, *The Shackleton Letters*, p.52.

12 Ted to Shackleton, 8 March 1907, Ibid., p.74.

13 14 October 1900. 'The Presidency [BMA] had been offered to me and I should have like to accept it but as a family man I did not consider that I was justified in undertaking the expense.' Dr E.T. Wilson, *My Life*.

14 Emily Shackleton became a girl guide leader and Cecily, a 'tomboy'.

15 Seaver, *Wilson of the Antarctic*, p.160.

16 Ibid., p.164.

17 Ted to John Fraser, included in Seaver, *Wilson of the Antarctic*, p.184.
18 Scott to Ted, Ibid., p.180.

Chapter 15

1 The Shackleton England affair is described in Daly, *The Shackleton Letters*, p.120.
2 Scott to Kathleen, 28 July 1906, MS1453/3/160;D SPRI.
3 Scott to Ted, quoted in Seaver, *Wilson of the Antarctic*, p.180.
4 Louisa Young, *A Great Task of Happiness: The Life of Kathleen Scott*. London: HarperCollins, 2014, pp.99–100.
5 Crane, *Scott of the Antarctic*, p.372.
6 Ted to John Fraser, from the North British Station Hotel, Edinburgh, 25 January 1909, MS1577/6/14;D SPRI.
7 Seaver 'Biography of Oriana', p.302.
8 Ted to John Fraser, 25 January 1909.
9 *The Times*, 2 September 1909.
10 Kathleen Scott/Kennet, *Self Portrait of an Artist, from the Diaries and Memoirs of Lady Kennet, Kathleen Scott*. London: John Murray, 1949, p.84.
11 Young, *A Great Task of Happiness*, p.98.
12 Young, *A Great Task of Happiness*, p.113.
13 Ibid.
14 Kathleen Scott/Kennet, *Self Portrait of an Artist*, p.386.
15 Seaver, 'Biography of Oriana', p.302.
16 Letter from Kathleen, 18 November 1908, quoted in Crane, *Scott of the Antarctic*, p.412.
17 Ted to Scott, 12 November 1908, MS1453/188/1-8;D SPRI.

Chapter 16

1 Seaver, *Wilson of the Antarctic*, p.179.
2 Mill, *Rejoice My Heart*, p.41.
3 Ted to Shackleton, 1–5 July 1909, Daly, *The Shackleton Letters*, pp.284–85.
4 Ted to John Fraser, 13 June 1910, MS 1577/6/21;D SPRI. Also included in Seaver, *Wilson of the Antarctic*, p.184.

5   *New York Herald*, 7 September 1909, cited in Robert M. Bryce, *Cook and Peary: The Polar Controversy, Resolved*. Mechanicsburg: Stackpole Books, 1997, p.376.
6   Josephine Peary, *My Arctic Journal, A Year Among Ice-Fields and Eskimos*. London: Longmans, Green, 1893.
7   Bryce, *Cook and Peary*, p.488.
8   Marie Peary, *The Snowbaby's Own Story*, New York: Frederick A. Stokes, 1934, p.252. Marie Peary found the impression of Shackleton's signature in the hotel blotting paper. Shackleton and Emily were on the same lecture circuit following the success of the *Nimrod* expedition, and must have been using the same hotels. She cut out the impression of her hero's signature and treasured it for life.
9   For Ted's thoughts on death see Seaver, *Wilson of the Antarctic*, p.171.
10 Ibid., p.171.
11 Ibid., p.170.
12 Ibid., p.303.
13 Ibid., p.195.
14 Ibid., p.184.
15 Soord also painted portraits of Ted's parents, Dr E.T. Wilson and Mrs Wilson, now at Cheltenham Borough Council and the Cheltenham Trust/The Wilson Family Collection.
16 Seaver, *Wilson of the Antarctic*, p.183.
17 Ibid., p.171.
18 Ibid., p.126.
19 Ibid., p.171.
20 Ibid., p.242.

Chapter 17

1   *EA Wilson – Journal*, 1 June 1910 to 27 February 1912 (including extracts from his letters and those of his wife), 1 June 1910, p.1.
2   Reginald Pound, *Evans of the Broke*. Oxford: OUP, 1963, pp.62–63.
3   Seaver, *Wilson of the Antarctic*, p.196.
4   Young, *A Great Task of Happiness*, p.103.
5   Ibid., p.114.
6   *EA Wilson – Journal*, 4 July 1910.
7   Ibid.
8   Anne Strathie, *Birdie Bowers: Captain Scott's Marvel*. Stroud: The History Press, 2011, p.86.

9   Bowers to his mother, Crane, *Scott of the Antarctic*, p.435.

10 Strathie, *Birdie Bowers*, p.86.

11 Crane, *Scott of the Antarctic,* p.438.

12 Ted to John Fraser, 25 January 1909, MS1577/6/14 SPRI.

13 Ory's letter of 26 August 1910, included in *EA Wilson – Journal*, p.70.

14 Ibid.

15 H.G.R King, *Edward Wilson: Diary of the Terra Nova Expedition to the Antarctic 1910–1912*. London: Blandford Press, 1972. From the original mss in the SPRI and the British Museum.

16 Ibid.

Chapter 18

1 Young, *A Great Task of Happiness*, p.113.

2 King, *Wilson: Diary of the* Terra Nova, 15 August 1910.

3 Ibid.

4 Ibid., 31 August 1910.

5 Ted to Ory, Seaver, *Wilson of the Antarctic*, p.267.

6 King, *Wilson: Diary of the* Terra Nova, 12 October 1910.

7 Young, *A Great Task of Happiness*, p.114.

8 King, *Wilson: Diary of the* Terra Nova, 12 October 1910, quoted in Young, *A Great Task of Happiness*, p.114.

9 Ibid.

10 Roland Huntford, *Scott and Amundsen: The Last Place on Earth.* London: Penguin/Random House, 1999, p.307.

11 Ory letter to Westal, 2 November 1910, included in Dr E.T. Wilson, *Edward Adrian Wilson: A Memoir by his Father,* 1995.550.36 Cheltenham Borough Council and the Cheltenham Trust/The Wilson Family Collection.

12 Huntford, Scott and Amundsen, p.309.

13 Ory letter to Westal, 2 November 1910.

14 Ibid.

15 Young, *A Great Task of Happiness*, p.113.

16 Bowers letter to Emily, 7 December 1910. SPRI 1/1/3/103.

Chapter 19

1 Debenham, F., quoted in Seaver, *Wilson of the Antarctic*, p.206.

2 Young, *A Great Task of Happiness*, p.113.

3   The Shackletons shared an intense love of poetry. Ernest could quote vast tracts of poetry and did so at the least provocation. Someone once asked him how long it took him to remember a poem. He told them that he read it once, then once again to check the punctuation. It was how he had won Emily. She needed poetry to leaven the saltier side of his character.
4   Rob Weir, 'Vagabond Abroad: Mark Twain's 1895 Visit to New Zealand', *The Journal of the Gilded Age and Progressive Era*, Vol. 8, No. 4, 2009, pp.487–514. www.jstor.org/stable/40542877.
5   Seaver, *Wilson of the Antarctic*, p.205.
6   Ted to John Fraser, 27 November 1910, MS1577/6/22;D SPRI.
7   King, *Wilson: Diary of the* Terra Nova, p.61.
8   Seaver, *Wilson of the Antarctic*, p.304.
9   King, *Wilson: Diary of the* Terra Nova, 28 November 1910, p.62.
10 Bower's letter home is quoted in Crane, *Scott of the Antarctic*, p.438.
11 King, *Wilson: Diary of the* Terra Nova, 28 November 1910, p.62.

Chapter 20

1   Lawrence Oates to Caroline Oates, 23 November 1910, quoted in Sue Limb and Patrick Cordingley, *Captain Oates: Soldier and Explorer.* Barnsley: Pen and Sword, 2009, p.121.
2   Ibid., p.134.
3   Young, *A Great Task of Happiness*, p.116.
4   Ibid., p.115.
5   Ibid., p.157.
6   Seaver, *Wilson of the Antarctic*, p.171.
7   Seaver, *Wilson of the Antarctic*, p.267.
8   Seaver, *Wilson of the Antarctic*, p.185.
9   Ibid., p.265.
10 Ibid., p.243.
11 Ibid., p.265.
12 Young, *A Great Task of Happiness,* p.116.
13 King, *Wilson: Diary of the* Terra Nova, 29 November 1910, p.62.
14 Seaver, *Wilson of the Antarctic*, p.77.
15 Young, *A Great Task of Happiness*, p.117.

Chapter 21

1 The Dennistouns were recent arrivals and their Boulton & Paul home was a bubble of old England in an oasis of quixotic greenery, and Emma Taylor kindly engineered a visit for me in 2011. They had chosen all the large window options the catalogue offered: bowed, boxed and window seated, sash, hinged. All of them looked out onto shaven English lawns. A grandfather clock still ticks peacefully in the hall.

2 Seaver, *Wilson of the Antarctic*, p.207.

3 Ibid.

4 Seaver, *Wilson of the Antarctic*, p.214.

5 Young, *A Great Task of Happiness*, p.118.

6 Ibid., p.119.

7 Cited in Juliet Nicholson, *The Perfect Summer: Dancing into Shadow in 1911*, London: John Murray, 2007, p.170. Nicholson gives an evocative account of this long summer of soaring temperatures and gaiety marked by the gathering storm clouds of world war as well as profound social and industrial unrest.

8 The journey to Cape Crozier in search of Emperor Penguin's eggs was undertaken in the depths of the Antarctic winter between 27 June and 2 August 1911. Cherry later described it as 'the weirdest bird's-nesting expedition that has ever been or ever will be' in his book *The Worst Journey in the World*.

9 A little-known expedition to the Antarctic (June–August 2011) visited the ruins of Oriana Hut close by the Emperor Penguin colony at Cape Crozier and confirmed the precise position.

10 Scott to Ory, 1 October 1911, Cheltenham College Archives.

11 Young, *A Great Task of Happiness*, p.123.

12 Seaver, *Wilson of the Antarctic*, p.267.

13 Ted to Westal, 16 January 1911, *EA Wilson – Journal*, 1 June 1910 to 27 February 1912 (including extracts from his letters and those of his wife), typed bound copy, p.153, MS715/2;BJ SPRI.

14 E.T. Wilson, *My Life*, 9 November 1911.

15 Ibid., 7 November 1911.

16 Seaver, *Wilson of the Antarctic*, p.281.

Chapter 22

1   E. T. Wilson, *My Life,* 21 January 1912.
2   King, *Wilson: Diary of the* Terra Nova, 22 January 1912, p.237.
3   Ibid.
4   King, *Wilson: Diary of the* Terra Nova, 28 January 1912, p.238.
5   Seaver, *Wilson of the Antarctic*, p.289.
6   King, *Wilson: Diary of the* Terra Nova, 29 January 1912, p.238.
7   Ibid., 4 February 1912, pp.239–40.
8   Ibid., 8 & 9 February 1912, p.241.
9   Ibid., 15 February 1912, p.243.
10 R. F. Scott, *Captain Scott's Last Expedition*, Max Jones (ed.), Oxford: OUP, 2006 17 February 1912, p.397.
11 King, *Wilson: Diary of the* Terra Nova, 17 February 1912, p.243.
12 Scott, *Captain Scott's Last Expedition*, 19 February 1912, p.400.
13 Ibid., 16–18 March 1912, pp.410–411.
14 Ibid., pp.393–400.
15 Ibid., 10 March 1912, p.408.
16 Young, *A Great Task of Happiness*, p.147.
17 *Captain Scott's Last Expedition*, 16–18 March 1912, p.410.
18 Ted to Ory. Probably written on 21 March 1912. As has been mentioned, Ory didn't keep the last letters Ted wrote to her. Reproduced from a number of sources in Heather Lane et al., *The Last Letters, The British Antarctic Expedition 1910–13*, Cambridge, The Scott Polar Research Institute: 2012, p.52.
19 Ibid., pp.53–54.
20 Scott to Ory, original letter is in the SPRI Collection, Cambridge MS2093. Lane et al., *The Last Letters*, pp.27–29.

Chapter 23

1   Letter from Ory to Mr and Mrs Smith 7th April 1912 SPRI MS 1330/7.
2   Ibid.
3   Ibid.
4   Ibid.
5   Ibid.
6   Ibid.

7   Ibid.

8   Ibid.

9   Telegram from Ory to the family at Westal, 3 April 1912, 2010.36 Cheltenham Borough Council and the Cheltenham Trust/The Wilson Family Collection.

10 Letter from Ory to Mr and Mrs Smith 7th April 1912 SPRI MS 1330/7.

11 Ibid.

12 Ibid.

13 Ibid.

14 Ibid.

15 Ibid.

16 Ibid.

17 Ibid.

18 King, *Wilson: Diary of the* Terra Nova, 20 July 1911.

19 Ibid.

20 Ory to Mrs Pennell, 7 April 1912, MS888/3;D SPRI.

21 Ory to Mrs Smith, May 2nd 1912 SPRI 841/13/1/13.

22 Ibid.

23 Ibid.

24 Amundsen had made a false start for the Pole, leaving Framheim, his Antarctic base, on 8 September at what he hoped was the beginning of the season, but the wintery weather conditions forced a hasty retreat and a later start date.

25 Ory to the Smiths. 7 April 1912 MS 1330/7 SPRI.

26 Seaver, *Wilson of the Antarctic*, p.237.

27 Ory to the Smiths. 7 April 1912 MS 1330/7 SPRI.

28 Kinsey to Scott, 11 March 1912, MS1453/127/1-8;D SPRI.

29 '[Ory] is full of suggestions for the furnishings and appointments of "Uncle Bill's Cabin." I am sure you will be pleased to hear that I purchased the Observatory hut from Pennell and have had it erected at Clifton … several alterations and additions to this, I hope to make a comfortable little cottage and home for Doctor and Mrs Wilson until they leave for England.' Kinsey to Scott, 10 December 1912, MS1453/127/4 SPRI.

30 Ibid., p.242.

31 Ory to Jim, 19 December 1912, from Christchurch, New Zealand. Cheltenham Borough Council and the Cheltenham Trust/The Wilson Family Collection. 1995.550.106.

Part 2 Prelim

1　*Wanganui Chronicle*, Iss. 12857, 11 February 1913, p.5.
2　Ory to Anne Hardy, 14 February 1913 MS64.1. Anne Hardy Collection, Canterbury Museum, Christchurch. It wasn't an anniversary and the *Terra Nova* wasn't due back until March.
3　Kinsey to H Brett Esq, c/o 'Star Office, Auckland, 2 July 1913 MS559/164;D SPRI.
4　Teddy Evans to Kinsey, 10 February 1913. Kinsey Collection, Alexander Turnbull Archive, National Museum, Wellington, NZ.
5　'God sent them to help me that day … I don't know how I could have got through that journey,' Ory wrote later, 'if the Dennistouns had not come up on the chance that I might be in the train.' (The Dennistouns caught up with the train somewhere between Geraldine and Ashburton.) Ory to Anne Hardy, 14 February 1913. Anne Hardy Collection, Canterbury Museum, Christchurch.
6　Seaver, *Edward Wilson of the Antarctic*, p.141.
7　Ory to Anne Hardy, 14 February 1913, MS64.1. Anne Hardy Collection, Canterbury Museum, Christchurch.

Chapter 24

1　Crane, *Scott of the Antarctic*, p.572.
2　Ted to Ory. Probably written on 21 March 1912. Reproduced from a number of sources in Lane et al., *The Last Letters*, pp.52–54.
3　Ibid.
4　Scott to Ory, March 1912, Ibid.., pp.27–29.
5　R.F. Scott, *Captain Scott's Last Expedition*, p.422.
6　Ory to Anne Hardy, 17 February 1913, MS64.2. Canterbury Museum, Christchurch, NZ.
7　Ory to Anne Hardy, 19 February 1913, MS64.2. Canterbury Museum, Christchurch, NZ.
8　Roland Huntford, *Scott and Amundsen: The Last Place on Earth*, London: Penguin/Random House, 1999, p.350.
9　Ory to Anne Hardy 14 February 1913, MS64 Canterbury Museum, Christchurch, NZ.
10　Lilian Burton to Cherry's mother, 18 February 1913, MS 1330/2 SPRI.

11 Sara Wheeler, *Cherry: A Life of Apsley Cherry-Garrard*. London: Jonathan Cape, 2001, p.151.
12 Ibid., p.154.
13 Young, *A Great Task of Happiness*, p.157.
14 The *Illustrated Western Weekly News*, 1 March 1913, cited in Huntford, *Scott and Amundsen*, p.353.
15 Scott/Kennet, *Self Portrait of an Artist*, p.123.
16 Ibid.
17 Scott to Kathleen, March 1912, Lane et al., *The Last Letters*, pp.15–25.
18 Young, *A Great Task of Happiness*, p.157.
19 Ibid., p.159.
20 Quoted in Chris Turney, *1912, The Year the World Discovered Antarctica*. London: Bodley Head, 2012, p.292.
21 King, *Wilson: Diary of the* Terra Nova, p.245.
22 Scott, *Captain Scott's Last Expedition*, p.377.
23 Young, *A Great Task of Happiness*, p.159.
24 *Marlborough Express*, Vol. XLVII, Iss. 52, 1 March 1913, Press Association.

Chapter 25

1 Captain Greenstreet to Joseph Kinsey, 13 April, 1913, Alexander Turnbull Archive, National Museum, Wellington, NZ.
2 Ibid.
3 Ory to Kinsey, March 20 1913, MS22 File 43, Alexander Turnbull Archive, National Museum, Wellington, NZ.
4 Ibid.
5 Undated letter from E. Wilson to Thomas Hodgson, MS1330 SPRI. In the ps of his letter to Hodgson, ET Wilson mentions: 'Have just heard that Ory is to have the Royal medal of the Geographical Society and perpetual free entrance to the zoo gardens.'
6 Scott, Captain Scott's Last Expedition, 10 March, p.471.
7 Quoted in Turney, *1912*, p.24.
8 Huntford, *Scott and Amundsen*, p.558.
9 Curzon's note from the RGS archives is quoted in Turney, *1912*, p.304.
10 Ory to Kathleen, 22 May 1913, MS 1453/190/3;D SPRI.
11 Letter from Ory to Sir John Murray, Wilson Museum DV 22/22A.
12 Ibid.

13 Ory to Kathleen, 10 May 1913, MS1453/190/1 SPRI.
14 Ory to Kathleen, 20 May 1913, MS1453/190/2 SPRI.
15 Ory to Kathleen, 10 May 1913.
16 Ory to Kathleen, 20 May 1913.
17 Kathleen to Teddy Evans, 27 June 1913, MS1453/153/1 SPRI.
18 Ibid.
19 Letter from exhibition manager to Kathleen, 8 July 1913, MS1453/153/2 SPRI.
20 Emily Shackleton to H.R. Mill, 26 January 1923, quoted in Mill, *Rejoice My Heart*, p.81.
21 13 February 1913, *The Daily Telegraph*, Roland Huntford, *Shackleton*. London: Hodder & Stoughton, 1984, p.354.

Chapter 26

1 Seaver, *Wilson of the Antarctic*, p.275
2 Apsley Cherry-Garrard, *The Worst Journey in the World*. London: Constable and Company, 1922, p.322.
3 Wheeler, *Cherry*, p.222.
4 Copy of letter from George V, signed by his Private Secretary, Lord Stamfordham to Ory, 19 July 1913, MS 952/1/3 SPRI.
5 Ory to Reginald Smith, 21 July 1913, MS952/1-4;D SPRI.
6 Ibid.
7 Ory to Reginald Smith, 11 June 1913, MS952/1-4;D SPRI.
8 Ibid.
9 Ory to Cherry, 13 September 1913.
10 Ted to John Fraser, 19 August 1909 MS1577/6/19;D SPRI.
11 Ory to Reginald Smith, 31 July 1913, MS952/1-4;D SPRI.
12 Ory to Kathleen, 6 November 1913, MS 1453/190/1-5;D SPRI.
13 Ibid.
14 List of articles by Cherry on *Terra Nova* headed paper, MS559/51;D SPRI.
15 Cherry, *The Worst Journey*, p.318.
16 Ory to Cherry, 22 May 1913, M559/143/1-25 SPRI.
17 8 November 1913, Dr E.T. Wilson, *My Life*.
18 Oriana Wilson to Apsley Cherry Garrard 8 July 1913. SPRI
19 Ory to Cherry, 3 May 1918, M559/143/1-25 SPRI.
20 Cherry's retrospectively annotated journal [October 1911] SPRI.
21 Ory to Cherry, 22 May 1913.

22 Cherry's notes on paper from Kathleen's house headed 174 Buckingham Palace Rd, final page MS 559/159/;D SPRI.

23 'Sympathy poured in on every side. It was help but nought can soothe the aching heart and it was long before the realisation of the noble self-sacrifice and devotion to Duty even unto death began to take the place of our own selfish grief.' E. T. Wilson, *My Life*, Vol. 2, 12 February 1913.

24 E. T. Wilson, *My Life*, 25 December 1913, p.410.

25 Ted to Alfred Soord, quoted in Seaver, *Wilson of the Antarctic*, p.183.

26 Ibid., p.171.

Chapter 27

1 'Dad' had pasted the pictures next to the references about Ted's Cambridge days. Dr E. T. Wilson, *Notes for a Life of Ted Wilson*.

2 Huntford, *Scott And Amundsen*, p543.

3 Ory's nephew, Michael Wilson, interviewed by his son David – recorded interview held at Cheltenham Borough Council and the Cheltenham Trust/The Wilson Family Collection, 2004.

4 Ory to Cherry, 18 June 1914.

5 Dr E. T. Wilson stage-managed the opening of the Cheltenham Museum in rooms next door to the Art Gallery. The Wilson, as the Museum was renamed in 2013, houses the Wilson family archive including Ted's skis, his snow suit and various artefacts on permanent display. 'Dad' opened it on 20 June 1907. 'Our museum [he said] should be no curiosity shop, in which dusty specimens of moth-eaten, ill-stuffed birds and animals, mummy cases, and ancient pickles shock more senses than one.' He was also adamant that the museum should have a 'diligent, energetic and knowledgeable curator who could make the dry bones live ...' The Wilson, cheltenhammuseum.org.uk.

6 There was some controversy over naming geographical features for 'girls'.

7 They are credited 'By king permission of Mrs Wilson. Dr E. A. Wilson, del.' Seaver, *Birdie Bowers*, pp.216–17.

8 21 February 1914, *The Times*.

9 REF World Register of Marine Species: WoRMS.

10 The importance of the letters to Ory comes across here: 'I shall always be grateful to you all, that you persevered in looking for the tent – for as a result of your search I have had the comfort and help of receiving the last words Dr. Wilson wrote to me and I am more

thankful to you all than I can say.' Ory to Tom Crean, 23 February 1913. Letter in Crean family ownership.

11 Charles S Wright, *Silas: Antarctic Diaries and Memoir of Charles S. Wright*. Colin Bull (ed.), Patricia F. Wright (ills), Columbus: Ohio State University Press, 1993, p.379.

12 Patricia Frances Wright (born in 1924) became an accomplished artist. The painting *Rain Clouds Fort Augustus* was bequeathed by Ory to her. Ibid.

13 'And he's lived up to his ideal', Ponting told the *Daily Chronicle*. 'To my mind it is the most touching thing of the whole tragedy.' Limb & Cordingley, *Captain Oates: Soldier and Exporer*. Barnsley: Pen & Sword, 2009, p.211.

14 Ponting. H. quoted in the *Daily Chronicle* 1913, Referenced in Limb & Cordingley, *Captain Oates*, p.211.

15 Ted to Mrs Oates, March 1912. This letter was written in Oates' diary, as was Wilson's final letter to his wife. 'Please be so good as to send pages 54 and 55 of this book to my beloved wife addressed Mrs Ted Wilson, Westal, Cheltenham. Please do this for me Mrs Oates – my wife has real faith in God and so your son tells me have you – and so have I.' Quoted in Limb & Cordingley, *Captain Oates*, p.221.

16 Dr E.T. Wilson, *My Life*, July 1914.

Chapter 28

1 Dad never saw the end of the war, he died of cancer of the lower intestine in 1918. Dr E.T. Wilson, *My Life*.

2 Ory to Alex H. Turnbull, 24 October 1915, MS papers, Folder 98, Alexander Turnbull Archive, National Museum, Wellington, NZ.

3 Quoted in Wheeler, *Cherry*, p.184.

4 Ory to Cherry, 13 December 1916.

5 Ory to Cherry, 4 September 1915.

6 Sara Wheeler, *Cherry*, p.172.

7 Ory to Dorothea G. Palmer, Wanganui 16 May 1916, quoted in *Wanganui Chronicle* Vol. LX Iss. 16704, 27 July 1916, p.6.

8 Ory to Cherry, 29 February 1916.

9 Ory to Cherry, 4 September 1915.

10 Ory to Cherry, 3 May 1918.

11 Even before the war Ory had wanted to be a nurse, 'What I would not give to be able to start nursing! But it is not to be – at any rate for the present', but at the time she would have been fully occupied

trying to secure Ted's scientific legacy. Ory to Cherry, 8 October 1913.

12 Seaver, *Wilson of the Antarctic*, p.55.
13 Ibid., p.299.
14 Quoted in Christine E. Hallet, *Veiled Warriors: Allied Nurses of the First Wold War*. Oxford: OUP, 2014.
15 Ory to Bertha Raynham, 31 May 1917, Private Collection.
16 Ory to Bertha Raynham, 21 July 1917, Private Collection.
17 Ory to Cherry, 13 April 1916.
18 Ibid.
19 Seaver, 'Biography of Oriana', p.302.
20 *Kathleen Scott Diary*, 29 December 1916, Kennet Papers. Quoted in Wheeler, *Cherry*, p.194.

Chapter 29

1 Seaver, *The Making of Books*, Chapter 18, p.149: 'Moreover [Kathleen Scott] was (like Ory, and both were daughters of clergymen) a confessed agnostic without assurance of hope in immortality; for whom the past was gone forever and death the final extinguisher of the lamp.'
2 Letter to Herbert Ponting, quoted in Wheeler, *Cherry*, p.182.
3 Ory to Bertha Raynham, 28 August 1917, Private Collection.
4 Ibid.
5 Mary Agnes Wilson to Bernard, 11 April 1918, Cheltenham Borough Council and the Cheltenham Trust/The Wilson Family Collection. Mary Agnes lived on in Cheltenham until 1930, cared for by Ida, who never married. In her will, she left Ory a sprung double bed with linen, a washstand and a piece of silver cutlery.
6 Ory to Cherry, 29 February 1916.
7 Letter from Ory to Cherry, 1918.
8 Mary Agnes Wilson to Bernard, 11 April 1918.
9 'Zeadequate' was the Telegram and Cable Address for the New Zealand Red Cross offices at 125 High Holborn and the Depot at 11 Southampton Row.
10 Ory to Bertha Raynham, 15 October 1917, Private Collection.
11 Margaret Bowen to Bertha Raynham, 3 March 1919, Private Collection.
12 Ory to Cherry, 3 May 1918.

13 Ory to Anne Hardy (undated) MS 64.6 Canterbury Museum, Christchurch.
14 Ory to Sir John Murray, 25 October 1933, DV22/22A Wilson.
15 Founder Emily Williamson maintained that 'Lady-Members shall refrain from wearing the feathers of any bird not killed for the purposes of food, the ostrich only excepted.' RSPB Rules 1899.
16 Conversation between Evelyn Forbes and Sara Wheeler, quoted in Wheeler, *Cherry*, p.278.
17 Ory to Anne Hardy, undated, Anne Hardy Collection, Canterbury Museum, Christchurch.
18 Ory to Dr AEL Bennett, 1 May 1919, MS 1346 Folder 224 Alexander Turnbull Archive, National Museum, Wellington, NZ.
19 Peter Speak, *Deb: Geographer, Scientist, Antarctic Explorer: A Biography of Frank Debenham, OBE*. Guildford: Polar Publishing, 2008, p.63.
20 Frank Debenham to Cherry, 2 June 1920, MS559/57/8;D SPRI.
21 Ibid.
22 Ibid.
23 Quoted in Crane, *Scott of the Antarctic*, p.503.
24 Debenham to Cherry's widow, Angela, quoted in Wheeler, *Cherry*, p.238.
25 'Debenham's grand daughter (Philippa Foster Back) ... thinks the SPRI was really inspired by her grandfather's love for Uncle Ted but named for Scott for reasons of protocol ... Uncle Ted would not have countenanced it being named for anyone other than Scott ...' David Wilson to KM 2018.
26 Frank Debenham to Cherry, 30 May 1920 MS559/57/10;D SPRI.
27 Frank Debenham to Cherry, 2 June 1920 MS559/57/10;D SPRI.
28 '[Debenham] was very clever to get her to part with all the paintings by having an art gallery designed and making special arrangements for them all to be hung (as per EAW's wishes that they shouldn't be hidden in a cupboard under the stairs, as he said that they would be at the RGS). Of course, they can't be today because of modern museum conservation requirements – which is partly why my brother and I published a big selection in the books – to help them be seen again.' David Wilson to KM 2018.
    (*Edward Wilson's Nature Notebooks*, *Edward Wilson's Antarctic Notebooks* by D.M. Wilson and C.J. Wilson, Reardon Publishing, 2004 and 2011 respectively.)
29 Frank Debenham to Cherry, 30 May 1920.
30 Ory to Cherry, 4 September 1915.

30 The Proceedings of the Zoological Society of London, 7 February 1899.
31 *The Annals and Magazine of Natural History*, August 1900.
32 Oldfield Thomas, 'LXVI.—A new bat of the genus *Miniopterus* from N. Australia'. *Annals and Magazine of Natural History*, Vol. 10, Iss. 60, pp.616–17.

Chapter 30

1 Ory to Anne Hardy, 20 December 1922, MS 64.5 Anne Hardy Collection, Canterbury Museum.
2 Ory to Ursula Bethell, 29 March 1939, MB558 124247 University of Canterbury Archives, Christchurch, NZ. Ory wrote a continual flow of letters to the charismatic Ursula who was at the centre of a fascinating and diverse group of cultural figures in Christchurch.
3 Ory to Ursula, 14 May 1931, MB558 124247 University of Canterbury Archives, Christchurch, NZ.
4 Young, *A Great Task of Happiness*, p.214.
5 Young, *A Great Task of Happiness*, p.214.
6 Apsley Cherry-Garrard, *The Worst Journey in the World*. (First published London: Constable, 1922), New York: Dover, 2010, p.233.
7 Ory to Anne Hardy, 20 December 1922.
8 Ibid.
9 Charles Baudouin, *Suggestion and Autosuggestion*. Eden and Cedar Paul (trans.), London: Allen & Unwin, 1920.
10 Ory to Oldfield Thomas, 1 April 1923, sent from Auckland NZ, REF:219 Natural History Museum, London.
11 Ibid.
12 Letter from Ory to Mr Kinnear, 28 October 1935, EA Wilson DF 230/65 Natural History Museum. Norman Boyd Kinnear was head of the bird section at the NHM and became Director in 1947.
13 I only found the bats when my godmother Jane Bannister, in Australia, found a reference to them on the Internet. It was news to the Wilson family. Good news.

Chapter 31

1 Thanksgiving service address given by Michael Wilson for his father, 3 June 1972, Documents of J.V. Wilson, MS 95.550.161 Cheltenham Borough Council and the Cheltenham Trust/The Wilson Family Collection.
2 Ethel Burnett, a school mistress, was ten years younger than Ory. She had been a teacher but she would 'dig hard and grub gorse' or set up a 'small shop in the bay for home-made cakes jams and pickles' as the family's financial situation demanded. She refused Ory's offer of money, and Ory responded by trying to help 'in various odds and end ways'. Ory to Isabel Smith, 24 January 1935, MS 559/145/2 SPRI.
3 *Evening Post*, Vol. CXI Iss. 104, 3 May 1926. 'Women in Print' mentions Christchurch Association of Overseas Women War Workers, p.13.
4 Ory to Ursula Bethell 23 April 1935 MB558 124247 University of Canterbury Archives.
5 Ory to Ursula Bethell, 12 October 1935 MB558 124247 University of Canterbury Archives.
6 Ibid.
7 Seaver, 'Biography of Oriana', , p.304.
8 *Evening Post*, Vol. CXI Iss. 104, 3 May 1926.
9 *Feilding Star*, 29 May 1918, 'Honoured' – paperspast.natlib.govt.nz.
10 Ory to Dr Bennet, 13 November 1929, MS1349 Folder 224, Alexander Turnbull Archive, National Museum, Wellington, NZ.
11 Frank Debenham to Kinsey, 8 January 1927, MS-Copy-Micro-528-41 (letter attributed 'g' in the inventory) Alexander Turnbull Archive, National Museum, Wellington, NZ.
12 Quoted in a letter from George Seaver to Ida Wilson, 19 September 1928, MS715/6/1-10;D SPRI.
13 Ory to Cherry, 15 January 1929, MS 559/143/1-25 SPRI.
14 Ory to Mrs Benton, 7 March 1934, from Kenya, 2006.39.2-4 Cheltenham Borough Council and the Cheltenham Trust/The Wilson Family Collection.

Chapter 32

1 George to Ida Wilson, 17th September 1928, (collection of 10 letters) MS715/6/1-107 SPRI.
2 Ibid.

3 Ory to Cherry, 15 January 1929.
4 Seaver, *Of the Making of Books*, p.123.
5 George to Ida, 17 September 1928.
6 George to Ida, 17 October 1928.
7 George to Ida, 17 September 1928.
8 Seaver, *Of the Making of Books*.
9 Ibid.
10 Seaver, 'Biography of Oriana', , p.300.
11 Ibid., p.300.
12 Ibid., p.301.
13 The copy of Cherry's *Worst Journey*, which Ory gave to George, is in the Seaver Archive.
14 George to Ida Wilson, 12 March 1929.
15 Seaver, 'Biography of Oriana', p.300.
16 Ibid.
17 George to Ida Wilson, 5 June 1929.
18 Ibid.
19 George to Ida Wilson, 24 October 1928.
20 Seaver, 'Biography of Oriana', p.302.
21 Ibid., p.301.
22 'frivol': a rather lovely Oryism. Ory to Ursula, 1 August 1931, MB558 124247 University of Canterbury Archives.
23 Ibid., p.302.
24 Seaver, *Of the Making of Books*, Chapter 8.
25 Ory to Bernard Wilson, 2 December 1928, Cheltenham Borough Council and the Cheltenham Trust/The Wilson Family Collection.
26 Seaver, *Wilson of the Antarctic*, p.289.
27 Ory to Bernard Wilson, 2 December 1928, Cheltenham Borough Council and the Cheltenham Trust/The Wilson Family Collection.
28 Ory was proposing to emigrate to Wellington and was considering giving Ted's pictures to the New Zealand Government, providing they had a decent gallery in which to house them. The SPRI building itself, designed by Sir Herbert Baker, was not ready until 1934, but when Deb offered to sort out the storage and insurance, and to create a permanent Wilson Gallery, Ory decided in favour of the SPRI.
29 1 March (Newspaper heading and date torn off the fragment), 2006.39.2 Cheltenham Borough Council and the Cheltenham Trust/The Wilson Family Collection.

Chapter 33

1 Ory to Bernard Wilson, 2 December 1928. The Wilson Collection, Cheltenham.
2 The Auckland-based *New Zealand Herald*'s headline on 6 February said it all: 'NAPIER LIKE YPRES'.
3 Ory to Cherry, 3 May 1918.
4 Seaver, *Wilson of the Antarctic*, p.304.
5 Author's conversation with Eleanor Bragge, Sherbourne, 2012.
6 Ory to Isabel Smith, 26 February 1935, MS559/145/4 SPRI.
7 Ory to Ursula Bethell, 8 September 1931, MB558 124247 University of Canterbury Archives, Christchurch, NZ.
8 General Register Office, Axminster, County of Devon DYD 278520.
9 It was clear when I met her at a nursing home in Salisbury that Eleanor Bragge, Constance's younger daughter, did not know how her mother had died. It seems that the girls had been taken in by neighbours so that they did not witness their mother's death. Ory, along with the rest of the family, had obviously felt it better not to tell the children. Her nephew, Nicholas Bantoft, son of Eleanor's older sister Elizabeth, had never discussed it with either his mother or aunt. We assume, therefore, that neither of the daughters ever learned what had happened.

Chapter 34

1 Ory in her letters often related stories to try to distract Cherry from his own demons, Ory to Cherry, 13 April 1916, M559/143/1–25 SPRI.
2 Ory to Ursula Bethell, 8 September 1931, MB558 124247 University of Canterbury Archives, Christchurch, NZ.
3 Ibid.
4 Author's conversation with Eleanor Bragge, Sherbourne, 2012.
5 I wondered how good Ory was at looking after her bereaved nieces; after all, she knew so much more about boys. I met Eleanor Bragge as a formidable six-foot lady of 91, leaning on two sticks instructing the gardener of her nursing home in Salisbury to move that clematis a little to the right for the best chance of afternoon sunshine. Eleanor, the only person I spoke to who had known Ory, described her as 'frightfully bossy [but her home was] very well furnished and cosy, a nice garden, what I call "a cosy house"'.

6 Seaver, 'Biography of Oriana', pp.303–04.
7 Ory to Jim Wilson, 13 October 1933, 1995.550.106 Cheltenham Borough Council and the Cheltenham Trust/The Wilson Family Collection.
8 Their mammal colleague Barrett Hamilton had been nicknamed 'The Splitter' for his tendency to split single species up in order to name-credit friends. Lowe and Kinnear found three others had pitched for Ted's bird but they pushed as hard as they dared.
9 Ory to Dr Lowe, December 1931, Natural History Museum, London.
10 George Seaver to Kinnear, 17 December 1936, NBK/ML Seaver Archive.
11 Ibid.
12 Michael Wilson talking to Dr David Wilson, recording at Cheltenham Borough Council and the Cheltenham Trust/The Wilson Family Collection, 2004. '… Ted appears to be smoother than in fact, he was.'
13 Ory to Isabel Smith, 24 October 1933, MS 559/145/1-5;D SPRI.
14 Ibid.
15 Newspaper reviews, October 1933.
16 'Jim broke down under the mounting stress, left Burslem and for three years was unable to work while he struggled with the tears and rage and the black depression which at times brought him to near suicide … But of all the reasons he subsequently gave for his recovery you can be certain of one – my Mother, whose capacity for absorbing stress and giving back love seemed inexhaustible. At the side of so many remarkable men you will often find an even more remarkable woman.' Thanksgiving service address given by Michael Wilson for his father, 3 June 1972, Documents of JV Wilson, MS 95.550.161 Cheltenham Borough Council and the Cheltenham Trust/The Wilson Family Collection.
17 Ory to Jim, 13 October 1933.
18 Ory to Mrs Benton, 7 March 1934, from Kenya, 2006.39.2-4 Cheltenham Borough Council and the Cheltenham Trust/The Wilson Family Collection.

Chapter 35

1 'Hut represents 'an indomitable spirit.' Quoted in 'Cabin link with Scott's Antarctic quest', *The Press*, 28 April 2012. www.stuff.co.nz/the-press/news/6821883/Cabin-link-with-Scotts-Antarctic-quest.

David and Valerie Crichton became custodians for the hut when they bought the piece on Kinsey Terrance on which it was situated. Realising its significance, they have worked tirelessly for it to be saved and donated it to the nation. Thank you.

2   The Wilson Picture Gallery opened with the SPRI in November 1934. Visitors were taken upstairs to the roof space where around thirty paintings were exhibited in natural light with plain frames and broad white mounts.

3   Ory to Isabel, 26 February 1935, MS559/145/1–5;D SPRI.

4   Ory to Isabel, 21 February 1935, MS559/145/1–5;D SPRI.

5   Ory to Ursula Bethell, 10 September 1938, MB558 124247 University of Canterbury Archives, Christchurch, NZ.

6   Ory to Isabel, 21 February 1935.

7   Ibid.

8   Ibid.

9   Ory to Isabel 9 January 1935, MS 559/145/1–5;D SPRI.

10   Ory to Isabel, 26 February 1935.

11   Letter from Ory to Alex H. Turnbull, Westal, Cheltenham, 24 October 1915, MS papers, Folder 98, Alexander Turnbull Archive, National Museum, Wellington, NZ.

12   Ory to the Kinseys, 6 March 1935, Alexander Turnbull Archive, National Museum, Wellington, NZ. Sir Joseph Kinsey died in May 1936, Lady Sarah Ann Kinsey, his wife, died in 1941.

Chapter 36

1   Oriana Wilson, Preface to George Seaver, *Edward Wilson: Nature-Lover*. London: John Murray, 1937, p.vii.

2   Ory really did seem to have taken Baudouin's autosuggestion seriously. What was she trying to get out of? 'I am convinced my ankle was done by my subconscious mind! I certainly got out of a position I didn't like, into one I did, by the breaking of it. My friends think I'm mad over this subject but as I see it in myself & all round me – I can't help drawing conclusions!' Ory to Ursula Bethell, 15 February 1937, MB558 124247 University of Canterbury Archives, Christchurch, NZ.

3   Anne Hardy Collection, Canterbury Museum, Christchurch.

4   Ory to Ursula Bethell, 6 August 1937, MB558 124247 University of Canterbury Archives, Christchurch, NZ.

5   Evelyn Forbes and Dr David Wilson, 11 August 1995, Cambridge. Recorded interview at The Wilson Museum Archives, Cheltenham.
6   Michael Wilson and Dr David Wilson, 2004. Recorded interview at Cheltenham Borough Council and the Cheltenham Trust/The Wilson Family Collection.
7   Letter from Ory to Sir John Murray Wilson Museum DV 22/22A.
8   Ted's three notable contributions to science are evaluated in Seaver, *Edward Wilson: Nature-Lover,* pp.206–208.
9   In an extraordinary coincidence I bought myself an edition of *Edward Wilson: Nature Lover* through Amazon and, of all the books that I could have bought, this very copy was posted to me. I noticed the dedication and was able to match the handwriting with archive letters containing Kathleen Scott's handwriting.
10 Images: MG 6569 SPRI (donated in 1983 by Peter Scott).
11 Evelyn Forbes and Dr David Wilson interview, 11 August 1995.
12 Ibid.

Chapter 37

1   Ory to Ursula Bethell, 6 August 1937, MB558 124247 University of Canterbury Archives, Christchurch, NZ.
2   Ory to Ursula Bethell, 9 May 1938, MB558 124247 University of Canterbury Archives, Christchurch, NZ.
3   Ursula's Salon (and therefore Ory's Wilson Arts Fund sponsorship) supported, amongst others, the writer Ngaio Marsh, the essayist M.H. Holcroft, the artists R.H. Field and Evelyn Margaret Page, the poets Blanche Edith Baughan and J.H.E. Schroder, and the musician Frederick Joseph Page.
4   Ory to Anne Hardy, 1 December 1938, MS 64.7 Canterbury Museum, Christchurch, NZ.
5   Tom Griffiths, *Slicing the Silence: Voyaging to Antarctica.* Cambridge, Mass: Harvard, 2007, p.172.
6   Evelyn Forbes and David Wilson, 11 August 1995, Cambridge. Recorded interview held at The Wilson Museum Archives, Cheltenham.
7   Ibid.
8   Apsley Cherry-Garrard, Introduction to Seaver, *Wilson of the Antarctic,* p.ix.
9   Ory to Sir John Murray, Wilson Museum DV22/22A.

10 Ory to Oriana Walker November 1941.
11 Seaver, 'Biography of Oriana', p.304.
12 Bowen Family Visitor's Book, Middleton, Christchurch, New Zealand, 25 April 1912.
13 Seaver, 'Biography of Oriana', p.304.
14 Ibid.
15 Seaver, *Wilson of the Antarctic*, p.299.
16 Seaver, *Wilson of the Antarctic*, p.299.
17 Ted to Polly, Christchurch NZ, 17 December 1901, 2015.29.7 Cheltenham Borough Council and the Cheltenham Trust/The Wilson Family Collection.

Postscript

1   King, *Wilson: Diary of the* Terra Nova, pp.151, 158.

Bibliography

UNPUBLISHED MATERIAL

Maarten Vandenberg's Souper family tree – private collection.

UK Incoming Passenger Lists 1878–1960 – Board of Trade: Commercial and Statistical Department and successors. National Archives, London, England.

Life of Copthorne Preparatory School taken from *The Old Copthornian School Chronicles*. Bernard Rendall, Ted's brother-in-law was headmaster.

Correspondence between KM and David Wilson 2008–18.

Hilton Parish Records – Mandate for Induction of Francis Abraham Souper, Ory's father.

Death certificate, Axminster for Constance Mary Bragge, Ory's sister, 31 August 1931, General Register Office, England.

Interview with Constance Eleanor Bragge, daughter of Constance Mary Bragge, Ory's sister, by KM, 21 March 2012 Sherbourne.

Letters from Constance E Bragge to KM.

Tribute at the funeral of Constance E. Bragge by her nephew Nicholas Bantoft, Yeovil Crematorium, 15 March 2016.

Conversation with Ralph Slater, the Old Rectory, The Green, Hilton, Huntington with author September 2012.

Noel Beaumont Souper 1878–1916 on memorial at Thiepval Memorial to the Missing of the Somme, Pier F11 D and on Hilton War Memorial, Huntingdonshire.

Letter from Gillian Painter to KM, 17 March 2013, regarding the Wilsons of New Zealand.

Ashburton Guardian, Saturday, 7 January 1989, 'Hardy's Stores catered for Everyone'.

Brixham British Seamen's Orphan Boys Home Records, Brixham Museum, Brixham, Devon.

Recording of interview between Evelyn Forbes and David Wilson, 11 August
    1995, 10 Summerfield, Cambridge. Cheltenham Borough Council and the
    Cheltenham Trust/The Wilson Family Collection.
Obituary of Oriana Wilson, *Polar Record*, Vol. 4, No. 30, July 1945, p.290.
MacInnes, K., *Love and Death and Mrs Bill*, A Play about Oriana, Wife of Polar
    Explorer Edward Wilson, UK, 2013.

Archives

Alexander Turnbull Archive, National Museum, Wellington, NZ
Bradfield College, Bradfield
Cheltenham College, Cheltenham
Royal Geographic Society, London
St Andrew's Prep School, Eastbourne
St George's Hospital, London
The Natural History Museum, London
The Scott Polar Institute, Cambridge
The Seaver Family Archive
The Wilson Family Collection at Cheltenham Borough Council and the
    Cheltenham Trust/The Wilson Family Collection, Cheltenham Trust and
    Cheltenham Borough Council
University of Canterbury Archives, Christchurch, NZ

PUBLISHED

Booth, Charles, *Life and Labour of the People in London*. Vol. 1, London: Macmillan,
    1902.
Bryce, R.M., *Cook & Peary: the Polar Controversy resolved*. Mechanicsburg: Stackpole
    Books, 1997.
Cherry-Garrard, A., *The Worst Journey in the World*. (First published London:
    Constable, 1922), New York: Dover, 2010.
Church, I.N., *Last Port to Antarctica, Dunedin and Port Chalmers: 100 Years of Polar
    Service*. Dunedin: Otago Heritage Books, July 1997.
Crane, D., *Scott of the Antarctic: A Life of Courage and Tragedy in the Extreme South*.
    London: Harper Perennial, 2012.
Elliot, George, *Scenes of Clerical Life*. London: Blackwood & Sons, 1857.
Evans, E., *South with Scott*. London: Collins, 1921.
Fiennes, R., *Scott*. London: Hodder & Stoughton, 2003.

Herbert, K., *Heart of the Hero: The Remarkable Women who Inspired the Great Polar Explorers*. Glasgow: Saraband, 2013.

Herbert, W., *The Noose of Laurels, The Discovery of the North Pole*. London: Hodder & Stoughton, 1989.

Huntford, R., *Scott and Amundsen: The Last Place on Earth*. London: Penguin/Random House, 1999.

Huntford, R., *Shackleton*, London: Cardinal, 1989.

Jones, M., *The Last Great Quest: Captain Scott's Antarctic Sacrifice*. Oxford: OUP, 2003.

Kennet, K., *Self Portrait of an Artist, from the Diaries and Memoirs of Lady Kennet, Kathleen Scott*. London: John Murray, 1949.

King, H. (ed.), *Edward Wilson: Diary of the Terra Nova Expedition to the Antarctic 1910–1912*. From the original mss in the SPRI and the British Museum, London: Blandford Press, 1972.

Leach, A.F., *A History of Bradfield College*, London: H Frowde, 1900.

Lee, L.G. (ed), Boulton & Paul Ltd: *1898 Catalogue, Rose Lane Works, Norwich*. Almonte: Algrove Publishing, 1998.

Limb, S., & Cordingley, P, *Captain Oates: Soldier and Explorer*, London: Batsford, 1982 (Pen & Sword 1997).

Nicholson, J., *The Perfect Summer: Dancing into Shadow in 1911*, London: John Murray, 2006.

Nicholson, V., *Singled Out: How Two Million Women Survived Without Men after the First World War*. London: Penguin, 2008.

Peary, J., *My Arctic Journal: A year among Ice-Fields and Eskimos*. New York: Contemporary Publishing Co, 1893.

Peary, M.A., *The Snowbaby's Own Story*, New York: Frederick A Stokes, 1934.

Richards, J., *Imperialism and Music: Britain 1876–1953*. Manchester: Manchester University Press, 2001.

Savours, A. (ed.), *Edward Wilson: Diary of the 'Discovery' Expedition to the Antarctic Regions 1901–1904*. From the original manuscript in the SPRI, London: Blandford Press, 1966.

Scott, P., *Observations of Wildlife*. Oxford: Phaidon Press, 1980.

Scott, R.F., *Captain Scott's Last Expedition*, M. Jones (ed.), Oxford: Oxford University Press, 2006.

Seaver, G., *Edward Wilson of the Antarctic: Naturalist and Friend*. London: John Murray, 1933 (26th reprint containing 'A Biography of Oriana' 1959).

Seaver, G., *Edward Wilson: Nature-Lover*. London: John Murray, 1937.

Seaver, G., *The Faith of Edward Wilson of the Antarctic*. London: John Murray, 1948.

Shackleton, E., and Robert, M.H., *Rejoice My Heart: The Making of HR Mill's 'The Life of Sir Ernest Shackleton'. The Private Correspondence of Dr Hugh Robert Mill and Lady Shackleton, 1922–33*. Santa Monica: Adelie Books, 2007.

Shackleton, E., *The Heart of the Antarctic, The Farthest South Expedition 1907–09*. London: Penguin 2000.

Shackleton, J., and MacKenna, J., *Shackleton: An Irishman in Antarctica*. Dublin: Lilliput Press, 2003.

Strathie, A., *Birdie Bowers: Captain Scott's Marvel*. Stroud: The History Press, 2012.

Strathie, A., *From Ice Floes to Battlefields: Scott's Antarctics in the First World War*. Stroud: The History Press, 2015.

Trollope, J., *Britannia's Daughters: Women of the British Empire*. London: Pimlico, 2006.

Wheeler, S., *Cherry: A Life of Apsley Cherry-Garrard*. London: Jonathan Cape, 2001.

Williams, I., *With Scott in the Antarctic: Edward Wilson, Explorer, Naturalist, Artist*. Stroud: The History Press, 2008.

Wilson, D.M. and Wilson, C.J., *Edward Wilson's Antarctic Notebooks*. Cheltenham: Reardon Publishing, 2011.

Wilson, D.M. and Wilson, C.J., *Edward Wilson's Nature Notebooks*. Cheltenham: Reardon Publishing, 2004.

Young, L., *A Great Task of Happiness: The Life of Kathleen Scott*. London: HarperCollins, 2014.

Journals

Antarctic, Quarterly publication of the New Zealand Antarctic Society, Christchurch.

Ashburton Guardian

The Evening Post, Wellington

Oamaru Mail

Whanganui Chronicle

MacInnes, K., 'Marriage by Post', *The Lady* lady.co.uk/marriage-post.

MacInnes, K., 'The Invisible Woman', *Cotswold Life*, November 2011.

MacInnes, K., 'Land of Ice and Snow', *Literary Review*, December 2012. literaryreview.co.uk/land-of-ice-snow.

Mankelow, S., 'Well Travelled Antarctic Cabin Rides Again', 20 March 2013, Conservation Blog, Department of Conservation. blog.doc.govt.nz/2013/03/20/ scotts-antarctic-cabin.

Nicholson, K. (MacInnes), 'Cabin link with Scott's Antarctic quest', *The Press*, New Zealand, 28 April 1912. www.stuff.co.nz/the-press/news/6821883/Cabin-link-with-Scotts-Antarctic-quest.

Index

IF YOU ENJOYED THIS TITLE FROM THE HISTORY PRESS:

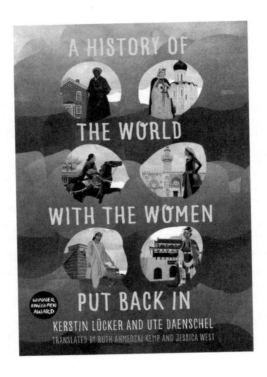

978 0 7509 8909 1

The destination for history
www.thehistorypress.co.uk